Hank Van Iersel has written for the *Weekend Australian Review* supplement, *Rhythms magazine*, *Country Update magazine*, *The Wanderer magazine* amongst others.

He has been a writer/full member of the Australasian Performing Rights Association since 1986 and has released five CD's of original songs. He has won the Tamworth NSW Star Maker Quest in 1985 and a Golden Guitar for Best New Talent in 1986.

He currently lives in Hervey Bay QLD.

THE BAKER'S SON

HANK VAN IERSEL

First published 2024 by Hank Van Iersel

Produced by Independent Ink
independentink.com.au

Copyright © Hank Van Iersel 2024

The moral right of the author to be identified as the author of this work has been asserted.

All rights reserved. Except as permitted under the *Australian Copyright Act 1968*, no part of this publication may be reproduced, stored in a retrieval system, or transmitted in any form or by any means, electronic, mechanical, photocopying, recording or otherwise, without prior written permission from the publisher. All enquiries should be made to the author.

Cover design by Catucci Design
Edited by Samantha Sainsbury
Internal design by Independent Ink
Typeset in 12/17 pt Minion Pro by Post Pre-press Group, Brisbane
Cover image credits are on page 297

ISBN 978-1-7636271-0-9 (Paperback)
ISBN 978-1-7636271-1-6 (epub)
ISBN 978-1-7636271-2-3 (Kindle)

For my daughters
Zoe, Mikahl and Erin.

INTRODUCTION

'Please don't make a fuss over my story,' said my father to Dutch author Jack Didden when Didden contacted Dad in 1985 to solicit wartime reminiscences for a book he was writing. The book was going to cover the years of German occupation of their hometown of Waalwijk in the south of The Netherlands during World War II. Mr. Didden was particularly interested to know whether Dad had been involved in any Resistance activities during that time. My father replied that it had been his own and possibly also Mr. Didden's experience that most people who had operated in the Resistance during that period were hesitant to shine much light on their war-time exploits on account of the dismal treatment meted out to them by the post-war Netherlands regime. There had been no official recognition of their efforts. In fact, they were being widely referred to as 'The Illegality' and sometimes 'terrorists' in an attempt to distinguish them from the royally decreed B.S., the *Binnenlandse Strijdkrachten*, the 'National Fighting Forces'.

Dad went on to tell Mr. Didden that, having been prodded

by his sons for some account of their father's dealings during the war, he had written a short, twenty-five page tale of his escapades, entitled *One Man's War* which he would send along if he liked, on the proviso it was returned to him.

In 1991, Jack Didden's book, *Provincial City During Wartime, Waalwijk and districts 1939–1945* indeed contained parts of my father's story as it related to Waalwijk, as well as reproductions of Dad's forged identity papers and inclusion on the Gestapo's list of wanted criminals. But it only scratched the surface and in fact whetted my own appetite to unlock more of the story only hinted at in Dad's *One Man's War*.

I did some research and was astounded to learn that some of the exploits in my father's account which merited but a brief mention had been, in reality, amongst the most renowned and significant moments of the history of the Resistance movement in The Netherlands during World War II. There was no way I could leave it at that. Many of my father's close compatriots during that time did not survive, but had since been honoured in books and films, on monuments and plaques, some even had streets in their home towns named after them. I concluded that because he had survived, my father had been forgotten. But not by me. I carry his name and I resolved to flesh out his story so that there would be a record of this remarkable man, if not for the wide world to know, at least for his offspring to be aware of who he was, what he did and how he lived his life.

So, why make a fuss of his story, when he strongly suggested we shouldn't? Why would this tale matter now, some eighty years after the events? Well, I think that firstly, it is imperative to view the events of World War II not just as grainy, black and white images of a historical period, but as the genuine experiences of people only one generation removed, real men and women; in the case of this book, folks within my ken. And in the context of World War II, we should acknowledge and remember just what human beings, potentially all of us, are capable of doing to one another.

Secondly, such brutal and cruel aggressions as occurred during World War II are happening again in our own world, as we speak. Russian president Putin's hostile and belligerent invasion of Ukraine, which he ironically characterises as being against the evil forces of Nazi ideology and for the defence of the purity of the Russian people, echoes with eerie similarity the evils of that time not eighty years ago.

Of course there are differences. The Ukraine president Volodymyr Zelensky, despite being so advised, did not turn tail and bugger off as did Wilhelmina, Queen of The Netherlands and her government in 1940, just days after instructing her loyal subjects to stay and fight as she would. Also, as opposed to what is occurring in the Ukraine, there was no flood of Dutch refugees fleeing the German Occupation, as there was simply no place to go. To the west was the North Sea, to the south, Belgium and France, already occupied by the Nazis. As a result, in The Netherlands during the years 1940–1945, people who'd run foul of the Germans, be they Jews, students, workers, Resistance operatives, mostly went 'underground'; they took shelter with other citizens prepared to hide them, often on pain of death. By the end of the Occupation, they numbered some 300,000, a simply astounding number.

It would come as no surprise that in The Netherlands at that time, especially amongst folks who gravitated to active

Resistance, the realisation dawned that royal families and national governments are comprised of people who may not have your interests at heart.

This is the tale of how my father survived that time.

CHAPTER 1
1945

He offered me a cigarette and reached across to light it. My file lay open on the desk in front of him. 'You know,' said the recruiting major, exhaling a billow of smoke into the regimental room, 'your record of resistance activities during the Occupation entitles you to be promoted to the rank of lieutenant.'

Lieutenant you say? Well, if I'm to be drafted into the army again for a couple of years, I may as well make some money for a change. I thought. A sergeant's pay didn't amount to much and at twenty-eight years of age, I had certainly not managed to cobble together anything remotely resembling a life. 'That's very heartening to know, major,' I replied, 'I'd be happy to be promoted to the rank of lieutenant.'

He took a long toke on his cigarette, blew a cloud of blue-grey smoke towards the ceiling and threw me a long, patrician glare. 'You must realise, of course, that you are a baker's son and a family background such as yours could be quite a disadvantage in dealing with your fellow officers,' he declared.

Were my ears deceiving me? Did he really just warn me

that even though I was technically qualified to be promoted, I would never really belong amongst the elite echelons of the officer class? That I'd be forever out of my depth, never more than just working class. How fucking dare he! The adrenaline that I'd only recently been able to subdue began rising in my blood at his vile utterance, threatening to explode into an action I may have come to regret. I leapt to my feet, "You can stick that promotion fair up your shining officer's arse Sir, I shall happily remain a sergeant thank you!" and without saluting the arrogant pig, stormed from the room.

A black rage shook the coffee cup in my hand as I took a table in the base mess hall and tried to calm myself. Rolling a cigarette I thought, *Here we go again!* It had not been two months since those god-forsaken Germans were finally driven off our native soil and already the privileged, self-righteous weasels of the governing classes had crawled out from whatever rock they were hiding under. They were nowhere to be found when it mattered most and expected now to just take up where they left off. I should have seen it coming when they appointed Prince Bernhard, that profligate playboy ex-Nazi husband of the Queen's daughter Juliana, to the position of Commander-in-Chief over all active resistance fighters. They'd marketed him as a partisan hero and sent him in behind the advancing Allies like some frontline tourist to ensure the royal family could preserve the privilege and power they'd enjoyed before the war. They didn't want their position challenged by what they saw as the Communist dreams and aspirations espoused by the armed Resistance organisations. Well, here they all were. The elites, the churches, the royal family, the old-school army officer hierarchy back as if nothing had happened. As if all the sacrifices, the betrayals, the deprivations, the suffering, the double dealing, the decencies, the fortitude and cowardice of ordinary people caught up in extraordinary times had been for nothing. It felt as though the cold-blooded execution of my friends Wim and Pedro, lined up and shot dead in a paddock only weeks before we'd been liberated, had been in vain. I couldn't tell whether the tears falling in my coffee were tears of fury or of sorrow; all I knew was that these thoughts would prove to be as difficult to dislodge as the nightmares that now made sleep for me as elusive as the promise of a new and fairer Fatherland. How on earth had it come to this?

CHAPTER 2
1935

WHEN LIFE GIVES YOU lemons, go play some music. There's something in the act of strumming a stringed instrument, the wood reverberating against your chest, that can actually interrupt the inner monologue of the mind and refocus it on the natural heartbeat of one's body. It can make your consciousness dance. Feet begin to tap as you lighten up, crack a smile and shed those storm-cloud thoughts that threaten to derail your happiness. Yeah, times were tough; in the mid-1930s our town of Waalwijk had certainly seen better days, but we could still ease on down to our favourite cafe, lubricate our throats with a couple of *borreltjes* (the Dutch brandy and sugar beverage much loved in our southern province of Brabant) and rattle the rafters with renditions of popular songs of the day.

My musical co-conspirator in these spontaneous jam sessions was usually Tom Brokken, a larrikin and fine guitarist who I'd known since we were kids. His solid rhythm style and wide repertoire were the perfect foil for my mandolin noodling and no moping misanthrope was safe from our instrumental assault. It wouldn't take much before we had folks singing along to songs like 'I Got Rhythm', 'Pennies From Heaven', 'Begin the Beguine', 'Daar Bij Die Molen' ('There, by that windmill'), 'Dat Moet Naar Den Bosch Toe' ('Better go to Den Bosch') and my personal favourite, 'Silver Threads Among The Gold'.

Everybody knew these songs because, like us, everyone listened to the radio. That glowing piece of furniture held households in thrall, softening to some extent the realities of a hard-scrabble life of wage-slaving or worse, joblessness. When a town is dependent on one main industry for employment and for whatever reason that particular industry suffers a dramatic downturn, the deleterious effects on that community can be considerable. And so it was with the shoe and leather factories for which Waalwijk had become widely known. The trade had begun as a cottage industry of farmers in the district tanning cow hides over the long, savage winters. The advent of industrial sewing machines saw economies of scale grow the trade to levels previously unimagined. Over time, the region transformed into the nation's foremost centre for footwear production. Instead of the rural pace of working with the seasons, the majority of townsfolk now clocked on and off in enormous, noisy factories where they were at the mercy not of mother nature, but the caprice of wealthy owners. The bosses were determined to keep wages low and conditions tight and they would brook no dissent or any form of worker mobilisation. There had been attempts to form fellowships amongst the factory workers, usually along denominational lines, but a principled stand is difficult to maintain when there are mouths to be fed and one's livelihood hangs by the barest thread. Throw into the mix the ruinous spectre of the 1929 Great Depression that still hung like a low mist in dales of the region, waiting in vain for an economic headwind to dissipate its cold effect, and a degree of desperation could not be avoided. Folks could use a little cheering up.

To my mind, being under the thumb of less than benevolent overlords, not to mention the fire and brimstone religious shepherds of both Catholic and Protestant persuasions, made people rather too docile and subservient. I was young, opinionated, possibly a little belligerent, but eager to avoid such shackles and keen to be a little more adventurous, although just how adventurous, indeed perilous, my life would become, I could not have foreseen.

Call it ego or delusions of grandeur, which my parents certainly did, but Tom and I began entertaining thoughts of escalating our music making out of the rough and tumble bar room jams we'd been used to and catapulting our talents onto an actual professional stage with a musical review. Sprinkle a little show-business buzz on the town. Shine a spotlight of song to cut through the gloom and doom of everyday life, if only for an hour or so.

Our two cinema houses were doing it tough because folks really couldn't justify spending money they didn't have on frivolous pursuits like going to the movies. One of them, the 'Musis Sacrum' had operated in the past as both a music hall and theatre due to it being furnished with a decent-sized stage, usually disguised behind the silver screen. Maybe the owner could be persuaded to turn over a slow Saturday night to Tom and me to stage a modest musical extravaganza, at no cost to him, out of which he might even turn a small profit. Having nothing to lose and perhaps a little to gain, he agreed to let us have an upcoming Saturday night to put on our show.

Feeling a little like flash entrepreneurs with one foot in the door to show-business success, it was time to put our music where our mouths were. The venue secured and the date locked in, there remained only the small detail of building a show that people might actually want to attend. Despite sporting a repertoire of popular songs that were sure to go over well with our expected audience, the sad truth was that neither Tom nor I could remotely be described as having tremendous 'stage presence', of possessing the looks and allure of the style icons of the day. We were going to need some help.

It came in the shapely form of two young ladies with whom we'd traversed the testing terrain of high school. Margriet and Dineke were what you'd call 'lookers', the kind of girls to turn heads if they walked into a bar. They had about them an aura of availability, of knowing they were attractive, but coupled with a certain aloofness that suggested they did not suffer fools, especially foolish men, gladly. And they could sing and dance. Committed to pursuing the arts rather than academia or sport, they seemed favourably disposed to the proposition of joining the show we were in the process of putting together. They were confident performers and terrific fun in rehearsals and when Dineke mentioned that she was a more than capable seamstress and would be happy to sew stage clothes for us all, I seriously considered marrying her.

At our first full dress rehearsal on the stage of the Musis Sacrum, it was obvious that the girls' influence in design and presentation lent the production the theatricality it so critically needed. Dineke had outfitted Tom and I in white shirts and slacks with a sash belt of colourful material and casually knotted neckerchiefs that suggested a couple of strolling players from some gypsy caravan. The girls themselves looked radiant in white, bubble sleeved blouses atop free flowing skirts that billowed with vibrant colour as they danced. Margriet had decorated the stage with potted plants, a black cloth covered cube centrepiece and a backdrop of an oversized national flag of red, white and blue, pinched and draped so that it resembled a tri-coloured smiling mouth. Dineke's father, keenly supportive of his daughter's artistic endeavours, had arranged for a friend of his, a photographer who worked for the local newspaper, *De Echo Van Het Zuiden* (*The Echo of the South*), to attend our dress rehearsal to take a few publicity photos. This shutterbug subsequently managed to wrangle one of them onto an article in the paper about our upcoming gig with the welcome result of us getting a decent roll up of people to our show.

The night itself went swimmingly. The audience seemed happy to be swept up in the colour, movement, not to mention music, emanating from the stage, to the point where, towards the end of the show, they were heartily singing along to the more uptempo tunes we'd saved for the finale. We had a pretty good success and were for a day or two, almost, the talk of the town.

Not long after our modest triumph at the Musis Sacrum, a gentleman who had attended the show visited and introduced himself as working for the local radio station. He'd thoroughly enjoyed the night, he said, and wondered if perhaps we would be willing to have our music recorded for broadcast over the wireless. Does the Pope wear a frock? Do bears defecate in the woods? I was sure I spoke for the rest of our little troupe when I answered in the affirmative and before long we'd arranged daytime access to the theatre for him to set up the equipment to record our playing. The radio guy rigged his microphone, and we began to play.

He had donned earphones to monitor exactly what was being committed to tape but did not look happy. He stopped us mid song to say that my mandolin because of its high-pitched tone was cutting across the more mellow sounds of the guitar and upsetting the balance. We played around with various placings until the solution was found whereby I played out in the middle of the empty hall and Tom played guitar on stage in order to strike a better mix of sound. Slightly primitive but it worked.

What a surreal thrill it is to hear oneself played on the radio. It's a near out-of-body experience to hear sounds so intimately familiar that are, at the same time, almost detachedly alien. I couldn't help but wonder just how widely the broadcast might reach, how many other people were hearing me at that exact moment.

My parents, of course, reacted with that strange attitude of, 'don't get your hopes up', 'that sort of thing doesn't happen to people like us' and 'it will only cause disappointment down the line'. I was no starstruck fool, but did allow myself a small, delicious dollop of possibility that a musical career might present an escape from the seemingly pre-ordained destiny of life in a factory town. As it turned out, musical prowess, such as it was, would indeed come to alter my life, but certainly not in the manner I then envisaged.

CHAPTER 3

As a subject of polite conversation, politics, much like religion, is usually best avoided. Common ground is remarkably difficult to come by. Safer are topics such as sport and music where, personal preferences aside, some level playing field may be enjoyed. Bar-room banter between my friends and I had been mostly along those lines: how our local football clubs were fairing, had we heard the latest Benny Goodman tune, who was that girl in the red dress.

But as the winter of 1936 was giving way to spring, sinister echoes of world events were beginning to insinuate themselves in ways that could not be ignored. Chief amongst those were the antics of that creepy, hysterical little man with the sawn-off moustache who was whipping up unrest and violence in Germany, just across our eastern borders. He seemed to be taking delight in stirring up diplomatic tensions, ignoring Germany's obligations under the Versailles Treaty by remilitarising and stationing troops in the Rhineland near the border with France.

THE BAKER'S SON

The press reports in *De Echo* newspaper chronicling his ever more belligerent rants about the new Germany needing more *lebensraum* (room to live) for its pure Aryan people did not make for comfortable reading. I knew our country had managed to remain neutral during the hell years of the Great War, but would that again be possible if the worst-case scenario of another conflict should rear its ugly head? Slowly, almost imperceptibly, world politics and our own place in it were beginning to consume the national dialogue and eat into our complacency. I was beginning to seriously dislike that puffed-up little poser for sowing angst into the calm of the community and for potentially disrupting my glorious ascent into a musical career.

Ugly divisions began to appear like cracks in the mirror of how we saw ourselves. The simmering, ultra-nationalist fanaticism of that rabble of malcontents, the *Nationaal Soccialistiche Beweging*, the NSB, became more emboldened with every development in the Third Reich. Since their inception some years prior, they seemed to have attracted every misfit who had a chip on his shoulder and who dreamed of revenge on the neighbours who had slighted them. We had our share of them in Waalwijk, their fawning over everything German and aping of the worst excesses of the Nazis managed to put most everyone offside. Dark clouds were gathering on the horizon of world affairs, and they could very well be blowing our way.

In March of 1937 I was nineteen years old and any notion I may have harboured of playing music for a living were crushed with the arrival of my call-up papers for the army in the mail. I was to be wrenched, kicking and screaming, from the relative comfort of my teenage life into the compulsory regimentation of the military for a period of five months. Now, it didn't say much for the state of preparedness of our armed forces that I was asked to supply my own boots and underwear. *Oh really? Should I search the shed to see if I might rustle up an old blunderbuss? Should I bring my slingshot? What about an armoured bicycle? Should I see if Mother can spare some crockery or if Father has a district map folded up in his desk?* Facetious these thoughts may have been but as it turned out, they were not all that far from the reality of a grievously undercooked army.

I was to make my way to the army base in the city of Utrecht, some fifty kilometres to the north, for induction and training. Lads from all over the south of the country had been similarly summoned and, like me, were now being prodded and poked to assess our fitness for service. There were plenty of stout farmer's sons who could be depended on to do some heavy lifting, some student types that might possibly end up in stores or supply and young men, myself included, who had not yet embarked on any meaningful trade or vocation. I'd played football for the Waalwijk Catholic Youth Organisation as goalkeeper so I was relatively fit and passed the army's physical examination without a problem. I wasn't gay, had no fallen arches or impaired eyesight, and so I was sent on to the next department where I would be questioned regarding my background and previous experience so as to be placed in a unit commensurate with my capabilities.

'I see here that you play the mandolin; is that correct Private Van Iersel?' asked the interviewing major.

I thought maybe I might end up in the regimental band. 'Sure do, sir.' I replied eagerly.

'Very well,' he said, 'you'll go to the Communications Unit to be trained as a radio signaller. To be able to play a musical instrument means you must have a strong feel for rhythm, and that, what with morse code and the like, is what's needed to become a signalman.'

Not quite with the band, I thought, but certainly preferable to being posted as canon fodder to the infantry which would have been the alternative. It seemed my musical ambitions might, after all, conspire to change the course of my life, however subtly.

I was in; I was now a soldier and had the rough, scratchy, grey-green uniform of a rather hand-me-down quality to prove it. The uniform and the obligatory haircut were of course designed to wean one off the trappings of individualism in order to better blend in with the subservient, homogenous whole of the armed forces. But rather than having a sense of pride in serving my country, I instead felt more than a little resentful at having been forced so rudely out of my prior life, however unfocussed that may have been.

There were eight of us, all conscripts like myself, being trained to operate radio senders and receivers and learning to be fluent in manipulating the dots and dashes of morse code. It was definitely more interesting than the rifle drill and shooting practice that would have been my lot in the infantry. We learned quickly and were soon able to fart out messages in morse code while sitting on one of the long wooden tables in the mess hall for amplification. This was of no practical use to the war effort but it amused us greatly.

In a relatively short amount of time, I was promoted to the rank of sergeant, a surprisingly brisk elevation which carried with it a modest raise in income. But before I could allow myself any smugness at this minor triumph, I realised that this meant a further four months of service, which put rather a damper on my promotion. So there I was, locked into the armed forces for the foreseeable future, while, if one listened to the radio or read the newspapers, the world was inching inexorably closer to war. And I couldn't see that we were in any way, shape or form ready for it. We were an army of raw recruits, being trained by a seriously depleted professional officer class who, to be honest, appeared out of their depth. They did not instill any great level of confidence that they would be ready for armed conflict should it, god forbid, ever eventuate.

Their reckless haste in establishing dependable command structures may indeed have been a factor in my rapid rise through the ranks. It was a promotion, it goes without saying, that entailed greater responsibility in being involved in training newer recruits. This task was made more difficult by the distinct shortage of the radio transmitters and receivers that were our tools of trade. It was a situation I could not fathom. The Dutch firm Philips, situated in the southern city of Eindhoven, was the largest producer of such equipment in the world; why could they not adequately supply our armed forces? I could only surmise, and my army experience so far seemed to bear it out, that, since our country's neutrality during the Great War, a fully equipped and staffed armed forces had not been a priority, possibly because our government felt that we could maintain such a stance in any future conflict. A naive notion. Sure, we were a small country, but in the belligerent boasting of that maniac to our east versus the unwavering bulldog to the west, we were destined to be the meat in the sandwich.

Where previously the radio had provided our entertainment as we listened for the most recent Duke Ellington tunes, now in barracks, my comrades and I huddled around it for the latest news bulletins. And these were mostly ominous. In March of 1938, Herr Hitler's Third Reich declared *Anschluss* with Austria, a shackling on of that sovereign state within one Germany.

Not content with such a seemingly effortless invasion, he now set his sights on taunting Czechoslovakia to give up the Germanic peoples of the Sudetenland along the German border. All this sabre-rattling was making us nervous. After all, if the shit did hit the fan, we'd be the ones in the firing line. Because of their mutual military support arrangements with Czechoslovakia, France and Great Britain were now being drawn into these altercations with Herr Hitler. When our newspapers featured that infamous, front-page photo of the British Prime Minister Chamberlain alighting his aircraft on home soil after the Munchen Agreement with France and Germany, waving a piece of paper he asserted to be an undertaking by Hitler to go no further, and indeed, signified peace for Europe, only a few of us breathed a sigh of relief.

My mother had a saying, 'Go tell the cat; he might believe you!'

Hate is a strong word, but I was beginning to seriously loathe, detest and abhor that killer clown with the toothbrush moustache creating such a stink on the other side of our eastern border. I hated him not least for the fact that when he did invade Czechoslovakia in October of 1938, now that I was a sergeant I was ordered to remain in the army indefinitely. Some twenty-first birthday present.

By March of the following year, all of Czechoslovakia had been overrun by the Wehrmacht. Now facing the reality of a dangerous and deteriorating political crisis in Europe, our government and army hierarchy began finally to confront the facts that: A, war was coming; B, we were in its way; and C, we weren't ready. To those of us recently corralled into uniform, this last fact had been bleedingly obvious, from being asked to bring our own underpants to the embarrassment of the ancient, nineteenth century weaponry with which we were expected to defend the Fatherland. And if our superiors weren't befuddled enough, our ranks soon swelled by some fifty thousand men, when in August all leave and furlough was cancelled. Admittedly, our communications unit was not as drastically overrun with raw recruits as was, say, the infantry, but with no input from the commissioned officers, the other couple of sergeants and I had a devil of a job getting them onboard. We had to beg, steal and borrow enough uniforms to dress them and somehow find a sufficiency of bunks for them to sleep in. And then we had to knock them into some sort of battle-ready state.

I suppose desperate times call for drastic measures and we were not spared them. On 28 August, all Dutch men who had ever been conscripted between 1924 and 1939 were recalled into the army, resulting in us being inundated with another one hundred thousand men. Utter chaos and mayhem ensued. Executive decisions were being made without any contingency planning, leaving non-commissioned officers like myself to sort through the shit. Thanks a lot. Then, as if things could not get any worse, on 1 September, Hitler, the megalomaniac that he was, invaded Poland. He could not have done anything more provocative or insane, and if he figured that France and Great Britain would not risk getting involved, he sadly miscalculated. Two days later, both countries declared war on Germany.

The faeces was now definitely about to make contact with the oscillator.

I had been ordered to the town of Middelburg in the south-west of The Netherlands to take charge of the radio transmitting station belonging to the commandant of that region. There were eleven regions in all throughout the country, each with its own commander and radio station operating under the General Command which had its headquarters in The Hague.

Getting to Middelburg was a mission in itself; I humped my cumbersome kit bag through three changes of train, each station crawling with young men, their luggage and often their families waving them off, in transit to the army base to which they'd been assigned. The atmosphere sullen and hectic; there was little in the way of train travel's sometime allure, only sombre adieus as fathers, sons and brothers headed into a future which seemed anything but rosy.

Arriving in Middelburg, there was no opportunity to appreciate the town's historical legacy evident in the many buildings dating back to the 16th and 17th centuries when this was an important centre for trade with Africa and the Far East during the heyday of the Dutch East India Company. It was no social visit. Briskly, I made my way to the army base and presented to the sentry post at the front gate of the compound. The soldier manning it was faffing about like a greasy spoon cook with too many orders to fill, answering the telephone, sorting papers and god knows what else. It took some effort to get him to notice me. When he finally did and had perused my orders, he waved me through and onto the base with an impatient, non-directional wave of his arm, I guess pointing out the building to which I needed to proceed.

The garrison was a hive of activity with none of the orderliness usually associated with such a working community of bees. Utmost care needed to be taken walking its rough avenues as vehicles of all kinds zoomed around with an unfocussed urgency that bordered on the anarchic. The regimented discipline one would rightly expect to find on an army base was conspicuous by its absence. More by luck than design, I located the administration building and entered, looking for a responsible officer to whom I could report with my orders. Here too the pace was hectic, personnel of varying rank strode purposefully up and down the building, in and out of side rooms, on missions of apparent importance, some perusing paperwork, others smoking cigarettes as they walked.

In a vestibule off to the side of the main entrance stood a solid wooden desk overflowing with teetering piles of correspondence that threatened to engulf the black bakelite telephone ringing insistently on its deck. The private, whose job it seemed was to answer its shrill call, was in animated conversation with a sergeant standing next to him, leaving him unsure and rather flustered at who to deal with first, the impatient implement or the superior officer. Figuring this guy to be a sort of concierge, I thought it best to hang back a little before burdening him with yet another enquiry. I lit a cigarette and waited.

After the sergeant had marched off and the telephone's receiver was finally cradled, it was my turn to bother the private to ascertain where I might find the relevant officer to whom I could present my orders. He um'd and ah'd as he absentmindedly shuffled papers about on his desk before directing me to the third office on the left down the long, main corridor, where he said I should speak to a Major van der Berg. The corporal

THE BAKER'S SON

in the third office on the left down the long, main corridor informed me that the good major was not in and that it was unclear as to where he was or when he might return and that I should probably check in with a Lieutenant Brouwer, whose office was upstairs on the first floor. This I did but he also was not in attendance. After another two wild goose chases I chanced upon a Lieutenant Koopmans who took pity on me and actually scrutinised my orders.

'Ah, Sergeant Van Iersel, so you're to be our new radio operator. Headquarters has been promising us one for weeks. Glad you're here.' He knew enough to inform me that the job and, indeed, the radio room, were classified 'Top Secret' and as such, I was to be billeted off-campus with a civilian family nearby. My immediate superior, he told me, was located in the nearby town of Vlissingen where I should go once per month to pick up my pay and travel vouchers. We then climbed into his staff car and drove to a smaller, nondescript building off to the side of the electricity substation for the base, housing the radio room.

A 'Top Secret, Unauthorised Entry Forbidden' sign graced the front door. Inside was an ante-room sporting a table and chairs and a small gas stove for brewing coffee. There were a couple of ashtrays, some cups and a reasonable supply of coffee and sugar, I was pleased to see. A rather solid door opened into a windowless space filled with radio equipment, morse code sets and a filing cabinet. Home was never like this. I was to maintain twenty-four-hour radio contact with headquarters in The Hague while listening in to radio chatter coming in off the North Sea. Koopmans bid me adieu and said to contact Major van der Berg if I had any problems. And that was it: there's the deep end, lad; let me throw you in.

Stashing my kit bag in a corner, I poured myself a strong, black coffee and got comfortable in front of the array of scanners, receivers and radio senders stacked on the desk against the far wall of the radio room. Clamping on a set of headphones and positioning the microphone and morse code keys within reach, I threw a switch which brought the equipment humming, beeping and flashing to life. I was ready to listen to night on the North Sea. German U-boats prowling the offshore depths needed to surface in order to be able to use their radios to receive orders and transmit reconnaissance, a task they usually reserved for nighttime when they were less likely to be spotted. And like an insomniac scanning their radio dial to find music worth listening to, I began sweeping the radio frequencies hoping to ensnare enemy broadcasts. My headphones crackled with varying intensities of white noise, interference and otherworldly sounds, until, like a mosquito flying suddenly close to one's ear, a burst of morse code would materialise and I would try to decipher the message, holding the frequency as long as possible. The task was then to ascertain whether it held any importance before passing it on to headquarters in The Hague. If it was indeed of German origin, it would be in code, so probably made no literal sense but I sent it along just the same.

There is a degree of sensory deprivation that occurs when seated in a windowless, darkened room, hunched over dimly lit equipment and concentrating only on auditory input. The thin line between one's own thoughts and the pervading influence of only one of the senses blurs, time evaporates and some part of you seems to be virtually skating the layers of night air above an ink-black ocean, alert for action.

It was only the jolting realisation that I was beginning to

converse with an ex-girlfriend from my home town who was plainly not present in the room that forced me to confront my deteriorating mental state. It was not pretty. I was shocked to discover that three days and nights had passed, and I was well on the way to becoming delirious with exhaustion. I was spent and almost hallucinating. That 'Top Secret, Go Away' sign on the front door was proving highly effective; no-one had come near me or given me a moment's thought for a full three days. Time to ring Major van der Berg.

The weight of a world at war seemed to be heavy on the good major's mind when at last I managed to get through to him.

After telling him my name, he said, 'Right. Refresh my memory, who exactly are you?'

Desperately trying to maintain decorum, I blurted out, 'I am the top-secret radio operator who is about to expire due to having been stuck in the radio room for three days and nights without relief of any kind!'

'Well, pull yourself together, lad. None of us are having an easy time of it,' came his terse reply. 'Leave it with me and I'll see what I can do.'

It wouldn't do to tell a major in the army to go fuck himself so I zipped my lip and hung up.

The following morning, however, following a brusque rapping on the front door, I was pleased to discover that the old man had indeed sent reinforcements in the shape of a corporal and private from the army reserves. I could have kissed them. I wasted no time bringing them up to speed on the requirements of the job and the rudiments of operating the equipment, after which I literally threw myself onto the floor of the tea room, using a rolled-up overcoat for a pillow, said go for it, lads, wake me if you get stuck and finally pulled the switch on my overtaxed brain.

It was nigh on twenty-four hours before I opened my eyes again. My new assistant operators had gotten through the night without any major dramas and had now, god bless them, managed to rustle up some fresh bread, butter and cheese to go with the coffee percolating on the stove. I liked them already. They were older than me but seemed to share my disenchantment with the army brass and their rather worrying lack of decisive leadership. We knew we'd sooner be anywhere else than in uniform but could not resile from the fact that our Fatherland was heading into mortal danger, and we had to do our bit.

Taking stock of the current situation, it became clear that, due to the 'top secret' status of our radio room, we were a hermetically sealed crew of three, operating independently of base command, our only caveat being to monitor radio signals and maintain round the clock contact with General Command in The Hague. I would need to travel once a month to the nearby town of Vlissingen to pick up our pay and free travel passes from the commandant there, but apart from that, we were on our own. With no official oversight, we rostered ourselves eight-hour shifts but wrangled it so that we would each have at least one weekend off per month. This worked very well, free time, free travel with no-one the wiser, not a bad way to be in the army.

But of course, world events were still unfolding. Herr Hitler was wreaking havoc in Poland and gambling that Great Britain would not thwart his territorial ambitions towards Russia. In late 1939 I was ordered to Rotterdam to take up the position of sergeant-in-charge of a class of university students who had previously been passed over for recruitment into the army, but because of the changed circumstances of Britain and France declaring war on Germany, were now to be drafted into service. What a surreal situation. With my own academic achievements limited to senior high school, here I was teaching university students who were not only older, but a lot more knowledgeable about radio equipment than I was. But, the army is the army, and I was the sergeant-in-charge and the sergeant knows best. Actually, they turned out to be really good blokes and we managed to get along famously. It was a state of affairs that was not destined to last.

CHAPTER 4

I MUST HAVE BEEN DREAMING. A bucolic stroll in woodland countryside had turned suddenly threatening after I had inadvertently bumped into and dislodged a soccer-ball-sized beehive. The until then industrious insects had taken umbrage and mobilised at once into a menacing, buzzing swarm that rose like toxic smoke from their downed domain. My legs bolted and carried me darting through the undergrowth before even my brain caught up, the dangerous, droning surge of bees in hot pursuit and closing fast. What to do? With the aggrieved insects nearly upon me and their intimidating whir growing louder in my ears, I suddenly spied a wide creek in my path. Leaping from the bank headlong into the air, I hit the water and ... awoke with a start.

The room was pitch black and I was panting and perspiring; it was three a.m. It took me a minute to compose myself, but if I was awake, why was I still hearing the drone of swarming bees? A cold jolt of recognition revealed that these were not insects but aeroplanes, lots of aeroplanes. Clambering clumsily into clothes, I ran outside and against the clear night sky, I distinguished dozens of aircraft flying low overhead, disgorging skydivers all over Rotterdam. A rain of sinister mushroom shapes were descending on the city. It was 10 May, 1940, we'd had no declaration of war, no formal notice of Germany's intent to invade, yet here they were, falling out of the sky and no doubt rolling across our borders, a hostile assault that plainly broadcast Herr Hitler's intent to never play by the rules of war.

The pre-dawn air reverberated with the roar and thrum of revving aircraft engines interspersed with machine-gun fire as it appeared fighter planes of the Dutch Airforce were attacking the incoming enemy with darting, strafing sorties in and around the German formations. Running towards the Veemarkt buildings in the city where my unit was headquartered, it seemed that most of the action on the ground was centred on the southern bank of the river Maas. Searchlights had begun probing the still-dark sky and tracer bullets from anti-aircraft batteries were spewing noisily heavenwards, most likely emanating from the Waalhaven Airfield situated there. To add to the cacophony, I could hear light artillery fire coming off the river itself. The streets were beginning to fill with pyjama-clad burghers spilling onto footpaths to see what the hell had so rudely interrupted their repose.

With no bombs yet falling, I reached the Veemarkt unscathed, only to be confronted by another kind of mayhem altogether. One might have expected a military command post to be a model of disciplined, orderly efficiency, soberly executing plans to deal with the emergent crisis. Wrong. Decapitated chickens running loose in the yard would have offered more cause for confidence. High-ranking officers were shouting random demands at subordinates who seemed unsure of how to respond.

'Where the fuck is Colonel Scharroo?' yelled one, referring to the commander of all Rotterdam's military forces. No-one knew.

Another was berating the lieutenant in charge of breaking out weapons and ammunition for being too pedantic: 'Lieutenant, we do not need to have every soldier sign for every gun and bullet; we are at fucking war, just give them out for god's sake!'

Telephones were demanding to be heard as soldiers took messages which they either scribbled hurriedly down on scraps of paper, or else shouted across the room to whichever officer might listen.

'Planes have landed on the river, sir. German soldiers are using rubber boats to reach the Noordereiland,' bellowed one.

'Waalhaven airfield is in danger of being overrun, sir!' shrieked another.

An officer demanded of no-one in particular, 'Do we have any troops defending the Maas bridges?' Rotterdam had been built on two sides of the river Maas, with the city centre on the north bank, residential, industrial districts and the military airfield Waalhaven to the south. Connecting the two and spanning the water were two impressive structures, one carrying the railway, the other, the Willemsbrug, vehicular traffic. Stretched underneath the bridges and just parallel to the southern bank lay the Noordereiland, a narrow, longish island, a residential and shipping precinct. These were surely the primary targets of the German attack now taking place. A command of those bridges would open access for their forces to storm through to The Hague, the seat of government and the queen her big, bad self. Alas, the answer to the officer's query was that no, we didn't have any troops defending the bridges. This resulted in frantic phone calls to the barracks of the Marine Corps, housed in another building in the city and home to the most experienced fighters at our disposal to get them down there as soon as possible.

When another sergeant and I were then ordered to take a rifle and sixty rounds of ammunition each and proceed to a northern zone of the city to defend two minor bridges, a lenient person may have concluded that in the frenetic atmosphere of the moment he had gotten confused as to which bridges he was referring. I just thought he was fucking bonkers. We were trained radio operators, not riflemen and the weapons with which we were supplied couldn't kill a cow at one hundred metres. And they were heinously slow to load. After each shot, the breech would need to be emptied before another bullet could be inserted, by which time you'd probably be dead. How we were supposed to defend two even minor bridges from attack was beyond me but, orders are orders, so off we went.

As we headed north through the city streets, the sun was already ascending a clear spring sky and a cool breeze made me glad I'd taken time to don my army overcoat. From behind us it seemed the anti-aircraft guns on the Waalhaven Airfield had grown ominously silent, suggesting they had in all likelihood been overrun, and there were no longer any of our fighter planes streaking across the sky. Bad signs further clouding our current mission. The strange quiet of thoroughfares normally abuzz with Friday morning traffic was pierced here and there with the shrill clamour of sirens wailing but also sharp retorts of intermittent small-arms fire. A police patrol we encountered told of emboldened German nationals who had been recently sent in ahead of the invasion, opening fire on unsuspecting citizens in order to spread panic amongst the population. The officers were themselves in the process of rounding up members of the Dutch National Socialist organisation, the NSB, who had been preparing to throw in their lot with the invading Huns.

With hearts sinking fast, the other sergeant and I reached our intended goal. A single span, mechano-set looking structure supported twin train tracks, while next to it, a simple bridge sported a two-lane, bitumen roadway. The bridges traversed a minor canal only big enough for non-motorised barge traffic. Not really impressive thoroughfares by any standard, but a daunting prospect to have to defend against rampaging enemy hordes armed only with our antique weaponry.

This was bullshit. Just a random posting in place of being part of some coordinated defence or counterattack. Yet here we were, radio operators with no line of communication unless we bothered the locals to see if we could use their telephone. A situation that was laughable if it wasn't so goddamned serious. Speaking of locals, the lady of the house of an adjoining farm must have noticed our plight and taken pity on these poor, lost, bedraggled little soldiers, for here she came, bless her, with bacon, eggs and coffee, a welcome breakfast before battle.

We seemed for the moment to be clear of any German advance, so we took time to set up positions that afforded untrammelled views of each bridge approach while still offering some protection from incoming fire. Behind us, about ten kilometres to the south, I could see German paratroopers still raining down out of a crisp, blue sky on what I presumed was the area around the airfield south of the city, reinforcing the fact that our chances of defending these bridges were about zero.

Despite the decent breakfast, a ball of dread lodged tight in my guts as the minutes dragged on. It was clear that on this day, some seismic shift had occurred to tip the axis of the world into a new dimension of uncertainty, danger and doubt, where previously comfortable concepts and beliefs counted for nothing, where the script of our lives was suddenly subject to change without notice. This was going to be one crap summer.

After a tense couple of hours watching for signs of German activity on the far banks of the canal, the sudden rumble of diesel engines from behind our positions shot adrenaline through our blood like a junkie pumping heroin into his veins as we reeled around in time to see a column of trucks pull into view. We cocked our ancient rifles in their direction and prepared to fire. This time the slowness to load these almost useless implements worked in our favour when the realisation dawned that this was a platoon of our own Dutch infantry. Men from the town of Gouda apparently sent to take over defence of these bridges. They were maybe not fully trained professional soldiers either, most likely recent conscripts like ourselves, but infantry nonetheless and we very gladly handed them the job.

On the way back though the city to our Veemarkt headquarters, we hunkered close to buildings due to the feverishly busy activity of German aircraft in the air not far above us. There was now little evidence of any of our own planes being involved, only darting, arcing Stuka fighters circling around and firing on targets in and around the river. The air reverberated with the concussion of bombs exploding south of the city sending billows of menacing black smoke rising threateningly into what was, in essence, a cool, blue, springtime sky, that season of growth and new life now desecrated with the blasphemy of war.

The relieved sergeant and I safely reached our headquarters where it was painfully clear that order and discipline were unravelling like a badly knitted jumper snagged on a nail. Colonel Scharroo, the rigidly upperclass and authoritarian commander of the military forces in Rotterdam, was in heated exchange with his Marine Corps counterpart, Colonel Von Frijtag Drabbe.

'I am the supreme authority here!' Scharroo was yelling. 'You and your marines will bend under my command, is that clear?'

'What is clear, colonel, is that you are a pompous, puffed-up little man and you can go to hell. I'd no sooner submit to your command than I would the tea lady in the mess hall. You have no jurisdiction over me and never will,' bellowed the Marine Corps commandant.

Scharroo was now visibly quaking with rage, his face reddening like a dyspeptic drunkard having a heart attack. 'How very dare you, you second-rate matelot! I'll see you court-marshalled for this!' He was shrieking, his voice straining for a higher octave.

Von Frijtag Drabbe was losing his cool too, clenching his fists with fury and frustration until he suddenly unholstered his pistol, pointed it squarely at Scharroo's face and spat out, 'Fuck you, colonel! I am taking my men and we will do what is needed to defend our country and leave you here to sulk in your little sandpit!'

Everyone within earshot stood in suspended animation, shocked at this fraught altercation. The air crackled with menace as Von Frijtag Drabbe stormed from the room, boots clunking on the hardwood floor. It was not until they'd faded that breaths were taken, and the room returned to a more sedate hubbub. Scharroo retreated to the sanctuary of his side office, ordering several of his staff to follow. They emerged soon after, barking shrill orders for myself and several others to go outside and dig trenches around our headquarter's perimeter. Embarrassment at our supreme commander's petulant outburst was now obviously needing to be assuaged by having us perform, what under the circumstances, were nothing more than absurd, menial tasks. Moral fibre, strong resolve and intestinal fortitude seemed to have deserted our leadership like snakes fleeing a burning cane field, leaving those of us under their command badly exposed to the full ravages of the invading enemy.

Stepping outside into the mid-morning air, acrid smoke from relentlessly exploding ordnance assaulting our senses, it was immediately apparent that our mission to dig defensive trenches around our headquarters was not only futile, it was downright suicidal. Mortar grenades being fired from the Noordereiland across the river were whistling into the city, deadly shrapnel slicing through anything in their way. A hundred metres down the street, one detonated above some trees, stripping them of leaves and upper branches in one fell swoop, like birthday candles being blown out by the gods. There was precious little opportunity for digging as we threw ourselves flat onto the pavement or into doorways and porticoes each time an arrow of death came whistling our way. What the fuck were we doing here, lined up like ducks in a fairground shooting tent? No prizes for guessing that our ringmaster had lost the plot and was simply buying time to plan his escape from this rapidly crumbling scenario.

The cruelty of our predicament on the pavement must have piqued the conscience of at least someone amongst the officers, for we were at last ordered back inside. Sad to say no sanity had yet taken hold and pandemonium reigned in place of any order or discipline, like an asylum where the inmates have been left to their own devices. Desperation to appear decisive saw two other radio signallers and myself be ordered to take rifles and ammunition and make our way to the Maas Station, the railway terminal on the northern river bank not far from where the rail bridge entered the city, to join a detachment of marines dug in there keeping the rampaging Huns at bay.

It was by now mid-afternoon and the situation on the street was even more dire than before. The air clattered with the sharp retort of small-arms fire, interspersed with bursts of rattling machine-gun salvoes as we headed towards the river, hugging buildings and dodging the *tzing* of ricocheting bullets.

We entered the more open terrain beside the river and outside the station, trees all around disintegrating with mortar-fire shrapnel, eyes stinging with smoke and grit. We then suddenly realised that we were under fire, not only from across the river, but also from positions behind us in the city. We were caught in a deadly crossfire from which there was little protection. With the Maas Station dead ahead, there was no option but to sprint in a zig-zag pattern as fast as our adrenaline-fuelled legs could carry us, across the eighty metres or so of open space before diving headlong onto the floor of the station building. Miraculously, none of us took a hit. We made it in but were sure as hell not getting out in a hurry.

'Don't look now, men, but I think our reinforcements have arrived!' sniggered a marine sarcastically. Pointing to our rifles, he said, 'Did you fellows call into an antique store on the way here to arm yourselves?' Hearty laughter rang out as we picked ourselves up from what was admittedly a rather inelegant entry. A small contingent of marines clad in their distinctive dark blue overcoats were defending this eastern end of the station and had obviously provided cover fire for our desperate dash to safety in their midst.

'Well, thanks for your warm welcome,' I told them, 'but we're radio signallers from the Communications Unit, who, for reasons known only to our superiors, have been outfitted with M95 rifles instead of transmitting equipment and sent to join you here to see if we can be of service. It would seem that noble birth and upper-class distinction are no guarantee of intelligence and that when the shit hits the fan the high and mighty cannot be depended upon for knowing what the fuck they're doing.'

'Amen to that,' said the marine, obviously well acquainted with such sentiments. 'I know exactly where you're coming from.'

With the interdisciplinary ice broken, he gave me a rundown of the state of play at the station, punctuated by sporadic gunfire from his comrades and incoming rounds from across the river. He and about seventy marines had been roused from their barracks in the city at six that morning and ordered to reinforce the one sergeant and seven soldiers then guarding the Maas Bridges. The Germans were already occupying the Noordereiland, having landed on the river in floatplanes and had reached the southern end of the bridges shortly thereafter.

'The bastards got as far as setting up a machine-gun nest on this side of the railway bridge which we haven't yet been able to neutralise and about fifty of them are holed up over there in the National Insurance building directly opposite the entrance to the Willemsbrug. That and the constant firing from the Noordereiland across the river means we're pretty much pinned down here in the station. You lads were lucky to make it in unscathed. It's a pity though, that you haven't got any radio equipment with you instead of those useless rifles because our only communication with the outside world, the telephone lines, are out of action.'

The great vaulted roof covering the several tracks and platforms echoed with near constant gunfire as he spoke. 'There's about twenty of us holding the western end of the station and another group dug in on the riverbank. We've so far managed to stop the mongrels taking the bridges, but Christ knows for how long. You guys should make your way to the main waiting room where Lieutenant van der Krap, the only officer who didn't bugger off, has set up a command post of sorts and he'll soon put you to work. And keep your heads down if you don't want them blown off your shoulders.'

Situated off the main platform in a red brick building richly adorned with Art Deco tiles portraying Rotterdam's rail and river trade was a cavernous space where the wooden benches normally supporting waiting train passengers had been shoved aside to accommodate a stack of boxes and crates. It was mercifully out of any lines of fire, a welcome respite. A short, stout man of Indonesian complexion was sorting the pile into some semblance of order.

'Bloody hell,' he exclaimed as he noticed us enter the waiting room, 'those carnival sideshow rifles won't do you much good around here. You couldn't shoot a sick woman off a piss pot with those.' Quaint turn of phrase but I had to agree with him. 'I'm Douw van der Krap, lieutenant and captain of a river gun boat, the MS Balder, which is unfortunately in dry dock undergoing maintenance. This morning when I saw the German planes landing on the river, I ran down here and, finding no officers on deck, as it were, sort of took charge. These marines are all good men, well-trained fighters who know what they're doing. I've divided them into three groups, one each on the east and west sides of the station and another contingent on the riverbank directly opposite the Noordereiland. Seeing as you lads won't be of much use with those antique rifles, you can be runners between here and the marines, supplying ammunition and keeping me informed as to how they're coping. How does that sound?'

'No problem, sir. Seeing as we don't have any radio equipment we're happy to do whatever helps.'

Having given us a basic grounding in the types and calibers of ammunition the marines were using, we spent the rest of the afternoon dodging incoming rifle fire while ferrying fresh supplies to the guys on the front line.

Come nightfall, the fighting abated somewhat but the sky to the south of the city, out past the island, took on a sinister red glow as a result of the destruction wrought from battles that must have raged there throughout the day. Its reflection on the Maas water seemed to turn it into a river of blood. An ominous end to an apocalyptic day.

'I'm off to organise a couple of night patrols so the rest of the men can get some well-earned sleep,' said the lieutenant. 'You lads should bunk down here, wherever you can, just make sure it's under cover. I'll see you in the morning.'

The bunched-up benches against the far wall of the waiting room seemed the best bet. Being out of any line of possible fire but no wider than a church pew, they were at least above the unforgiving chill of the floor tiles. With my rolled-up army overcoat as a pillow, it was time to get horizontal and give the body up to gravity. What a fucking day! It almost felt as if I'd lived a lifetime. As soon as I'd dared let go, a fatigue uncoiled itself into my carcass like dye staining a beaker of water. And in that state between consciousness and the opium of sleep, thoughts became portents. The world we knew was gone. The fundamental principles that governed our lives no longer applied; suddenly, matters of life and death trumped manners and the rule of law. Why, not twenty-four hours ago, this station would have throbbed with the comings and goings of thousands of commuters, the tracks alive with the snorting and sneezing of multiple locomotives pulling convoys of carriages, and now … now, the eerie, empty cavernous silence only punctuated with the slashing cut of ricocheting bullets. Maybe by this time I was inured to their sound, maybe I was more tired than I realised, but sleep nevertheless descended and rendered me non compos mentis until morning.

The quarrelsome rattle of machine-gun fire startled me awake. My back rebelled when I attempted to move, and I almost toppled off the narrow wooden bench on which I'd slept. It took some moments for my rousing brain to get a handle on where the fuck I was. My mouth felt as if I'd been gargling sand while my eyelids strained to defeat the grit and gunk threatening to clamp them shut. I wanted coffee. This hankering was destined to not be fulfilled as reality began slapping me in the face. Just as well it did, because the short walk to the toilets further down the platform was no stroll through the tulips, as an alert German in the National Insurance building across from the station might appreciate some target practice in the early morning light.

The lieutenant was already up and about, taking stock of just how much ammunition was left. It was doubtful he'd even slept at all.

'Morning lads,' he said, watching us stir in the gathering gleam of sunlight. 'Munitions are holding up reasonably well, but what we don't have are rations and food supplies. This is a problem. There is no way we are going to get any, so I want you lot to go out and scour the station for anything that's edible or drinkable and drag it back here. Understood?'

'Yes, sir, we'll see what we can find.'

My posting to the Radio and Electrotechnical School had not afforded much time to explore Rotterdam and I had definitely never set foot in the Maas Station, so this exploration was starting from scratch. Disappointingly, there was no elegant, first-class dining room, such as ones I'd seen in larger stations, that may have been stocked with fresh and frozen food. This was a terminus for rail lines coming into Rotterdam from the outlying cities of Utrecht and Gouda. It was not a transit centre. Catering to such clientele, however, we found a snack bar and a clutch of vending machines amongst the tunnels connecting the various platforms, so we raided them. There were heaps of chocolate bars, packets of chips, some rapidly deteriorating packaged sandwiches and soft drinks, all of which we ferried back to the lieutenant's headquarters.

'No nasi goreng?' he asked sarcastically as he perused our booty. 'Oh well, it'll have to do if that's all we've got.' He set about rationing it out to make it stretch between all the men.

The difficult part was not knowing just how long we were going to be holed up inside this station.

Fighting dragged on relentlessly into the day in a kind of dangerous, dynamic stalemate; our marines kept the German troops confined to the southern approaches to the bridges and prevented those in the National Insurance building and on the Noordereiland from making any moves. Meanwhile, our own efforts to advance or attempt to blow up the bridges came to nothing because of the constant enemy fire directed at the station. There was likewise little chance of any reinforcements or supplies reaching us. We were just this ramshackle enclave of resistance intent on thwarting the Nazi desire to overrun our country, oblivious to the wider state of play because the army favoured using the telephone system to communicate and surprise surprise, the lines were down. We could have been the last line of defence left in the country; there was no way of knowing.

Early afternoon. I'd just schlepped a weighty strongbox of bullets and ammunition belts to the guys at the western end of the station when above the near constant clangour of small-arms fire suddenly rose the deep-throated burping of anti-aircraft artillery. Through the pock-marked sky above the river, three roaring, low-flying bombers were heading towards us. Our lads.

They were soon over the bridges, bomb bays open, disgorging lethal projectiles that whistled and exploded in deafening detonations not far from our position. Shock waves buffeted the air as we dived for cover from flying shrapnel. Thick, dirty smoke spread rapidly, stinking of gunpowder. The bombers swerved up into the sky, accelerated and disappeared, leaving us wondering what damage they might have inflicted.

Much to our chagrin, the clearing smoke revealed the hump-backed metal spans of the railway bridge and the rectangular cage of steel girders supporting the Willemsbrug to be intact and unscathed. How the hell had they missed them? A couple of direct hits would have totally stuffed the German advance, not to mention have taken the heat off us for a while. To make matters worse, the few bombs that hit the Noordereiland seemed to have landed in the residential section and not the German positions there. What a demoralising body blow.

There was no disguising the fact that the mood in the station was sagging and may possibly have sunk into a measure of despondency if not for the unflagging drive of the lieutenant to keep us on course.

'Yeah OK, that wasn't the result we wanted,' he berated us, 'so what. This is fucking war; you win some; you lose some. Get over it and get back to work, we're not done yet.' He was right; there was nothing to be done except stay the course. Aye aye, captain.

With night descending, he'd initiated a rotating roster of night patrols to guard the riverbank. Van der Krap had seen the Germans use inflatable rubber dinghies to reach the Noordereiland so there was every possibility they'd attempt to cross the river under the cover of darkness to infiltrate our position in the station. He called me over.

'I know your rifle is rubbish over any sort of distance, Henk,' he said, 'but at close quarters it might be of some use. I want you to join the night patrol going out to the river at two a.m. so try to get some shut-eye until then.'

Bunking down on my favourite back-breaking bench, I tried but failed to zone out into sleep. My stomach gurgled in protest at not having been fed, my brain leapt off at tangents like spit on a hot griddle and my beating heart did its best to pump warmth through to the extremities of my weary body. Before I knew it, I was being roused to join the night watch on the riverbank.

The Maas Station was situated on what was known as the Eastern Quay, a docking facility for foreign ships to disgorge and take on cargo trade. Its water's edge was built up some two or three metres above the river, depending on the tide and was separated from the station facade by a broad open roadway some twenty metres across. Directly across the water lay the eastern point of the Noordereiland. The marines who had been defending this side of the station had built a barricade of wagons, trolleys and even requisitioned motor lorries along the edge of the quay to afford cover from the incessant fusillade of enemy fire and as shelter for returning broadsides.

On this clear but moonless night, we scurried across the roadway as unobtrusively and silently as possible to relieve the crew who had been there since dusk. They were more than happy to see us and reported relatively little enemy activity during their shift but cautioned that the calm conditions on the river could be an incentive for the Germans to try something during the night. We thanked them and dug in.

After about an hour and a half, I thought I heard the sound of sloshing water unlike that of the river's normal cadence. It just sounded wrong. Alerting my compatriots, we strained an ear to the water only to discern muted, but distinctly German mutterings, as well as the rhythmic splashing of oars hitting water. Despite the night's gloom, a careful scan through binoculars exposed the presence of about six inflatable rubber dinghies with four men in each, steadily rowing towards our position on the riverbank. The sneaky bastards. Really, the only thing they had going for them was the element of surprise, now thwarted, as we were in a far superior position both defensively and offensively. Being well above them and behind good cover, we waited patiently until they drew within range. As soon as they were, we let them have it, a full barrage making every shot count. Even my own antique rifle added its sting. In the first salvo and before they could organise return fire, we managed to destroy four of the boats and several of their occupants. The other two dinghies turned tail and began to furiously paddle back from whence they came, trying at the same time to drag wounded soldiers onboard from the scuttled craft. We continued firing until both boats had slipped out of range. There was no repeat attempt during the remainder of our shift.

It was a long night peering out over the ink black waters of the Maas and I was glad to be relieved as dawn began cracking the sky. The Germans on the island vented their displeasure at having been shot at during the night by lobbing a couple of mortar grenades in our direction. Luckily the lorries under which we were sheltering took most of the brunt and before they could reload, a short, sharp sprint saw us back inside the station building. I never would have believed that a hard wooden bench could appear inviting, but in circumstances such as these, its unforgiving surface beckoned as if bedecked with eiderdown.

I must have nodded off and slept until well into the afternoon but snapped awake when a distant rumble in the sky crescendoed to the thundering peal of low-flying aircraft.

Shouted warnings rang through the station, 'Luftwaffe! Take cover!'

Seconds after they passed overhead, to the accompaniment

of machine-gun fire loosed from our lads on the quay, strings of detonations lacerated the air in percussive bursts that pounded our eardrums. Most of the damage was evidently done to the south of the city, where ugly black billows of smoke could be seen growing skywards, but behind our position, some buildings in the downtown area had also been hit and were on fire. From what we could make out it seemed one of them was the marines' headquarters. The stand-off here at the Maas bridges was obviously beginning to seriously piss off the Germans as at the same time frustrating the bejesus out of our own forces at not being able to move to destroy them.

The following day dawned with no resolution in sight. Tension was high but supplies were running decidedly low. I liked chocolate but having to survive on small quantities of it instead of, oh, I don't know, bacon and eggs, maybe a steak or even some chips with mayonnaise, was a cruel thing to do to a stomach in danger of forgetting what food felt like. And, to use a regrettable turn of phrase, I could have killed for a cup of coffee. At least our ammunition was holding out, for the moment. The lieutenant was doing an exemplary job of maintaining morale, flitting from post to post, spurring us on to keep fighting and not back down. Did that man ever sleep? It could not be denied, however, that many of us, myself included, were quietly wondering just how long we could hold out until events spiralled out of control and on to some inevitable and dreadful conclusion.

Around mid-morning, fierce fighting suddenly erupted around the northern approach to the Willemsbrug. Heavy fusillades were spewing from the German positions on the upper levels of the National Insurance building and from a machine-gun nest near the end of the railway bridge. Although there was no way of knowing, much yelling in Dutch seemed to suggest that other of our forces might be staging an attack on the bridgeheads. From behind the barricades on the western extremity of the Maas Station, we could do little more than direct fire onto those German strongholds, hoping to at least provide cover for whatever assault was taking place. After about an hour or so, however, the furious shooting eased to more sporadic salvoes, giving the impression that neither side had made any significant headway, that we were back to the same grim, dismal stand-off as before.

Another dangerous, uncomfortable night gave way to one more deadlocked morning. For four days now, we had been pinned down inside this cavernous hulk of a train station reverberating with the deadly din of ricocheting bullets, no food or drink, no communication with the outside world, the hope of any resolution in our favour dwindling as rapidly as the depleting stock of ammunition at our disposal. A sense of impending doom hung heavy in the air. The situation was not sustainable; something had to give.

Thirteen hundred hours. The sinister drone of aircraft engines approaching from the east began filling the air, growing in intensity moment by moment. These were distinctly not ours. The Netherlands did not possess that many planes and even if we did, they would not be flying in from that direction. Holy fuck! Not good! A white-hot shiver of alarm shot through me as if being suddenly confronted with my imminent demise, fully expecting to have the course of my young life flash before my eyes in that nanosecond of recognition signifying the end. The bombers were overhead, their cacophony now punctuated with the shrill whistling of plummeting projectiles as I snapped back to reality in time to witness the arched girders of the station's great span blow up and crumble like the caved-in ribcage of some momentous beast. The blast threw me to the ground under a shower of grit and shards. Dazed and deafened but not dead, I staggered to my feet to find I'd entered what seemed like some extra-sensory twilight zone, a realm with no sound but terrible fury, a parallel universe of malevolence so fierce that it negated all thought, substituting animal instinct for rationality.

Bombs do not drop individually; they're shat out of bomb bays in a diarrhoea of death that befouls great swathes of territory below. The line of detonations next hit a train abandoned on tracks leading into the station, lifting its snake-like string of carriages into the air before dumping it, broken and burning, crashing to the ground. I ran. I bolted as fast as my legs could carry me, not hearing, but buffeted by the percussion of relentless explosions ripping asunder the very fabric of reality. Buildings around me came apart in some satanic mime of destruction as the deadly deluge continued from above.

With the restoration of some hearing, a further level of hell insinuated itself as human howls of pain and terror pierced the unabated pandemonium of a city being wilfully blown apart. Body parts and blood flew through the air with the bricks, glass, smoke and debris of homes obliterated and lives no longer lived. As I was running, I saw it all but couldn't take it in; the images and perceptions were too painful and surreal to process. My brain filed them away to no doubt haunt my quietude for years to come. If I survived. And that was a very big 'if'. Flung to the ground by yet another fiery burst, my eyes were sandpapered with grit and smoke. I struggled to my feet, relieved they were still there and operational and blindly resumed running. A treadmill in Hades. I neither knew nor cared where I was headed, only some deep-rooted instinct for survival drove me on.

Bombs continued whistling to the ground, cratering the city scape and rendering entire neighbourhoods unrecognisable, as I zig-zagged dementedly through burning streets. At one stage, the inferno was so intense that the sleeves of my overcoat caught fire and I had to roll on the ground to extinguish them. Yet I ploughed on, eyes, nostrils and throat burning with the superheated fetid air, bereft of rational thought, for god knows how long until I somehow came to a small lake on the outskirts of the city. I splashed my face and felt the cool relief, a shocking sensation that rattled the remnants of my brain into the realisation that I was alive and had outrun the clutches of certain death by the slimmest of margins. Behind me Rotterdam lay burning, but, raising my head, I was staring into the barrels of guns pointed my way by a squad of German soldiers.

Like a rude awakening, they were suddenly everywhere, as if their merciless, ferocious levelling of the city had finally unblocked some stubborn stoppage of sewer and unleashed a backed-up tide of effluent to flood forth. After being thoroughly searched, I was prodded onto the canvas-covered back of one of their trucks to join the dozen or so Dutch soldiers already squatting there. Small talk was out of the question; these lads were as dazed and spent as I. We merely sat there, heads bowed, shoulders sagging, dejected in defeat, wondering how we'd survived and what further hell might now be in store.

The Germans drove us back into the city through swirling fogs of dust and thick smoke, over rubble-strewn streets and past bewildered, wailing civilians wondering what was left of their houses and lives. Fire brigades battled block-wide, raging infernos with all the effectiveness of drunks pissing on a forest fire, while Red Cross trucks were already carting cargoes of the dead out of the city. We passed German cars, motorcycles, various heavy vehicles transporting prisoners and bizarrely, German soldiers posing in front of flattened buildings, having their photos taken like battlefield tourists. Finally we halted outside a school in a part of town spared the worst of the destruction. Here we were herded into classrooms to join other captured Dutch military personnel. With the adrenaline, exhaustion and deprivation of the previous four days and nights still reeling through my body, I was relieved to notice that hammocks had been provided for us in which to kip. Luxury!

A quick scan of my fellow inmates revealed no familiar faces from the train station but to counter thoughts that they may not have survived the bombardment, I convinced myself that this was likely not the only location around the city housing prisoners of war. Suddenly, however, my peripheral vision snagged a pair of dark shapes slumped against the far wall of the classroom clad, if I was not mistaken, in the distinctive dark blue overcoats with double rows of bright metal buttons that distinguished the Royal Marine Corps. These guys were in some state. Their hands and faces were singed and sooted from having come through fire, neither were wearing trousers underneath their overcoats, one was only wearing one boot while the other's footwear appeared ready to disintegrate.

'You fellows look like shit,' I said by way of introduction.

'Yeah, well, have you checked yourself in a mirror,' came the reply. 'You're not exactly an oil painting yourself, you know.'

I guess he had a point, my own hands were covered in burns and the dried blood from various cuts and a cursory wipe of my face revealed thick cakings of dirt but a distinct lack of eyebrows or hair, only singed stubble.

When asked, they confirmed that they were indeed marines who had been part of an attempted assault on the northern approach to the Willemsbrug the previous day.

'Well that would account for the fierce firefight we heard from our positions in the railway station,' I told them.

'There was not much more we could do except provide covering fire.'

'It was a doomed operation from the start,' they lamented.

What had been left of the military's High Command in Rotterdam was apparently greatly concerned that a major German Pantzer Division was gathering strength on the southern extremities of the Maas bridges, so decided to unleash an infantry battalion onto the city side to either hold back the enemy or destroy the bridges, my new friends couldn't be sure. However, in a by now familiar story of incompetence and confusion, the unit tasked with leading this assault arrived late in Rotterdam, leaving the marine brigade, to which these lads belonged, to carry out the attack, despite the fact that they, too, had already been fighting for three days and nights along the riverbank west of the bridges.

'It was supposed to have been a pincer movement, with a similar force attacking from the eastern side, but the orders were vague at best,' they said.

No useful intelligence had been gathered and communications coordinating the onslaught were, due to reliance on the crippled telephone system, non-existent. As a result, the two flanks of the manoeuvre were not synchronized in any meaningful way, leaving these lads to attack with no fire support or reinforcement.

'It was a bloodbath. As we climbed the stairs from the river's edge to the roadway at the entrance to the Willemsbrug, the Germans in the National Insurance building opposite picked us off one by one until only the two of us were left alive. Miraculously, we found a manhole in the deck of the roadway that led into a tight crawlspace under the road. We slithered in and dragged ourselves along while the bullets ricocheted off the tarmac above us. Piet here, as you can see, had been shot in the arm, but we just laid low while the battle raged on above us.'

The quieter of the two men was indeed holding his arm where a tear in the sleeve of his dark overcoat revealed a weeping wound.

'What happened to you when the bombs began falling this afternoon?' I asked them.

'Well, after what seemed like endless hours cooped up in that metal coffin, when all hell broke loose above us, we decided we were not going to die inside a tin can and crawled out of the manhole to leap bodily off the bridge and into the river. We surfaced only to be met with sprays of machine-gun fire so we swam back under the cover of the bridge and dragged ourselves onto the bank.

'Having just ditched our sodden uniforms and wearing only our overcoats, we were abruptly arrested by a bunch of smug German bastards. They led us back onto the roadway in time to see Colonel Scharoo and a subordinate, who was carrying a white flag, hand themselves over to the German officers who'd finally crossed the bridge. We just stood there shivering with our hands in the air, witnessing the capitulation of our forces. That was it. That was the moment we lost the war. The German officer who seemed to be in charge marched over to us. For a fleeting second I thought he might shoot us, but he wanted to know just how many Dutch marines had held back the might of his conquering forces for four days and nights. When I told him how few, he shook his head in seeming disbelief and proclaimed us to have been *"Zwartze Duivels"*, or, "Black Devils", on account of the dark overcoats we wore. I thought I detected a begrudging note of respect.'

'Black Devils he reckoned hey, well they certainly put us through hell this afternoon, the callous bastards. That was a city of unarmed civilians they obliterated. They'll get no respect from me.' I was tired, and I was angry.

And hungry. Our captors brought round a large kettle of soup and a supply of tin cups. We were fed a greasy gruel that may or may not have had a previous acquaintance with vegetables, it was difficult to tell. At least it was warm and wet, but I couldn't help but think that if this slop was also what they fed their own troops, it was going to be a short war.

At around seven p.m. the Germans turned on a radio in time for us to hear a national broadcast from the Dutch commander-in-chief, wherever he was hiding, calling on all Dutch armed forces to destroy their weapons and surrender. Yeah well, a bit late to surrender seeing as how we'd already been taken prisoner. A fresh hell of occupation awaited but I was too drained for any further thought so slung myself into a hammock and surrendered my carcass to gravity, lullaby undulation and the morphia of sleep.

The following day dawned with the noxious, acrid smell

of smoke from a still-burning city heavy in the morning air. Conditions in the school where we were being held were spartan, but there was at least facility to splash my face awake. No coffee of course, but a few of the soldiers still had tobacco and were kind enough to let a bedraggled and bereft soul like myself roll himself one and as I sucked the sweet, blue-grey smoke deep into my already-singed lungs, I savoured that cigarette as if it were an opulent breakfast. It was clear from the temporary amenities that this school served only as a mustering station for rounded-up prisoners of war and that it wouldn't be long before we'd be herded onto trucks and trains to be taken to Germany where they could put us to work or worse. Not a fancied prospect.

Strolling the grounds, mingling with the other prisoners, it seemed the campus was not heavily guarded. Only a solitary German soldier was stationed at the school entrance. Manoeuvring slowly closer, I could see that he was just a young, probably conscripted soldier only recently thrown into battle. Taking a deep breath and with calculated nonchalance, I ambled over and asked in somewhat basic and broken German if I might be excused for one quick moment to duck out and buy some cigarettes. To my relieved surprise he answered in the affirmative, as long as I didn't go far and remained in his sights. No problem I said, I'll be right back. There was no way he could, or would dare, leave his post, so I sauntered down the street until the first corner, around which I suddenly darted and began running for my life, figuring young Heinz would sooner lose one prisoner than abandon his duty.

Being careful to avoid any German patrols, I made my way to the house of some friends which, I was pleased to see, had mercifully not been pulverised in the blitzkrieg of the day before and, briefly explaining my situation, asked if they would hide me.

'For sure Henk, come in off the street. My god, you look terrible, if the queen could see how you've treated your uniform, she'd have you court marshalled. A moot point, of course, seeing as how she's already buggered off to England.' My friend was possessed of a sardonic sense of humour as well as being not overly fond of the royal family.

'What do you mean she's pissed off across the Channel?' I asked.

'Yes indeed. Last week when we were being invaded, she was on the radio exhorting her loyal subjects to stay put and do our duty and that she and her government would do likewise, then two days later, off they all fucked to England. Anyway, never mind that now, let's get you cleaned up and the dear lady wife will rustle up some food.'

Bacon, eggs and coffee never tasted as good as they did that morning. I was starting to feel almost human after a bath and the change of clothes my friends supplied. A radio played nonstop, as it apparently had done since the previous Friday, these folks, like the rest of the population, struggling to come to terms with the reality of being thrust suddenly into a state of war and thirsty for reports of the latest developments. An announcement was broadcast that all of the armed forces in The Netherlands had capitulated, that documents to the effect had been signed that morning. It was stressed that only the armed forces had surrendered, not the country itself. Well, that was a blessed relief, except for the fact that the Germans were now here and our government and royal family not here, but in England.

My friend offered to bicycle past the school from which I'd escaped to see what was happening. He returned with the sombre news that all prisoners were being loaded onto German army trucks to be deported to parts unknown in the Third Reich. Christ! Skin of the teeth. The chilling realisation hit me that I'd now gone 'underground' and become a fugitive. I had no way of knowing it then, but this was only the first of several times in the months and years to come that I'd have to do so.

Jan was a lecturer at the N.E.H., the technical university where I had been teaching radio signalling, while his wife, Renee, worked in the operating theatres of Rotterdam Hospital as a specialist scrub nurse. The university was apparently no longer standing, but by some miracle, the hospital had come through the bombardment of the city intact and was now virtually overrun with thousands of maimed and injured citizens needing urgent medical attention. Renee had returned home just long enough to wash and eat before going back in for yet another gruelling shift tending to the hapless victims of the barbaric onslaught that had crippled an entire city. She told of the Red Cross struggling to construct makeshift morgues to handle the hundreds of bodies that were being pulled from the rubble. A catastrophic toll of human suffering. Jan sent her off with a thermos flask of hot soup to tide her over until morning.

When Renee had left, Jan poured us both a brandy and lit me a cigarette as we sat and talked, trying to make sense of how our lives had been so violently ripped from reality and into a tumult heavy with menace and foreboding. A bed had been readied for me with soft pillows and a warm blanket, but, try as I might, the slow-motion replay of recent terrors would not relinquish its grip on my brain, defying gravity's pull on my exhausted body.

THE BAKER'S SON

My hosts could not have been kinder. In the face of sudden enemy occupation, they shouldered the danger of sheltering a fugitive with grace and good cheer, nothing was a bother to them. I'd been in their home for five days, when on 21 May, the radio, now totally given over to German propaganda, broadcast an announcement to the effect that, Herr Hitler, having been supposedly impressed by the gallantry shown by our armed forces, had decreed that all Dutch soldiers were now to report to wherever their units had been on 9 May. I could show my face again!

Renee had done a fine job of washing and patching my uniform, bringing it almost up to parade ground inspection standard and I was much obliged to them both. We said our goodbyes as I headed into the city to search for my platoon. It had been a week since the bombardment and still fires raged through entire city blocks, the choking, smoke-filled air now featuring an added element, the unmistakeable and almost unbearable stench of death. It stung the nostrils like a punch in the face, leaving one gagging and fighting the urge to heave the contents of one's stomach onto the pavement. God knows how many Rotterdammers lay buried still and decomposing under the mountains of rubble that once constituted their neighbourhoods. The traumatised living were congregating in the few cleared areas and, having nowhere left to live, were busy building shelters out of salvaged timber, even furniture and tents provided by the Red Cross. German soldiers on the scene seemed incongruously cheerful, lolling about as if sightseeing or visiting a theme park, a sort of Rotterdammerung perhaps. The vain pricks loved to photograph themselves, showing off their Aryan bravado to the folks back home.

I was glad of the handkerchief Renee had given me, folding it on the diagonal and tying it to cover my nose and mouth gave some relief from the suffocating reek of smouldering ruins as I made my way to the Veemarkt where my unit had been headquartered.

It was gone. Not one brick remained on top of another, the entire building flattened beyond recognition. A disheartening search through the wasteland of a once thriving and bustling port city for remnants of my unit took up most of the day and was proving fruitless until I fell in conversation with a couple of other Dutch soldiers on a similar quest. They had heard talk of some military remnants taking refuge in undamaged precincts south of the city proper. I needed to go check it out.

The Willemsbrug and the Maas Railway Bridge stood intact, the bastard Krauts having been careful not to compromise their access routes into our country, preferring instead to lay waste the city's unarmed civilian population. Crossing over, as still more Germans drove north, I couldn't help but wonder the extent to which their invasion may have been sabotaged had we managed to blow these bridges early in the piece.

By mid-afternoon, I finally tracked down what remained of my unit, huddled in a church not far from the river. There was little joy in the reunion, we were basically a decimated, leaderless rabble trying to make sense of a surreal situation beyond our control. We were put to work helping clear some burnt-out parts of the city in a forlorn gesture of usefulness. It was like clearing a rockslide with a dessert spoon. Bulldozers, trucks and other heavy equipment were needed that just weren't there. It was a sad and futile pursuit that we play-acted for a couple of days until the order came to demobilise the Dutch army.

THE BAKER'S SON

We were dismissed. And just like that, after three years in uniform, I was out on the street, an ordinary burgher, an empty vessel, wondering what the hell had just happened and, more importantly now, what hell was yet to come.

CHAPTER 5

In winter, the boughs, trunks and denuded branches of the tall old trees lining both sides of the Stationstraat, the street where I lived in Waalwijk, my home town, seemed like they were standing guard, ready to defend the neighbourhood against unforeseen evil. But, coming on to summer, their green foliage transformed the thoroughfare, dappling the entire street in playful, filtered light. When I was a kid, I thought it was the perfect way to live in a forest and the best way to have the forest live in town. They never held a deeper allure than when I alighted the train that day in late May of 1940 and strolled under their caring canopy to my home at number 90.

Mother, stoic as always, almost shed a tear as she embraced her prodigal son. I had not been a prolific letter writer these past three years.

My father muttered, 'You could use a shave.'

I guess it was easier than telling me he loved me and was glad that I was alive. Over coffee I gave them a somewhat sanitised account of my recent tumultuous history; there was no need to share all the graphic details. They listened with quiet consideration. Mother then took out her little rectangular snuff box made from hollowed-out bone, snapped open the lid and, shooting a small pinch of the bitter brown tobacco powder up each one of her nostrils, sighed and began to fill me in on the changes the war had already wrought on our town's way of life.

'Ach, Hendrik,' she said. My name is Henk, only my mother calls me Hendrik. 'People are afraid, confused; they don't know what's going to happen. There aren't many Moffen [a derogatory term for Germans] stationed in the town as yet, but we regularly see platoons of them passing through. Just last week they demanded food from Andre van Hilst's shop and then stole six trucks that disappeared in the direction of Germany. The *Echo van het Zuiden* [the *Echo of the South*, our local newspaper] has to publish all their new regulations that are making life more and more difficult. Hans Vermeulen from around the back had to kill all his homing pigeons, the ones he's been raising and racing for years, in case he might use them to send secret messages to England.'

A stout, upstanding woman who never suffered fools gladly, Mother was succinct in her summation of the temperature of the town. 'A lot of people are unhinged, sort of lost and taking succour where they can. The churches are full every Sunday. The same for the cinemas, even though the English and French films are banned, and you can only watch German propaganda. For most folks, I think their fear makes them want to just keep their heads down and accept whatever is happening around them and out of their control.

'We've had to put our clocks forward by one hundred minutes so we'd line up with German Summer Time. Everything for

Germany! Beer is to be reserved for them; they want our horses; they want our shoes. We can't go out at night anymore; anyone caught gets fined. We have to make sure no light escapes from our windows at night so that the Tommies can't see us when they fly over. No streetlights shine anymore. There are patrols that make sure we are in the dark. Things will get worse before they get any better. Already the only way to get coffee and tea is by coupon. This is just the start, Hendrik. And of course,' she added, 'Those miserable bastards in the NSB are imagining their time of glory is at hand and are beginning to throw their insignificant weight around at every opportunity.'

Her last comment came as no surprise. The *Nationaal Socialistische Beweging* (the National Socialist Movement;, we just called them NSB'ers) had already been spruiking their lapdog admiration for all things Hitler since the early 1930's, publishing their rants in pamphlets and periodicals and strutting about in pseudo-military uniforms. Since they tried but failed to win any significant number of seats when elections were held in 1937, their hatred of 'Jews, Marxists, Masons, Jesuits and Traitors' took on a shrill tenor that bordered on hysteria. They were, in turn, hated by almost everybody. They were, in effect, pathetic Pecksniffs who'd probably grown up bent under the perceived slights of childhood and had, as a result, matured into adulthood rather paranoid, with accompanying delusions of superiority and a propensity for revenge. Here in Waalwijk they congregated regularly at cafe/bar De Roestelberg on the outskirts of town where they would presumably drown their sorrows, drink to future glory and plan their mighty ascension to power. Now that their hero Hitler had overrun our Fatherland, they felt their sap rising and their destinies becoming manifest.

THE BAKER'S SON

Even before I was called up into the army, I'd had a run in with one of their number, Piet de Bont, when I wanted to go out with his younger sister. He had ranted and raved that I was only a baker's son and certainly not worth her attention. She was a lovely girl, but the tension in her household over entertaining any amorous inclinations towards a lowlife such as I made things just too difficult, and our friendship faltered. People like him, though, are a sour lot and tend to hold grudges, as I was later to find out.

But for now I was home, dismissed from the army and armed only with my skills as a radio operator, skills for which there was distinctly not much call. My two younger brothers were already helping our father in the bakery and business there would be anything but booming for the foreseeable future, so, to say that I felt adrift on the sea of uncertainty that was the Occupation, would be somewhat of an understatement. I was, in fact, seething with anger towards the Aryan bastards now strutting our countryside, trampling on our sovereignty like it was some kind of weed.

Their arrogance was hard to stomach. Amongst other restrictions, they demanded all beer be reserved for them, the conquering heroes. A demeanour more condescending than ruthlessly intimidating, it has to be said, but irritating nonetheless. The popular illustrated magazines gracing our newsstands were picturing German soldiers sunning themselves, swimming and relaxing, the enemy as tourist, if you like. Such manufactured pap and propaganda certainly didn't wash with me. There was no forgetting the ferocity with which their compatriots had only very recently flattened an entire city, callously dispatching hundreds of Dutch citizens to the afterlife. Me nearly amongst them. A velvet glove over the iron fist. I was never going to be seduced by the false face of these 'Moffen'. My fellow townsfolk, by contrast, seemed merely inconvenienced and rather relieved at how benign war had seemed until then, thinking it was probably not going to be all that bad and hopefully not last long. Good luck with that.

Twenty-nine June was the birthday of Prins Bernhard, husband of Juliana, Queen Wilhelmina's only daughter. His real name was Bernhard von Lippe-Biesterfeld, a minor German royal who was, until his marriage to our country's heir apparent, a member of the Nazi Party, the cavalry SS and the SS motor corps. He was known as a profligate high-flyer with a taste for fast cars and fast money whose family fortunes were faltering, while Juliana, no ravishing beauty, it has to be said, had been proving difficult to unload onto a fitting suitor.

After what seemed nothing more than a marriage of convenience, in 1937 he'd been granted Dutch citizenship and the ego-enhancing right to be referred to as 'His Royal Highness'. He was a self-serving, not to be trusted turncoat, revelling in the enhanced notoriety, not to mention business opportunities, that membership of The Netherlands' royal family afforded him. There was a lot to dislike about him, not least of which was his ostentatious penchant to never be seen in public without a bloody great big, white, carnation pinned to his lapel.

My opinion was not a prevalent one. Most Nederlanders, a trusting lot, had blithely accepted the Prins's inveigling of himself into our royal family with remarkable tolerance and had now decided to mark the occasion of the royal consort-in-waiting's birthday with the spontaneous and widespread wearing of white carnations. Lapels and blouses suddenly sprouted the favoured blooms, while orange bunting and flags were unfurled all over the town and, it was reported, in many other regions of our occupied country, as a restrained up yours to the enemy and a not so discreet sign of solidarity with the House of Orange, our royal rulers. An outpouring of frustration at having been overrun by a foreign force, albeit one that had, up to that point in time, appeared relatively lenient. A power that was not to remain restrained for much longer.

The day became known in the press as 'Carnation Day', the first visible surfacing of resistance to the Third Reich. It was reported subsequently that it had coincided with a visit to The Netherlands from Joseph Goebbels, the German Minister for Propaganda, who had most likely come to see what might be plundered from our fair land. He'd apparently been so furious at this display of affection for our monarchy and love of Fatherland, that both Seyss-Inquart, the Reichskommisar for Occupied Netherlands and the SS and Police Chief Rauter were summoned to Germany to be hauled over the coals by Herr Hitler. They were demonstrably embarrassed, not to mention pissed off, at this indignation, to the point where they soon began to show other, more sinister sides to their personalities. The velvet glove came off. What some had termed the 'white bread weeks' of occupation were now consigned to history.

Almost immediately, a slew of new edicts and decrees suppurated from the open wounds of their lacerated egos. References to the Dutch royal family in the monikers of buildings, organisations, institutions, clubs, streets etc., were to be excised post-haste upon pain of swift and decisive retaliation from our Aryan overlords. Any mention of royal doings were proscribed in the press. They were, in fact, to restrict their coverage of events in our land to only those which shed positive light on the wonders of the Third Reich. The General Dutch Press Office (the *Algemeen Nederlands Persbureau* or ANP) began to be referred to by irreverent burghers as 'Adolph's Newest Parrot', a sad indictment on the truth of the situation. Our libraries were ordered to purge their inventory of any literature deemed detrimental to, or in any way critical of, Nazi ideals. This is the way of totalitarianism, control of all information and the elimination of all contrary voices. If you asked me, having failed in their attempt to annex and align The Netherlands to the National Socialist dogmas of their own country, the Moffen were now turning nasty, showing at last their true colours and beginning to tighten the thumbscrews on a population less pliant than they'd presumed. I'd seen what they were capable of right from the start; no savagery or cruelty was too much when they didn't get their way.

We belligerently referred to Reichskommisar Seyss-Inquart as *zes en een quart* (six and a quarter). He had confected an image of himself as the concerned conqueror when he had very publicly visited Dutch as well as German war wounded. But he now mutated into the ice-cold psychopathically brutal and bloodthirsty pig he had probably always been. He saw red, but what he didn't want to see was orange, the House of Orange, to be precise. He promptly banned anyone from listening to Radio Orange, the voice of our government in England, or in fact, any broadcast emanating from the BBC. How he was going to prevent anyone turning on their wireless sets wasn't made clear, really the only way would be to confiscate all radios, an idea that had not yet occurred to them.

Fresh directives spewed forth to further restrict and punish our day-to-day existence. Horses had to be handed over to the Moffen; bicycles were not to be ridden more than thirty kilometres from home; civilian cars were not to be driven at all. The Sicherheitspolizei and SS Chief Rauter took control of all police forces, an action which left our constabulary deeply conflicted and compromised, now having to decide whether to continue to serve the townsfolk or do the enemy's bidding. Likewise, local town mayors would now be overseen by the Moffen, which led in some instances to the installation of puppet NSB'ers to the post. Fortunately in Waalwijk that was not the case, our mayor, Mr. Moonen, an ex-army officer, was allowed to retain his position. Some considered him too authoritarian, but to me he came across as a fair-minded and grounded man who had the community's wellbeing at heart, traits that would be sorely tested in his dealings with such a devious foe as the Moffen.

Plunder and control had obviously been the driving forces behind most of the regulations enacted so far, but a proclamation printed in the *Echo of the South* newspaper in early July hinted at a hidden agenda not yet articulated. All non-Aryan foreigners living in Waalwijk who had left Germany between 1933 and 1938 had eight days to register at the police station with their passports and identity papers. This could only be directed at local Jews who had fled the anti-Semitic rhetoric of the burgeoning Nazi regime as they assumed power. We had welcomed them into the community. Living alongside Jews wasn't a big deal; we never gave it a second thought. This new decree had the stink of depravity about it and did not augur well for the future.

One of my closest friends besides Tom Brokken was, in fact, a Jewish lad named Herman Nasch who worked in a leather factory named De Amstel where his father was one of the directors. We three would meet regularly in the Hotel Royal where, over a few sugared brandies, the ramifications of the rapidly evolving state of the Occupation would inevitably be the prime topic of conversation. It was clear that the sequence of recent events had now conspired to force all citizens into adopting one of three stances. Remaining on the sideline was no longer an option.

One course of action was to just go with the flow, keep your head down and above all, don't rock the boat. This seemed the preference of most Nederlanders, a trusting and mostly accommodating folk.

A second possibility was collaboration, luckily only adopted by a relative soulless few, in our town mostly represented by the arse-licking, grovelling German lovers, the NSB.

And finally, resistance: the conviction that the occupying Huns were to be thwarted and fought with every possible means, be they symbolic, defensive, active or even armed. We instinctively gravitated towards the third option.

Our ruling class had already buggered off and were clearly not to be trusted, so it was obvious that we had to do this ourselves; not for the patriotic defence of Fatherland, but for our own survival. There were no immediate plans to organise any subversive activities; we would just remain open to possibilities of protest as they arose. Open and alert, because times were now changing at an alarming rate, and there was no room for complacency.

Herman's situation being a case in point. His family's shoe and leather business had been grappling with some seriously conflicting issues. There had been orders placed across the

Waalwijk leather industries for the delivery of one hundred thousand pairs of boots, a deal that represented a substantial boost to their bottom lines. The spanner in the works was that those boots were destined for the German Wehrmacht. On the one hand a major kick along for the local economy but one that could also be construed as a collaboration with the enemy. A serious moral and financial dilemma. And speaking of finance, Herman revealed that agents for the enemy had already twice made overtures to buy the family firm. Suspect German company representatives had approached Herman's father with belligerent demands to take over the business. 'You are going to lose your business anyway, so why not sell it to us cheaply and we will ensure it is repatriated to you after the war' was their sales pitch. It was rejected out of hand, of course, but left a bitter taste in the mouth, a sinister omen of German intent towards Jewish businesses, not to mention the Jewish people themselves.

With various such dark clouds besmirching our firmament, it was understandable that folks in town were rather looking forward to letting their hair down at the upcoming annual distraction that was our Town Fair, what we called 'Kermis'. In those years, the concept of taking actual vacations was, for workers in Waalwijk, an alien one. It simply did not exist. In its stead, once a year, usually late in July, all factories would close their doors for one whole week and townsfolk would flock to the cafes and dancehalls for nights of uninhibited revelry. A much-needed letting off of steam from the rigours of factory life.

During the day, families would partake of all the fun of the fair on the rides and attractions that had been set up in the town square. But now, in the altered universe of the Occupation, it seemed we were to be denied this much anticipated outlet for our frustrations because the provincial commissioner had deemed it inappropriate, given the circumstance of there being a war on. As might be expected, voices of protest were raised in the Town Council, arguing that precisely due to the vexations being suffered by the citizenry, the holding of Kermis would represent a much-needed boost in morale. Mayor Moonen appeared sympathetic and agreed to parley with the commissioner with a view to rescind the ban on Kermis.

His powers of persuasion had apparently proven equal to the task because the local newspaper, *The Echo of the South*, reported the mayor announcing that a modified Kermis would indeed be held from the fourteenth to the twentieth of July. 'Modified' in that the usual rides and attractions would this year not be present in the town square, but extended opening hours would be allowed in the cafes and dancehalls, provided they not overly transgress the blackout regulations. The *Echo* added its own editorial, urging the populace to remain calm, behave with decorum and above all, refrain from overtly political discussion. Yeah right. Besides banter concerning the fairer sex, political discourse was the main staple when Tom, Herman and I sat down with our *borreltjes*, a custom we were not in any hurry to curtail.

Curfew and blackout regulations meant that a repeat of the cabaret evening Tom and I had previously put together was out of the question. Still, with Kermis there was nothing stopping us from dragging instruments down to the Hotel Royal in order to amuse ourselves and perhaps entertain the other punters.

Whether it was the booze or the momentary release from having to put up with all the shit that the occupation forced on us, or a combination of the two, I couldn't say, but the place soon filled with raucous singing and laughing. Pop tunes of the day were given a spirited workout, followed by good old drinking songs as the alcohol flowed, until some half-pissed patron launched into a stirring rendition of our national anthem, 'Het Wilhelmus'. It started off in reverent tones befitting such a seriously nationalistic air, but Tom and I kicked it up a couple of gears until it swung like a well-oiled gate, with everyone singing along and dancing as if it was the latest hit from Duke Ellington. Man it felt good. Everyone was smiling and grinning like the drunken fools we were, except for that miserable NSB'er Piet de Bont, sitting in a far corner, whose eyes seemed to say, 'Brother, I'll get you somehow'.

Kermis came and went without any major disturbances, just a few revellers fined for staggering home drunk after curfew. The people who still had jobs went back to work. Tom came by later that week clutching a copy of *De Echo*.

'Henk, get a load of this!' he exclaimed, folding the paper over to the page that published letters to the editor. He pointed out a missive credited to our old pal, de Bont, who had apparently been highly offended by the way some *'two-bit musicians and their drunken hangers-on in one of the town's less than salubrious saloons'* had so desecrated the National Anthem as to render him ashamed and embarrassed. '*It was only due to the generosity and benevolence of the Third Reich that we were given the freedom to hold Kermis in the first place,*' he thundered, '*and that freedom must be earned, not by bespoiling our beautiful "Wilhelmus" in some den of iniquity!*'

'Can you believe this guy?' said Tom incredulously. 'Who does he think he is?'

'He's a low-life would-be if he could-be suckhole to the

Germans,' I ventured. 'I reckon I might have to draft a letter of reply to the snivelling little gobshite.'

Three days later, my riposte reached the letters page.

Dear stuffed shirt, grovelling German lover, I wrote, *If you cannot stomach a spontaneous welling up of national pride in the form of a spirited singing of 'Het Wilhelmus' in a public house, then perhaps you'd best be crawling back into whatever little hole you and your sour lot call home. In the meantime, may I wish you back itch and arms too short to scratch it.*

Not particularly withering, but our little exchange did have the effect of shaking loose a more widespread hostility to the sell-out sentiments of Meneer de Bont and his band of quislings, evidenced in further letters to the editor questioning their loyalties.

Newspaper publishers are known to sometimes court controversy as a way of inducing emotional responses in their readers, resulting in wider sales. The more mercenary amongst them may even be guilty at times of confecting differences of opinion for purely profit motives. The editor of *De Echo* was not one of those. He made it clear in print, that however much the NSB pressured him to publish their pap as news, he considered it nothing more than treasonous propaganda and would not be dignifying it with any column inches while he was in charge. This sent them off in a spiteful, vindictive huff from whence they resolved to take matters into their own hands.

Before long, the NSB began printing and distributing on the streets of the town, braying, bellicose pamphlets of rampant admiration for all things German and paranoid, deep-seated disdain for anything *De Echo* might deem to publish. It became impossible to negotiate the sidewalks without a wad of their handbills being thrust rudely into one's clutches, resulting in quite a littering problem as folks merely scrunched them into a ball and sent them flinging to the gutter.

They weren't making many friends. As a matter of fact, their antics had the opposite effect of turning people against them, and of convincing townsfolk the NSB were nothing more than traitors to their country. We wanted nothing to do with them. So when three eminent gentlemen in The Hague announced the formation of a 'movement' which would be distinctly not a political party but an attempt to unite national sentiment for social justice and a renewed push for a fairer Fatherland, a lot of people took notice. Their stance seemed antagonistic not only towards the NSB, but also against the stifling class and religious constraints that had poisoned our society for far too long. Their organisation was called 'De Unie' or 'The Union' and I liked the fact that they seemed to forego any empty patriotic invoking of the royal family or our government in exile. As far as I could see, they operated outside the influence of any of the established political parties. The question was, how long would our Nazi conquerors allow them oxygen. Not mentioning the House of Orange obviously let them off the hook for a while, but their insistence on pamphleteering on the streets of Waalwijk drew them into direct conflict with the NSB goons' handbill territories. It was not a pretty sight, even if entertaining in a way. Name-calling would inevitably deteriorate into fisticuffs after which the local constabulary, and luckily not the Gestapo, would be forced to step in and restore order. The warring factions were ordered forthwith to maintain a distance of three hundred metres on their sidewalk positions. As if there were no more pressing battles to confront.

Like the humourless jellyfish they were, a plan was soon concocted at the Roestelberg Cafe to nocturnally paste the walls of the town with posters of their preposterous pontifications. And so we woke to find walls and hoardings besplattered with glued-on manifestoes and hoarse harangues about the need for the population to succumb to the inevitable advance of National-Socialist superiority and control. Such vandalism, of course, served only to intensify the hatred we felt for these betrayers of our country. *De Echo* weighed in with an editorial, lambasting these pasters of posters and lamenting the fact that they had disturbed the traditional peace of a work-free Sunday with people now having to scrape and peel the offending placards from walls and fences.

The paper itself was, of course, not permitted to print any actual news regarding the course of the war or, especially, the actions of the royal family or our government in England. It had to restrict itself to publishing the new regulations and protocols demanded by the Occupation, notifying which goods were available by coupon, for example, but its editor could not resist the kind of anti-NSB comment which managed to, predictably, inflame that rabble into waging an ongoing vendetta against its owner.

Mother had little time for what she called 'that fiddle faddle', and so was apt to take no interest in reading the local rag. However the ramifications were that one time she missed the published date of when butter would be available on the coupon and as a result had to go twenty-four days without it. Mother loved her butter. The reality of the distribution was that goods were becoming scarce and the staples of life rigidly rationed. Already bread, flour, coffee, tea, shoes, butter, margarine and

THE BAKER'S SON

lard could only be procured on the coupon. Soon would be added soap, meat, eggs and cheese. This was proving a genuine hardship for households as, usually the mother, struggled to keep up with distribution times in order to keep food on the table. This made the distribution card about the most important document in the house.

I told Mother that I would go to the distribution office to try to wrangle access to some butter outside of the given date.

By chance, the director, Arnold Verwiel, was manning the front counter.

'You're Peer Van Iersel's son, aren't you?' he asked.

'Yes, sir, I am indeed.'

And we got talking. He knew that I'd been in the army and asked me what position I'd held. When I told him that I'd been a sergeant in the Signal Corps, he offered me a job as clerk on the spot, saying that he was finding it difficult to recruit suitably qualified personnel to cope with the rapidly expanding distribution duties. I gladly accepted the position, happy to have something meaningful to do and pleased to perhaps line my pockets with some welcome cash. My job was to be a travelling collector of ration cards from the villages surrounding Waalwijk and to distribute to them, by bicycle, the coupons their people would need. This suited me fine. Getting out into the countryside was infinitely preferable to being tethered to a desk in some office. So I returned to my mother butterless but employed, a situation she knew was for the best. There was, however, no way she could have foreseen how this job at the distribution office would, in time, conspire to alter the course of my life.

CHAPTER 6

The pillowy eiderdown of freshly fallen snowflakes smothering the polders in virginal white was almost enough to make one think the world was new again, clean, unsullied and unmolested. This was until the eyes strayed further, to the mangled, jutting joists and girders of the blown-up bridge lying half submerged in the icy waters of the river Maas. It was bloody cold, my exhaling breath swirled like smoke in the sharp, keen air. The rhythmic pumping of the pedals on my bicycle, though, kept the blood pulsing and the muscles warm, affording time, on these trips to the outlying villages, to reflect on the rapidly evolving course of the war and my place in it.

A lot had happened. Since September, Waalwijk had had to suffer the poisoned privilege of hosting an entire Infantry Division of jackbooted German troopers catching their breath from subjugating the hapless French army and trampling Belgium underfoot. They'd insinuated themselves into the town with all the subtlety of a fertiliser cart crashing into a beauty salon. Four or five months of heavy fighting had stripped them of whatever decorum they may previously have exhibited as happy-snapping enemy tourists, to the point where they were now arrogant, pugnacious, often drunk and in our face. They could not be avoided. The nighttime curfew obviously did not apply to them as we would hear them staggering drunkenly past our house at all hours, yodelling out of tune versions of all manner of Germanic Liederen and splintering random windows like the uncouth vandals they were.

And what really pissed us off was that while food and the necessities of life were becoming prohibitively expensive or impossible to procure for us, the occupying Huns were swimming in coupons and so well provided for that they were sending food parcels (of our food) back home to the folks in Germany. Goose-stepping goons with too much money, too much time and too few manners. The feeling of impotence at having no avenue of reprisal gnawed at my marrow like some rodent pest, strengthening my resolve to stay alert for possibilities of resistance, for means of sabotaging these bastard foreign interlopers.

Annoying as it was to have to endure the thuggery and boorish behaviour of the rank-and-file German troops stationed in the town, of greater concern was the increasingly sinister tone of the decrees that emanated from their superiors. We didn't know it at the time, but Reichskommissar Seys-Inquart was a Jew-hating Austrian who had already made quite a name for himself as the savage persecutor of communists, intellectuals and Jews in Poland. His fanaticism, still somewhat restrained, was beginning to be incrementally unleashed on our Jewish population.

In September he'd ordered all Jewish public servants to register at the Town Hall and declare the names of their parents and grandparents as well as full details of their income and assets. The true intent of that edict became clear in October, when those who had complied were summarily sacked, rounded up and transported to work camps in Germany. Waves of shock and disbelief washed through the community to see neighbours we had grown up with and worked alongside prodded onto the back of trucks at gunpoint clutching only meagre belongings and being driven away. It was a sight that sent a sobering and disturbing chill through my bones like an early onset frost foreshadowing a winter that would be anything but mild.

The joy was sucked right out of this year's Christmas season. Of course the churches would be packed on Christmas Day, filled not so much with rejoicing as fervent prayers for the war to end. Our usual outdoor celebrations of the feast of Saint Nicholas and New Year's Eve came and went with most everyone staying home where it was warm, relatively safe and where we didn't have to interact with those detestable Moffen lousy about the town. We seemed to have ended the year stranded on some malevolent planet that bore little resemblance to our old benign one, robbing us of the comfort of certainty and the solace of familiarity. Our moral compasses would struggle to show true north in the face of such dissociation. Perilous headwinds buffeted our transit into the new year.

The slow, unrelenting crackdown on our Jewish friends and neighbours showed no signs of subsiding. Already in January the town's two cinemas, continuing to do a roaring trade despite the meagre filmic fare on offer, testimony to the great need of folks for mindless diversion, were ordered to no longer admit Jews.

No big loss, according to my friend Herman. 'Who would

want to pay to watch Nazi propaganda dressed up as entertainment anyway?' he said.

What did trouble him deeply, however, was the proclamation, in February, for all Jewish people to register at the Town Hall where their identity cards would be stamped with a prominent, white 'J' on a black background square. This was a move designed to keep track of the whereabouts and movement of all Jewish people in our country. Tom and I discussed with him the possibility, that if the shit hit the fan and the Germans began rounding up Jews for deportation, we could smuggle Herman out of town and find a sympathetic farmer in some outlying district who might be willing to hide him. With a not totally convincing laugh, Herman told us his father was keeping a close ear to the ground and had a plan, should the situation become too dangerous, of sending him away to stay with family friends. We knew that his father was well connected so we let things be for the time being.

'Ja, from me they can go burst themselves!' vented Mother as she slammed her coffee cup to the table with the authority of a judge pounding his gavel. She had just heard the broadcast of the new German demand for all copper, bronze, silver and gold coins to be handed in to them. Not content with the mere occupation of our land, it seemed they were now beginning to turn their attention to appropriating anything of benefit to the Third Reich. We weren't particularly overburdened with valuable currency, but Mother took what we had and stashed it where only she could find it. That this latest ordinance was not met with universal compliance would be an understatement. Folks hid their coins, hoarded them, anything to avoid handing them over to those greedy, mongrel Huns. One resourceful fellow we knew, melted down his gold coins to fashion into a cigarette case. Mrs de Jager from down the street was reported to the local constabulary by a friendly neighbourhood NSB'er for wearing one of her gold coins as jewellery and not only had it confiscated but was fined into the bargain. Such vindictive and puerile dobbing in of their fellow citizens to the Germans, not to mention their persistent pamphleteering and poster-daubing, pissed us off no end and got so up the noses of some locals that retaliation in the form of whitewashed swastikas and anti-NSB slogans began appearing on doors, walls and pavements near their haunts. Juvenile antics to be sure, but they betrayed an awakening level of civil disobedience, of a subtle shift from reticence to action. The NSB in turn, ran crying to the police, the mayor and, of course, the Moffen. Their shrill bleating at being hard done by and ignored by *The Echo of the South* newspaper annoyed just about everybody, even the Germans who, probably to shut them up, ordered *The Echo*'s editor to henceforth publish their drivel.

Whether it was the oxygen of subversion or the smell of lime in the whitewash, I couldn't say, but our nocturnal brush wielders soon began extending their repertoire to include massive white 'V's painted liberally about the town on hoardings, walls and roads. Of late, the BBC had been belligerently broadcasting a recurrent 'V' for 'Victory' signal across the airwaves, pumping out the morse code equivalent, three dots and a dash, coincidentally the first four notes of Beethoven's famous fifth symphony, inspiring our whitewashers to follow suit in their chosen medium. Heady with success and giddy with the rush of their seditious splattering, they soon expanded their range to include the letters 'OZO', which stood for *Oranje Zal Overkomen*. 'The

House of Orange (our royals) Shall Overcome'. All good and well, but such patriotic vandalism soon had the town centre looking like it had been shat upon by a flock of incontinent storks. The easily offended enemy countered by stringing up banners spruiking their own version of 'V', something like 'Ve Vill Win, Ja!', which it didn't take locals long to deface.

Kermis was again allowed in 1941, although without the traditional rides and attractions in the town square, only some relaxed opening hours in the cafes. But there was just no mood to celebrate; after more than a year of enemy occupation, not many people could muster the enthusiasm to let their hair down. Life was tough, money tight and the deprivations slowly sapping the community's spirit. Even though Tom and I still played music from time to time to amuse ourselves, there was no question of taking instruments down to the pub for a sing-along. It was going to take more than summer's clement weather to evaporate the pall of despondency that lay on the town like a suffocating doona.

A fresh wave of defiant daubing accompanied what would have been, in normal times, the celebration of Queen Wilhelmina's birthday on 31 August. Brazen exhortations to 'Get rid of the Germans' and 'Ditch the NSB' accompanied the more tried and tested 'V's and 'OZO's on fences, sides of buildings and sidewalks, while orange flowers and badges blossomed on many a truculent lapel. The onset of autumn, however, saw cold realities begin to blow across the landscape, with hopes of better times tumbling like the dying leaves now flittering to the ground.

Herman came to visit. His usually upbeat demeanour seemed to have deserted him as he revealed that his father was sending him to stay with some trusted friends in Tilburg.

'I don't really want to go, but things are becoming just too dangerous for us Jews. He wants me out of sight and somewhere safe.' He went on to explain that his father's company had been ordered to accept a German overseer, what they called a 'Truehander', who was, in fact, a representative of a German firm preparing to just blatantly purloin the entire enterprise.

'And when that happens, anyone Jewish in the company will likely be carted off to some dismal work camp in Germany.'

The air crackled with foreboding and unspoken emotion as we hugged and said our goodbyes, vowing to keep in touch, despite being aware that the odds of doing so would be slim indeed. Watching him walk away, I seriously wondered whether I'd see Herman again. The gross injustice being perpetrated on Jewish friends and neighbours rankled deeply, firing up a powerless wrath for which I was at some stage going to have to find an outlet lest it devour my psyche. There was now no disguising the true intent of the Nazis; if our land could not be persuaded to seamlessly meld into their doctrine of National Socialism, it would simply be ransacked, plundered and emptied of Jews. And they would brook no opposition.

In September, thanks to the incessant whining and bleating of complaint from the NSB, *The Echo of the South* was forced to silence its printing presses, stranding us yet further out from any anchorage of trusted information. They had already been heavily compromised in their reporting but had still managed to consistently provide a familiar, local voice. Yet another page out of the totalitarian handbook; muzzle all sources of information bar the ones you control.

'De Unie' was likewise shut down and disbanded as being too anti-Nazi and anti-NSB, along with all other unions, committees, organisations and societies, whatever their affiliations. Even the Boy Scouts were deemed too British an organisation and had to strike camp and go home. Only the NSB was permitted to exist, an exemption that puffed up their pathetic egos, but served only to alienate them further from the rest of the population. We hated the bastards.

In October we got word that the German firm that had so threatened Herman's father's business had been duly appointed as its new proprietor. The entire enterprise was stolen from underneath the rightful owners simply because these were of Jewish extraction and Germans held the reins of power. The bitter injustice of it was galling. It was not to be, of course, the end of the matter. All Jewish employees, including the directors, were summarily sacked in December and, manifesting what had been Herman's deepest fear, deported in January by train to work camps in Germany. At the time, no-one could have imagined what that entailed. No rational human being could have conceived of the barbarous, downright diabolical plans then being hatched by the Third Reich to literally eradicate all Jewry from the face of the earth. We were just appalled at the treatment meted out to folks we had long considered our equals, our neighbours, part of the fabric of our society. It felt very much like an attack on us all, you crucify my brother then you crucify me. More and more, seeds of defiance grew amongst fair-minded people; we will do what is right, not what we are commanded.

Winter set in, and it was a savage one. Deep snow fell early in the season and bedecked our burgh like an oppressive kindness. Hoary frost whiskered those foolish enough to venture out. Severe shortages of food, materials and fuel for heating were now a fact of life, on account of it all being requisitioned to Germany. At the Distribution Office we would daily hear tales of woe from folks genuinely struggling to get by. The upheaval in the factories being taken over by German firms had already resulted in fewer jobs and plummeting wages. What few goods not on the coupon were heinously expensive and thus unaffordable for just about everybody. We could only refer those people in desperate need to the soup kitchens set up in town by some public-spirited citizens. I was fortunate that on my official rounds to the outlying villages, it was possible to transact a little meat and some vegetables from friendly farmers to take home to a grateful Mother.

It is often said of the Dutch that we are a resourceful lot, methodical and efficient, but our arrogance can sometimes leave us blind to possible adverse outcomes of our innovation. From the beginning of January, everyone over the age of fifteen had been commanded to carry their identity card with them at all times. So now it meant that if you were Jewish or on the wrong side of German benevolence, it would be that much harder to escape their scrutiny. The SS had settled on this particular identification certificate because of how difficult it was to counterfeit. And they had been designed by two Dutch government officials so fucking pleased with themselves that any untoward implications of their work seemed to have completely escaped their conscience. Good old Dutch ingenuity.

Such naive dutifulness was again in evidence when in May, civil servants in the council were ordered to compile a list from the county records of all Jewish citizens in the town, a task they performed with alacrity and alarming attention to detail. I could not get my head around the fact that a person could so conscientiously comply with such suspect orders and not for one minute consider the consequences of their actions. That attitude of 'I'm only doing my job; the fact that it will result in people being carted off to die has nothing to do with me' stuck in my craw like a sideways fishbone. It was just such a monumental cop-out, such a lame, cowardly excuse.

No-one, not even the most naive and clueless municipal pen pushers, could have missed the gist of the latest humiliation of our Jewish friends when the SS and Polizei Chief Rauter let it be known that henceforth, all Jewish people were to wear the Star of David stitched prominently on their clothing. This then was the Nazi intent all along: degrade the Jews, demonise them, isolate them and finally, neutralise them, which in this case meant deportation. After they'd been robbed of all their earthly possessions, of course.

The expulsion of Jews on the council lists that had been so meticulously provided to the SS began in early July. It sent shockwaves of trepidation shuddering through our communities nationwide. Surely something could be done. Both the Catholic and Protestant Church hierarchies sent stern letters of protest to Seys-Inquart and Rauter which were then read out from the pulpits in their respective houses of worship. The SS, in turn, maintained the lie that these Jewish folk, which in truth, they actually considered to be 'undermenschen', or 'less than human' were only being sent to work camps, when the reality was that a range of extermination facilities had been built and readied for their arrival. Auschwitz I, Auschwitz II, Birkenau, Sobibor, Treblinka, Madjenek; these names have come to represent humanity's darkest depravity. These camps were already in operation, a fact we had no way of knowing when the trains with their sad cargo began rolling out of Westerbork, a town in the north-east of The Netherlands, the main marshalling depot for Dutch Jews being deported to Germany.

But of course, such matters never have quite as much impact as when they come knocking on one's door and forcing their way in. Simon Horschfeldt was the workshop foreman at the metal manufacturing business of Tom's father. He was a single man, a few years older than Tom and myself, who had become a close personal friend of the family. He was also a Jew listed on the municipal roll to be deported. It couldn't be allowed to happen. Tom explained that his father had submitted a deposition to the SS authorities in s'Hertogenbosch, our nearest city, elucidating the fact that Simon was an indispensable member of staff in a business vital to the German war effort, and as such should be excused from deportation. The answer shot back was curt and unambiguous; if you can't run your business without this man, we will come and run it for you.

With no room for further negotiations, it became clear to Tom and me that Simon's only option was to disappear, vamoose, go into hiding. Some of the more isolated farmers I'd met on my rounds for the Distribution Office had been most kind-hearted in sharing some of their fresh produce and I wondered if they might now be persuaded to secrete a Jewish fugitive on their property. It was worth a try. We were in no doubt that it would be a hard sell; please hide this person of a religious persuasion other than your own, upon pain of death to you and your family should they be found out, for no other benefit than the feeling of doing good. We cycled out to investigate the possibility.

One of the first farms we visited was owned by a stout, tall, hardworking man named Cornelis van Erp. Over coffee we explained the reason for our visit. He listened quietly, then told us his story. His wife Els and he had six children, the second oldest of which, a son name Hans, had his mind set on becoming a police officer rather than take on an active role in running the farm. Cornelis and his wife had reluctantly acceded to his wish and Hans had gone off to do the necessary training. After graduating as a constable, he had been posted to the main police station in Rotterdam. Cornelis showed us the photo of a proud young man looking dapper indeed in his police uniform.

On 14 May in 1940, he'd been on active duty in the city when the hell on earth that was the German bombardment levelled the town centre. His body had been found under the rubble of a blown-apart building. Apparently he'd been attempting to shepherd a group of women and children to what he'd hoped was safety. An involuntary shudder wracked my body at Cornelis' telling of this sad tale, as if some punk spectre had just kicked its way through my soul, undoing all the effort I'd expended to keep that nightmare at bay.

Bringing a broad, hard-knuckled hand to his face to wipe away the tears threatening to melt his usually stoic composure, Cornelis confided that he could never forgive the Germans for what they did, so, yes, he would be prepared to hide our Jewish friend on his farm. He had a loft area in his big hay barn that he said would be a discreet place to keep Simon from detection. My work in the Distribution Office meant that I should be able to wrangle extra food coupons to ease the burden of their family having an additional mouth to feed and with that, the deal was done and Simon could disappear for a while. We all shook hands and Tom and I cycled back to town, aware that we'd now crossed that line between indulging in mere rhetoric and perpetrating actual resistance activity. Of course, we weren't alone in this, around the country many similarly concerned citizens took to finding safe places where persecuted Jews could be hidden from the murderous SS, a process that came to be called in Dutch *Onderduiken*, 'Diving under', or going 'Underground', and all these folks were going to need some help.

CHAPTER 7

In common with most organisations and office environments, the Distribution Office in Waalwijk was prone to interpersonal politics. Few workplaces can ever boast a completely harmonious cohort of personalities actively striving towards a collective goal. One thorn in my side was the presence amongst the tally of clerks, of a rusted-on, dyed in the wool NSB'er, a co-conspirator of the grudge-bearing Piet de Bont, that miserable cur who had it in for me. Fortunately, my job kept me out of the office a lot of the time and this guy's desk was situated in a back room of the building, so I had, thankfully, little actual contact with him.

Arnold Verwiel, on the other hand, was a man with whom I got on fine. He was the office chief, the man who had hired me and someone whose quietly anti-German stance resonated with my own sentiments. Harry Didden, the office cashier responsible for balancing the books, was a sympathetic soul who could be relied upon to supply surreptitious extra coupons that would not be discovered as discrepancies. And then there was Henk

Romeijn. He was a bespectacled, tousle-haired, slim, somewhat sickly young man four years my junior, who was employed as a bookkeeper. He suffered from tuberculosis and had been away in a sanitarium for treatment and recovery but had returned to Waalwijk to again take up his position in the Distribution Office. In conversation we discovered that we had more than just our Christian names in common. We both hated the Moffen, of course, but were equally dismayed by the cowardly conduct of our royal family urging us to stay and fight and then buggering off to England at the first shots fired. We shared a deep mistrust of authority, class privilege and of the sanctimonious denominationalism that had needlessly riven our society for much too long. Who gives a shit if you're Catholic or Protestant; just be a good person. We became firm friends.

Henk confided that while he was laid up in the sanitarium he'd made the acquaintance of a council clerk from the town of Ijsselstein named Jansen, who claimed to have contact with a resistance group in Amsterdam who were producing and distributing a clandestine and highly illegal newsletter called *Het Christofoor*. Henk seemed to think that this guy Jansen was sincere and not just big-noting himself so perhaps we should get involved. There was no question that a source of information from our side was sorely needed; any voice other than that of German propaganda had been ruthlessly shut down. It was one of the first tenets of Totalitarianism. They controlled all radio broadcasts (except for illicit BBC transmissions), cinema content and had forced the closure of *The Echo of the South*.

Speaking of which, one might be forgiven for the impression that even the Germans had gotten so utterly fed up with the puerile antics of the NSB that it was easier to shut the paper down than to have to deal with any more of their constant bleating about bias.

We came to agree that it was, indeed, time to take a stand, to do something. That to sit back and do nothing would be tantamount to collaborating with the enemy.

So Henk contacted Jansen and expressed our readiness to take part in distributing *Het Christofoor* in our neck of the woods. He said to leave it with him; he'd run our proposal up the line and get back to us.

Roughly a week later, Henk got a message for us to meet Mr. Jansen in Amsterdam in two days' time. It was a weekend, and we both had it free from work commitments so were able to catch a train to Amsterdam where we met up with Jansen in a cafe on the Leidsestraat. Over coffee, he said that he had arranged a meeting for us with a contact person for the resistance group from whom we would get a supply of their news bulletins for dissemination around Waalwijk. He handed me a book by G.K. Chesterton entitled, *What's Wrong With The World*, which I was to present to the priest in the confessional of the Catholic Church on the Admiraal de Ruijterweg. This is how we were to meet Father Sanders. For obvious safety and security reasons, the good priest told us little about the make-up and activities of the group but said that we would be welcome to approach him for further supplies of *Het Christofoor*. We thanked him and returned to Waalwijk with a couple of bundles of newspapers secreted in the overnight bags we'd brought along for the purpose.

We were young and there was no denying that we relished the exhilaration, the frisson of danger that disseminating such highly illegal pamphlets entailed but it did mean we had to be circumspect with whom we shared them. It wouldn't do, for example, to bring them to the attention of our NSB colleague at the Distribution Office, but we had no trouble finding a ready market of folks we could trust who were keen to regularly get their hands on them. Tom was happy to take a swag of them to spread amongst the employees at his father's workshop and my own dad took some to give to valued, regular customers.

With contact secured in Amsterdam for continued supply and clientele in place to receive them, Henk and I would take turns travelling to Amsterdam to collect the latest editions at irregular intervals so as to avoid arousing suspicion.

Father Sanders seemed pleased with our efforts. At our various meetings no questions were asked by him, or, indeed, by us, as the less any of us knew of the organisation, the safer it was for all. However, after several weeks of, thankfully, incident-free activity, the priest surprised me one day by enquiring about my background. He particularly wanted to know what I did for a living. His interest seemed to have been piqued when I told him both Henk and I worked in the Distribution Office in Waalwijk because he opened up somewhat and began to tell me a few things about the resistance group of which, it seemed, he was a prominent member.

The group had come into being earlier in the year, he said, when two brothers and two of their friends, university students all, began planning acts of sabotage designed to thwart the efforts of the Moffen to empty Amsterdam of her Jewry. Though not Jewish themselves, they had been personally affronted by the inhuman attack on a population which constituted such a vibrant and integral part of the culture and history of Amsterdam herself. Their codename was CS-6.

Amongst other disruptive activities, said Father Sanders, they had attempted to blow up the train tracks to Westerbork to stymie the flow of Jews to the camps in Germany. Also one of their associates had recently burnt down a Rembrandt Plein cinema renowned for exhibiting only rabidly anti-Semitic Nazi propaganda.

'The point is this,' confided the priest, leaning conspiratorially closer and looking me square in the eye, 'it is now almost impossible for the group members to obtain their monthly ration cards here in Amsterdam. Would you be able and willing to supply those from your contacts in the Distribution Office in Waalwijk?' He paused for some moments, as if to let his words sink in, awaiting and monitoring my reaction.

'Well, Father,' I replied, 'our director is staunchly anti-German, most of the staff have been eagerly reading the pamphlets you've supplied and the cashier is a trusted friend who is already furnishing me with under-the-table coupons for a Jewish guy we've managed to hide with a sympathetic farmer so, to answer your question, yes, I'd be more than prepared, and certainly able to source what ration cards your group might need.' As the words left my mouth, I knew they constituted another step deeper into the Resistance, one move closer to the eye of the hurricane.

Of course pilfering ration cards was a bigger deal than merely pocketing some extra coupons and I must admit to entertaining some doubt as to whether I could actually make it happen. I needn't have worried. Harry Didden, our office cashier, was totally onside, keen to help without wanting to know anything about what we were doing with them. His legerdemain with the ledger was legendary. He was constantly able to camouflage inconsistencies in the accounts to the point where they were never discovered, even as the number of intended recipients grew. And grew. The Amsterdam group had recruited several more key members as they set about broadening the scope of their activities. Soon our own commitment was further tested when, I guess as a sign of his strengthening trust, Father Sanders asked if we could hide some Jewish kids whose parents had been carted off to the camps.

This time in the company of Henk Romeijn, I again cycled out to the farm of Cornelis van Erp to see if it would be stretching the friendship for him to take on hiding a couple of Jewish kids alongside the great work he'd been doing secreting Simon Horschfeldt. After a quick consultation with his dear lady wife, he agreed to take two young lads and added that he had a trusted friend on a nearby farm who would, he was sure, also help hide some kids. Thanks again to Harry, I could promise to provide them with the necessary cards and coupons that would help offset the demands of extra mouths to feed. Done deal. It was fortunate that our trains and train stations were still mostly staffed with the locals who had worked there all along, with only minimal oversight from German troopers, so that, although tricky at times, we managed, two at a time, to ferry a total of eight Jewish kids from Amsterdam to their temporary homes on outlying farms.

With autumn beginning to colour the leaves of the Stationstraat's trees, word came that Father Sanders wanted both Henk and I to travel to Amsterdam on our next run with the ration cards. Following our now well-established protocol, we went to the Catholic Church on the Admiraal de Ruiterkade, lit a candle in front of the statue of Saint Anthony set in a recess to the left of the apse and waited. To pray would have been hypocritical for a lapsed Catholic like myself, but the reverend silence and lingering note of incense inspired, if not exactly religious awe, certainly a welcome calm. Father Sanders emerged from the sacristy on the opposite side of the altar, bade us welcome and said, 'Walk with me.'

We followed the cleric out of the church and down several city blocks, finally turning into the Corellistraat and stopping to ring the doorbell at number six.

'Corellistraat 6, CS-6,' expounded our reverend guide as the middle-aged lady who had answered the door led us down a sombre hallway to a door towards the rear of the dwelling. Behind it, steep, narrow stairs descended into a rectangular basement room some seven metres by three and a half. The air was somewhat stale as might be expected from an underground space, imbued with the stain of cigarette smoke and other, less easily identified odours of a possibly chemical nature. A couple of bare lightbulbs dangled from electrical cord, illuminating workbenches along the walls strewn with hand tools, bottles, jars and all manner of wiring and other paraphernalia.

At the back of the room, four men were seated at a large wooden table, who now rose to greet us as Father Sanders made the introductions. The two younger guys, who looked to be about Henk's age, were the brothers Gideon and Jan Karel Boissevain in whose parents' house we currently found ourselves. The fellow more my age was introduced as Jan Verleun and the older man, it seemed, was a neurologist from The Hague, a committed communist and activist named Doctor Gerrit Kastein. We shook hands all round and were invited to take a chair at the table.

Gideon thanked us for our efforts at supplying the group with ration cards and explained that he and the others present constituted the core members of their resistance group. There were also several other associates scattered about the city. Some were members of the banned Communist Party of The Netherlands, and others were students drawn to action by the rapidly turning brutal occupation and, especially, the now blatant persecution of the Jewish population.

We were given a proposition; the lads felt that as a result of the work we had so far accomplished for them, we could be trusted to be more deeply involved in the group's activities, if we were so inclined. I shot a glance across at Henk. The nod he threw me confirmed that he felt, as did I, that we had come this far, there was no going back, and we should continue our commitment to the group.

'Good,' said Gideon. 'Welcome aboard.' He reached into a drawer in the desk behind him and produced two pistols, giving Henk and I one each. 'Get comfortable with these; things will get a lot more dangerous before they get any better. If you guys can find an isolated and secure area where gunshots won't attract undue attention, Jan here, will travel down to Waalwijk next week with ammunition and give you shooting lessons and target practice.'

A bottle of Jenever, the Dutch gin, was put on the table, and its contents soon found its way into seven tulip-shaped shot glasses which were then raised, clonked together and drained, to toast the consolidation of our compact with CS-6. We then handed over the ration cards we'd brought with us and said our goodbyes.

Over the previous couple of months, I'd grown reasonably

comfortable travelling with illegal pamphlets and pilfered ration cards secreted about my person, but riding the train home that day, hand on the pistol in the pocket of my overcoat, required a next level steeling of nerves. Not that I wasn't yet ready to use the gun, but rather the realisation dawned that it signified elevation into serious issues of life and death. Make no mistake. The first order of business when I got home was to find a secure place to stash my newly acquired handgun. It was best my family knew nothing of my clandestine activities, so it was imperative they not stumble upon a pistol secreted on the premises. In a dusty corner at the back of our attic stood a long-disused, cast-iron coal burner stove which would do just fine. During the following few days, in the guise of cycling abroad on official Distribution Office business, I reconnoitred areas to the south of Waalwijk where low-lying polders gave way to dunes and sparse forests that were devoid of even isolated farms. There I found a place behind a significant hillock called the Roestelberg where I was sure the firing of guns would go unnoticed.

As arranged, Jan Verleun arrived the following weekend from Amsterdam and the three of us cycled south towards the Roestelberg. Fortunately, although overcast and verging on cold, the rain held off. We left our bikes hidden in some low scrub and tramped over the knoll to a suitable clearing on its far side. Until then, Henk had little experience with firearms, having been excused from army service on account of his tuberculosis, but he was certainly a fast learner. For me, it was mainly a question of mastering the loading technique and getting to the point of being able to do that quickly. I can't say that I was particularly comfortable manipulating such an implement of destruction but I realised, of course, that we were now involved deeply enough in the Resistance to where a pistol might just be a prudent accessory.

Jan was an intelligent and committed young man whose enthusiasm made him easy to get along with. He set some stones along the horizontal trunk of a fallen tree roughly fifty metres away and imparted tips on how best to hold the gun so as to absorb the recoil and maintain aim. We loosed quite a few rounds on the stones which, to begin with, were in no immediate danger of being blasted apart, but as the sensations of firing became more familiar our accuracy improved.

After a solid couple of hours reducing rocks to rubble, we trundled up over the scrubby tor, retrieved our bikes and pedalled back to town. We stopped at a small cafe along the way and bought Jan a couple of *borreltjes* as thanks for his patience and tutelage before we saw him to the train back to Amsterdam.

As the winter of 1942 began to throw its icy weight around, so too were we being snowed under by new rafts of untenable demands from our cold and calculating captors. It was not only Jewish businesses and assets they sought to confiscate; it was becoming abundantly clear they meant to ransack our entire country of her able-bodied men as well as anything else of value.

Waalwijk, along with most other regional centres, had an office of the *Gewestelijke Arbeidsbureau*, or GAB, the National Labour Exchange. The GAB looked after the ranks of the unemployed, but these were now suddenly appropriated to the jurisdiction of a Hitler appointee named Fritz Sauckel, the new General in Charge of Labour. A fanatical Nazi, he wasted no time expounding his mission. The GAB was to immediately supply him with sixty thousand men to be sent to Germany to bolster her depleted workforce. With so many men in uniform, German industries were experiencing difficulties supplying their war effort, so our occupied country was to make up the shortfall in forced slave labour.

It was now not only Jewish families being torn apart, the filthy hand of the enemy was set to strike at the heart of all of us; no household would be safe anymore. It was a very rude awakening for those folks who'd hoped to be spared the wrath of the occupying forces if they just kept their heads down. Maintaining a neutral position suddenly became impossible when the choice was either have that family member sent to an unknown but ominous fate in Germany or figure out some way to resist. And I don't think I was alone in lamenting the fact that such heart-rending decisions would be processed by our own clerks, many of whom were NSB'ers, demonstrating their good old Dutch efficiency and expertise.

There were options. If called up, you could register and get sent to a slave labour camp in Germany. You might not register and await the consequences. If possible, find a doctor to write a certificate saying you're unfit for work and see how that goes. A claim could be made that you work in a business essential to the German war effort. Or, as now more frequently occurred, go underground, go into hiding, disappear. I was fortunate. My position with the Distribution Office was deemed essential so I was spared having to register.

My good friend Tom was not so lucky. After being called up for work in Germany, he had failed to prove that his father's business, where he was employed, was indispensable to the Nazis. We mulled over the possibilities but came to the conclusion that there really was no alternative, he had to disappear. Tom's father reluctantly gave his blessing, saying it was only a matter of time before the Nazis shut down all businesses deemed unnecessary to their war effort, at which time they would all be liable to be sent to Germany.

I knew my friend Jansen from Ijsselstein had already been able to find safe underground locations for a few CS-6 associates who had needed to vanish so I contacted him to see what he could do for Tom. He assured me that he could find a friendly farmer in an outlying district who would take Tom if I could provide his monthly ration cards. I was in a position to do this, so I said farewell to another firm friend, hoping that fortune would favour him in the dark, difficult days ahead.

I couldn't help thinking that we Dutch were experiencing a widening moral dichotomy where some folks, who could not be ignorant of the consequences, were sending fellow countrymen into the bowels of the enemy, while a growing number of compatriots were prepared to take on the significant risk of harbouring fugitives from an increasingly barbaric regime.

Sauckel was livid that the GAB, despite their best efforts, could only cough up less than half of his mandated amount of factory fodder and, no doubt fearful of incurring the wrath of Der Fuhrer, redoubled his resolve to hunt down more Dutch workers. His shrill call for a further one hundred thousand men saw unprecedented numbers going underground. There grew a distinct mood of defiance amongst the townsfolk at this blatant plundering of our workforce, a simmering resentment that found expression in widespread willingness to help hide those hunted by the Nazis. This, of course, put tremendous pressure on the Distribution Office to surreptitiously supply ration cards and coupons, but from the director down, most of our staff, excluding, of course, the couple of NSB'ers in the back office, were happy to put in the effort.

As the winter winds began whipping their frosty veils of snow over the town, cold currents of dread swept through what was left of Waalwijk's industry, with the Moffen now compiling lists of 'positive' and 'negative' businesses. Those on the 'positives' roster were firms from which the Germans directly profited and, as such, were permitted to carry on operating. Larger shoe factories, for example, continued to churn out footwear which was sent directly to Germany. We mere locals had to make do with whatever shoes we already owned and had to improvise repairs if they began to fall apart because there was no way of getting any new ones.

On the other hand, companies on the 'negatives' list were now suddenly forced to close down, surrender all plant and equipment and present all employees, directors included, to be deported to the work camps in Germany. I was in the office one day when the mayor, Mr. Moonen, arrived to take a meeting with our director. Although ultimate authority for the Distribution Offices in The Netherlands was vested in the central office in The Hague, Moonen held responsibility for the ones in our immediate region and, as such, had the power to hire and fire employees. His discussion with Verwiel concerned the fate of a number of Waalwijk workers from 'negative' firms being forced to close. After wrangling with the logistics, the upshot of their meeting was that roughly fifty of those men would be immediately hired to work as extra clerks in our Distribution Office and thereby evade being press-ganged into some slave labour camp in Germany. That was a brave and benevolent commitment to make, one for which they would each have to wear personal responsibility if challenged by either Head Office or, indeed, the SS. My respect for both men grew considerably.

Great need stirs in some people an imperative to act, to contribute, to do something, anything, to alleviate the consequences of blatant wrongs being perpetrated by abhorrent bastards. And so it was that, not only in our own community but in all parts of the country, there appeared pockets of resistance to Sauckel's decrees that sought to aid and abet those choosing defiance over acquiescence. We Dutch tend to like nothing more than forming committees, so it wasn't long before a covert national organisation bloomed to coordinate just such a response.

On one of my trips to Amsterdam, Father Sanders related the story of a minister of the Reformed Church in the town of Heemse named Frits Slomp who had needed to go to ground in an ungodly hurry due to his impassioned, anti-German utterances from the pulpit having come to the notice of the Gestapo. His immediate reaction had been to traverse The Netherlands north of the big rivers making contact with those right-minded people willing to hide fugitives from the Sauckel Actions and thereby gradually establish a loose network of resistance cells. These had apparently evolved to the point where, by January of the new year, representatives of all these disparate groups would meet each Saturday in the north-east city of Zwolle in a kind of clandestine 'information exchange', where contacts could be traded as well as resources for helping *onderduikers*, folks needing to go 'underground'. One group might have farmers able to provide shelter, while another might have a member or two who needed to disappear and so on. In the spirit of this cooperation was formed the *Landelijke Organisatie Voor Hulp*

Aan Onderduikers, the 'National Organisation For Helping People Going Underground', which from then on we simply referred to as the L.O.

There was no further room for naivety. With literally thousands of men across the country suddenly opting to go into hiding, involvement in clandestine activities such as the L.O. exposed one, not only to a blunt and brutal reckoning from the SS if caught, but also a very real danger of betrayal by those 'wrong' Nederlanders keen to curry favour with the enemy. It was a mystery to me how anyone could choose to side with a dangerous, vindictive foe like the Moffen at the expense of solidarity with one's own community and countrymen. At least in Waalwijk we had some idea who they were: mostly NSB'ers like Piet de Bont and his crony in the Distribution Office. The NSB seemed to suck perverse pleasure from the fact that they were detested by the rest of the population, a loathing that only fed their self-righteous sense of superiority.

I had no doubt that even Seyss-Inquart felt a deep contempt for Anton Mussert their insufferable leader and considered him nothing but a lily-livered toad, but, being the psychopath that he was, he knew that it would greatly amplify the insult and revulsion felt by we Nederlanders if Mussert was to be promoted to a position of power over us. So that is exactly what was done. He announced in late December 1942 that Herr Hitler had anointed Anton Mussert to the position of 'Leader of the People of The Netherlands' who would be permitted to form a 'Secretariat of State', a shadow cabinet, which would begin operating in an advisory capacity to Seyss-Inquart from February 1943. If the intention had been to disparage and deeply humiliate our people, it could not have been more successful. Not only had our royal family and government turned and run at the first sign of hostilities, we were now to be slapped with the ultimate insult of the possibility of a National Socialist Government of homegrown treasonous bastards riding roughshod over us.

It came as no surprise then, to find this very prospect the subject of robust discussion when Henk and I met with the core of CS-6 in Amsterdam early in the new year. We had travelled north to deliver the latest batch of ration cards and coupons we'd been able, again with the help of Harry Didden the cashier, to pilfer from our place of employ. The air in the basement room of the Boissevains's house on the Corellistraat was tense, somewhat fraught and thick with cigarette smoke, defying the attempt of a small electric fan in the corner to dispel the gloom. All present agreed that the likelihood of a de facto NSB-led government was untenable, not to be countenanced and must be prevented at all cost. That inevitably led to the question of how to thwart it.

Doctor Kastein reached behind his back, pulled out the revolver tucked into his trousers, laid it down on the table in front of him. 'I say we liquidate the leaders, cut the head off that chicken rabble and let the rest run off bleeding and panicking,' he said.

Jan Verleun was quick to concur. Gideon and Jan Karel, the Boissevain brothers, argued that discretion might be the better part of valour, urged caution and, for the time being, restraint.

'We need to consider the details of escape plans and safe houses,' said Jan Karel, 'before we dive in and start shooting people. I'd feel better if we spent some time planning and preparing for what needs to be done. And in any case, the announcement of the actual composition of Mussert's

"Secretariat of State" is not slated until February so we won't really know who to go after until then.'

Father Sanders thought that a sensible approach and with his blessing drew the others into a consensus of wait and see. The group advised Henk and me to reinforce our vigilance and to remain alert to developments before bidding us farewell.

We hardly spoke at all on the train back to Waalwijk as we each strove to assimilate the life and death reality of now being as deeply involved in the resistance as it was possible to be. I had no illusions. I'd seen first hand the callous ferocity with which the Germans had rained death upon many hundreds of civilians in the merciless bombardment that had flattened Rotterdam. The realisation that some of our own citizens were prepared to throw in their lot with these murderers to gain jurisdiction over the rest of us made me sick to my stomach. Henk, for his part, had once imparted to me that, on account of his tuberculosis, he was not expecting to live to any ripe old age, so he figured that he was already in a life-or-death situation. We quietly concurred that however unpalatable future exploits might turn out to be, they had to be done.

CHAPTER 8

An indistinct sensation had been bugging me. Tugging almost imperceptibly at my subconscious. It was like a reverse tinnitus, an unspecified entity that should always be there but wasn't. A feeling like I'd forgotten to do something which I couldn't recall. Then suddenly it hit me with all the clarity of a pealing church bell; there were no more pealing church bells. For all of us born and bred in Waalwijk, and it would be the same in most villages, the pace of life had always been punctuated by the ringing of church bells sounding out the hours, calling the faithful to worship and, on special occasions, trilling a cheerful carillon. Their clean and clear reverberations had vibrated within us since birth, their rhythms a part of our lives like an outward biological clock. And now they were gone. Silence, like a palpable evil, which of course it exactly was, enveloped our town.

The Moffen, not content to empty The Netherlands of her Jews, working men, livestock and food, now demanded all of our copper, lead, tin, bronze, in fact any metal they could use and that included disembowelling our churches of their precious bells. The trucks and workmen of a collaborating firm of Dutch profiteers had rolled into town and pilfered these priceless artefacts, some of which were hundreds of years old, with a cold and callous contempt for what they might mean to the town. An only minor consolation was the feeling that these acts seemed dusted with desperation, hopefully indicating that the war was going badly for the Third Reich.

Had they not been so heartlessly stolen from us, the church bells may well have been clanging a cheerful chorus on the morning of Wednesday 20 January when both the BBC and Radio Orange announced that the Queen's daughter Juliana (who was riding out the war in Canada) and her loathsome ex-Nazi husband Bernhard had celebrated the birth of a princess they named Margriet. I suppose that in normal times, this news would probably have been met with a reasonably restrained joy, but it seemed now to act as some sort of catalyst for a very public outing of nationalist sentiment. A small dam of peoples' pent-up frustration and thwarted patriotism suddenly burst in a flood of whitewash vandalism. The bucket and brushes brigade launched into a feverish daubing of buildings, roadways and hoardings about the town, splattering slogans such as 'Long Live Our Margrietje', 'Long Live Our Queen' and 'OZO' which stood for *'Oranje Zal Overwinnen'*, 'The House of Orange Shall Overcome'. The town once again looked like it had been shat on by a mighty flock of migrating fowl.

That the Moffen were incensed would be something of an understatement, but it was mainly because we had learned the news from listening to the BBC and Radio Orange, an activity they had expressly forbidden since 1940. This time they would teach us a lesson by confiscating all the radio sets in The Netherlands. Good luck with that. Everyone I knew listened to the radio. Other than our heavily censored cinemas, it was our only diversion, even despite the barrage of German propaganda that polluted so much air time. News, of course, also consisted only of matters the Germans would allow us to hear, which was why so many still surreptitiously tuned in to broadcasts from England.

I was having breakfast on the morning of 4 February, fried eggs, a rare treat I'd recently been able to cadge from a friendly farmer, when the radio carried a news item regarding Anton Mussert, the NSB chief latterly elevated to 'Leader of the Peoples of The Netherlands'.

Mother blurted out, 'Bah, that no-good, posturing peacock, may he rot in hell!' And she moved to silence the apparatus.

'No Mother, wait,' I exclaimed. 'I'd like to hear this.'

'Oh very well, although why anyone would want to hear anything to do with that whining weasel is beyond me.' Mother did not suffer fools gladly.

The bulletin concerned the announcement of the make-up of Mussert's shadow cabinet, his 'Secretariat of State', which he had termed, with typical hyperbole, 'The Empowered'. What barefaced effrontery! 'The Traitors' would have been a more fitting name for them. There followed a roll-call of eight or ten self-important, supercilious, opportunistic cowards who were ready to betray with a Judas kiss their own kin for the worldly reward of pieces of silver dripping with the blood of a million slaughtered innocents. *Now it gets serious*, I thought to myself as I recalled how ready Doctor Kastein and Jan Verleun had been to deal the NSB a deadly blow.

THE BAKER'S SON

One of those summoned to Mussert's 'Secretariat' was a retired general, an upper class, career military man named Hendrik Seyffardt who had been head of the Dutch SS (there really was a division of the dreaded SS comprised of Dutch citizens) volunteer group, 'Volunteer Legion of The Netherlands'. His 'Empowered' post was to be 'Deputy For Special Services', whatever that might be.

The following day, 5 February, a radio news bulletin reported that Seyffardt had been shot and wounded. I was not so much shocked as sobered by the thought that, A, it was more than likely CS-6 who had carried out the shooting, and B, how swiftly they had swung into action. With this rude awakening came the realisation that I was now complicit in a dangerous game where remaining on the sideline was no longer an option; there was no sitting this one out. The pistol I had secreted in the old iron stove up in the attic was no longer just some chic, cool accessory; it was now proof of my total commitment to a front-row seat in whatever form resistance to the Occupation might take. The Moffen, judging by the tone of the broadcast, were as livid as the NSB hierarchy was shocked and quaking. According to the news report, the general, though seriously injured, had been able to identify his assailants as 'students', so with great bombast and affront, the *Sicherheidspolizeidienst*, or SD, the bulldog-off-the-chain of German law enforcement, announced the immediate commencement of raids on universities to seek out and arrest anti-German activists and student radicals. A day later came the news that the general had succumbed to his injuries and died.

That rather put a dampener on any self-congratulatory glow the NSB may have felt at their ennoblement to power over the populace, the fulfilment of their perceived destiny. That conceit was about to be further deflated when on 7 February, radio bulletins reported that the freshly installed 'Empowered' pooh-bah for 'Information and the Arts', a certain Mr. H. Reydon had been gunned down and wounded in an attack wherein his wife was killed. Christ, the lads had done their homework and were certainly not mucking about! In just a couple of days, Mussert's grand 'The Empowered' had been reduced to something more like 'The Vulnerable', a panicked, paranoid and traumatised rabble. To my mind, the SD held no great affection for the NSB and saw them as mere lapdogs, but they were *their* lapdogs and therefore the offence was personal. In a tenor just short of hysteria, they vowed to eradicate any and all anarchistic tendencies lurking in the community and ordered further razzias on any universities harbouring hotbeds of dissent.

Even though Waalwijk could boast no institutes of tertiary education, the escalating tension wrought by the SD's wrath and their reported reprisals elsewhere could not be avoided. Generally speaking, the townsfolk felt no sympathy for the NSB, but certainly stopped short of displaying any relish at their persecution for fear of cropping up on the SD's radar. Like my mother, most preferred to quietly despise them for being 'false' fatherlanders. Little did she know, of course, how close her son was to the actual liquidation of several of their leaders. It was not possible to underestimate the danger this constituted to her and the rest of my family and that ominous thought was never far from my mind. It needed to be there, upfront, whenever any future actions were planned. Henk and I would have to be even more circumspect in our illegal activities.

On my next visit to Amsterdam for a fresh batch of *Het*

THE BAKER'S SON

Christofoor, Father Sanders confided that it had indeed been Dr. Kastein and Jan Verleun who had perpetrated the assassination of both Seyffardt and Reydon and that those would not be the last.

Along with preying on recalcitrant student agitators, the Moffen had not given up their relentless hunt for Dutch workers to fill the labour camps, where 'work 'till you drop' was the literal philosophy and inmates were expendable labour units that would simply be replenished by freshly shanghaied suckers should they indeed drop and die.

In early March, Mayor Moonen paid a visit to the Distribution Office. We'd become used to seeing him there and had become reasonably well acquainted. His efforts with our director Mr. Verwiel in employing dozens of laid-off Waalwijk workers in our office to prevent them being sent to Germany had certainly impressed those amongst us who valued courage and righteous determination. This time, however, the GAB had demanded he select seven of our workforce for deportation to the slave camps.

'But don't fret, lads,' he reassured us. 'Verwiel and I will draft a letter explaining that there is just too much vital work being done here to allow us to part with even seven of you.' The force of his personality must have flowed through to his pen because no-one ended up being sent and we heard no more about it.

To say that by now, everyone we knew had had a gut full of living under the Occupation would be an understatement. Food and provisions were scarce or unobtainable; it had all gone to Germany; most folks were living at subsistence level or below. All of our Jewish neighbours, those people we had grown up with, had disappeared into the heart of darkness of the camps in Germany. Our men were being relentlessly hunted down to provide slave labour to prop up German industry. Students were forced to sign declarations of loyalty to the Third Reich (very few of them did). The endorsement of the despicable NSB to a position of power over us; the list was endless. Then came the straw that broke the camel's back, the bridge too far, the spark in the tinderbox. Herr Himmler, Reichsfuhrer of the SS came up with the big idea to recall all Dutch ex-military personnel into custody as prisoners of war, a move that would net him an additional three hundred thousand men to be put to work in Germany.

After our army's capitulation in May of 1940, Hitler had allowed all military men to be dismissed and sent home, me amongst them. Then, on Thursday 29 April 1943, we awoke to an urgent notice published in the newspaper. In terse, belligerent language, all members of the former Dutch Army were ordered to immediately present as prisoners of war for deportation to Germany. No mention of exceptions or excuses due to mitigating circumstances, just a hard and final decree. The rotten bastards! This was going to directly touch so many families across our country in ways that no previous edict ever had. The idea of keeping your head down hoping it'll all just go away was suddenly wrenched from us as an option. Evil intent was now kicking down the doors on a hundred thousand homes across the Fatherland. An unanticipated (to the Germans at least) wave of universal outrage and fury swept through the nation like wildfire through cane fields, igniting deep feelings of indignation and affront. People took this personally. How dare the 'Rot-Moffen', as Mother referred to them, reach so deeply into so many families to cause so much grief.

That very evening, the radio news bulletin reported that

THE BAKER'S SON

workers in the town of Twente had spontaneously gone on strike in protest at this latest insult to our nationhood. The following day, news of that incident spread like juicy gossip and impulsive, unorganised outbreaks of workers downing tools sprouted throughout the breadth of the land like mushrooms after rain. Here in Waalwijk, what shoe and leather factories were still operating shut down as their workers walked off the job. The post office closed its doors. Local dairy farmers refused to take their milk to the factories where it was normally all sent to Germany, giving it away instead, and in some instances we heard about, actually pouring it out onto the ground rather than having it benefit the enemy.

It didn't take much for Henk Romeijn and I to catch the mood of this growing national disobedience campaign and begin to harangue our fellow clerks at the Distribution Office to stop work in solidarity with those other strikers across the country. Generally speaking, from the director on down, most of our staff were strongly anti-German so we got quite a positive response. Only those in the back office seemed hesitant to join in. That made sense because that was where the NSB mate of Piet de Bont worked. Henk and I went to town on them, calling them cowards, traitors and German lovers, snivelling dogs who would betray their mothers in order to benefit from the blessing of their Nazi overlords. This rather infuriated our resident Hitler devotee.

His face turned progressively redder and steam seemed to rise from his starched collar as he bellowed, 'You, Van Iersel, are a miserable, no-good Communist bastard. My friend de Bont was right when he said you were nothing but a puffed-up, lowly son of a baker with delusions of grandeur, who thinks he's somehow superior to normal people.' His yelling had by now attracted a small audience from elsewhere in the office, including the mayor who happened to be there right at that time. 'When the Germans come down to break this strike, and come down they will, you mark my words,' he thundered, 'I'll personally make sure that your name is mentioned as instigator and that will be the end of you, my friend!'

'To begin with,' I countered, 'you're not my friend and you can do your worst, you insignificant turd; you are a disgrace, a lame excuse for a human being.'

On our way out of this low-life's lair, the mayor quietly motioned for Henk and I to follow him into the director's office. He sat us down and in a considered tone said, 'You'd both better be aware that this guy giving you up to the Germans is no idle threat. He wouldn't hesitate to report you up the line for revenge and the kudos there'd be in it for him. I've heard that the SD has already issued death warrants for strike inciters in some parts of the country, so there's no reason to believe they won't do the same here. I'd strongly advise the both of you to make yourselves scarce for a while and I'll have a strong word with Mr. NSB'er and convince him to pull his head in. Here's my personal telephone number. Ring me in a week's time and I'll be able to tell you if it's safe to return to town.'

Ruminating on the mayor's sobering assessment of the situation, Henk and I agreed that it would indeed be in our best interests to disappear for a while. The NSB's predilection for giving their own countrymen the kiss of death was legendary for good reason. I rang Father Sanders in Amsterdam to see if he had any connections where we might lie low for a week or so. He said for us to travel to Ijsselstein and make contact again with Jansen, the guy who had introduced us to CS-6 in the first place, and that he, Father Sanders, would ring to let him know of our imminent arrival.

On the way to the train station the next morning, we bought a newspaper and read that in several towns where major factories had shut down summary executions of strike leaders were already taking place. They'd been singled out and shot where they stood. It seemed that Rauter, the SD and Polizei chief was proving to be even more rabidly fanatical than Seyss-Inquart and was coming down on this impromptu outburst of national anti-German disobedience with all the terror and vengeance of a wounded demon. The article went on to threaten that his men had been ordered to fire on any grouping of five or more men and that death warrants would be printed daily for any strike instigators. It was a good thing we'd taken the mayor's warning seriously.

Jansen was expecting us and said that Ijsselstein had remained relatively subdued due to the absence of any heavy industry that might have attracted the attention of the SD. He took us to the farm outside of town where my friend Tom Brokken was still hiding out. It was good to see him. I thought he looked like he may have lost some weight but then I guess we all probably had; no-one in our fair land, excepting of course the Moffen, were living high on the hog anymore. I gave him what news of Waalwijk I could and asked how he'd been getting on. He said that a battered guitar borrowed from the farmer had helped beat back the blues of boredom and conversations with his host's teenage daughter had definitely lifted his spirits. We settled in to ride out the strike's reprisals.

The ferocity of Rauter's strike-busting savagery fairly well shocked the entire country and as a result, the peoples' uprising had mostly petered out by early the following week. In its aftermath it seemed that around eighty citizens had been arbitrarily executed and hundreds more wounded. Irreparable damage had been done to the nation's psyche; there could be no further pretense that things would be all right; they were clearly not. We were being lorded over by masochistic killers intent on stripping us of our dignity, and every other material thing they could get their hands on. From now on each of us would need to find their own response to deal with the feelings of impotence and anger that percolated within us when faced with such inhuman brutality. In both Henk and myself, it manifested in a hardening resolve to contribute as much as we could to the resistance activities of our friends in Amsterdam.

Back in Waalwijk, there were two factors acting in my and Henk's favour. The first was the deep integrity and force of personality of our mayor and the second was the fact that the head of the SD in s'Hertogenbosch, Heinrich Kuther, the German officer in charge of our region, was widely known to be more interested in personally profiting from black-marketeering than in strictly carrying out his duties. It was said of him that he would either become instantly ill or else simply disappear when faced with any taxing official tasks.

After about a week lying low, I borrowed the farmer's telephone to ring Mayor Moonen. The mayor assured me that our NSB friend's bombast and threats had fallen on deaf ears in s'Hertogenbosch and that he'd called the troublemaker into his office to elucidate certain home truths, after which the lad had faithfully agreed to pull in his horns and cause no further ruckus. The mayor didn't divulge the precise nature of what were obviously persuasive arguments, but their effect was clear and he reckoned it would be safe for us to return to Waalwijk.

I then rang Father Sanders to let him know that we were getting ready to return home to resume our regular activities, but he suggested we should first travel on to Amsterdam to be briefed on the current state of CS-6's campaigns.

The following day, Henk and I took the early train and made contact with the good Father in his church on the Admiraal de Ruiterkade. He told us that since the shooting of Seyffardt and Reydon it was no longer safe to meet in the Corellistraat. The various members of the group had been staying in a succession of safe houses around the city, a momentum of movement necessary to evade detection and arrest. We should make our way to an address in the Valeriusstraat, in the south-west of the city at midday, he said, where a meeting of the group was to take place.

Once there at the appointed time, we were shown to an expansive, low-ceilinged room in the attic of the building, where Jan Karel Boissevain, his brother Gideon and our friend Jan Verleun were already seated at a large, rectangular table. They bade us sit down and explained that Father Sanders was detained on church business and wouldn't be joining us. They then had the sad news to impart that Doctor Kastein had been arrested in The Hague in early February and taken to the Binnenhof Government buildings for interrogation. He'd apparently had a concealed weapon on him because he shot one of the SD'ers who were trying to pump him for information. He was then, in all likelihood, severely beaten but, seeing as there had been no further arrests, it seemed that he'd kept his mouth shut. The torture must have been intense, they said, because in desperation, the good doctor had leapt out of a second story window, still tied to a chair, and had subsequently died from his injuries. Christ, if we ever doubted the degree of danger we were committing ourselves to, surely the torture and martyrdom of a valued colleague such as Doctor Kastein served to dispel any illusions about what was at stake.

After a respectful silence, the talk then centred on how the previous killings of the two 'Empowered' NSB Secretariat members, although resulting in raids and arrests of student activists around Amsterdam and the death of Doctor Kastein, had had the desired effect of taking the wind out of the sails of the rest of the NSB upper echelon. Their 'born to rule' smugness must now have given way to a soul searching 'is it worth my life?' scenario.

More, of course, needed to be done. The group had drawn up a list of other high-ranking officials dangerous to the country, not to mention the Resistance, that they felt also needed to be liquidated. The preferred target was Anton Mussert, their craven, traitorous leader, but he was too heavily guarded to be effectively got at. Other of the 'Empowered' shadow cabinet ministers would be singled out instead, along with other prominent betrayers of our people.

One such decided on was a certain Dr. F. Posthuma, recently elevated to be the 'Empowered for Fisheries and Agriculture'. Another was a Dutch lieutenant of police in the pay of the Moffen, who, they said, was ruthless in pursuing fellow countrymen wanted by the Germans.

The attention of the group then turned to Henk and myself. We were asked, not ordered, to undertake the elimination of a Mr. H. Van Dijk, the police commissioner of Nijmegen, a city some fifty kilometres to the east of Waalwijk, near the border with Germany. Apparently, this colluding traitor was a high functionary in the NSB and had already been responsible for arresting several members of the local resistance whom he coldly handed over to the SD to be shot. It was also known that he had a list of students from Nijmegen University who were active in the Resistance. In short, he was a treacherous, ruthless man who could not be allowed to continue his hunt on people opposed to Nazi rule. For my part, the recent executions of strike leaders and the horrific death of Dr. Kastein had hit me hard enough to make the decision to agree to carry out the liquidation of Mr. van Dijk a relatively easy one, not purely for motives of revenge, but more a strong obligation I felt to maintain the fight, and to prove that their deaths had not been in vain. A quick look into Henk's eyes confirmed we were in accord.

'Good,' said Jan Karel as he proceeded to pour each of us present a glass of Jenever. 'To the success of your mission.' He then advised us to take some time to study the man's movements and habits so as to find the optimum time and location for the hit. The group would put us in touch with a student in Nijmegen, a trusted ally, who could help in planning an escape route out of the city once the deed had been done.

On the train home to Waalwijk, Henk and I quietly discussed how best to undertake the necessary reconnaissance of van Dijk's comings and goings. We'd have to travel to Nijmegen to find out exactly where his police headquarters were situated and, of course, where he lived. We would need to know how and at which times he travelled to work and the same for when he returned home. It was obvious that the timing of our excursions would be crucial to prevent arousing any suspicions at the Distribution Office, but we both had a reasonable amount of leave days up our sleeves to cover them. We figured that a month or a month and a half of preparation should be sufficient for us to have in place a workable plan for the elimination of Mr. van Dijk.

During the rest of May and into June, Henk and I made several forays into the city of Nijmegen, familiarising ourselves with the layout of streets and, of course, getting to know the addresses of van Dijk's home and office.

As promised, the group had organised contact with a student activist from Nijmegen University who was happy to place his local knowledge at our disposal. What he told us of the police commissioner's modus operandi certainly reinforced the group's assessment of this man as a threat and deadly menace that needed to be neutralised. According to the lad, van Dijk was a fanatical NSB'er who, since his accession to the post in 1941, had been instrumental in emptying the city of all her Jewish citizens, acquiring in the process a dubious reputation for stealing their jewelry and even selling off their furniture after having them hauled away to the camps in Germany. Our student friend knew to tell us that van Dijk's extreme zealotry had already alienated a great deal of his police force. Under the commissioner's predecessor, who had been imprisoned for his anti-German sentiments, those officers had apparently taken great pains to treat the city's population as fairly as the situation allowed. Some of those disgruntled constables had now turned to warning prospective targets of their commissioner's wrath and delaying or sabotaging their arrests, such was their disgust at the attitude and behaviour of their current boss. Having already handed over some eight or ten partisans to his masters in the SD to be shot, van Dijk now had his sights set on Nijmegen University where the academic leadership were seen to be noncompliant with the wishes of the Nazis. This guy was a particularly nasty piece of work.

We watched him going about his business and returning to his genteel, middle-class home. He seemed outwardly calm, confident. But we knew his story, we could see the aura of evil he carried with him even as he endeavoured to maintain the exoskeleton of respectability that his ego was convinced hid his true nature. And we knew what we had to do. The task sat heavy on my conscience, its import tending to distract somewhat from the everyday, the thought of it consuming quite a considerable chunk of my attention. At night it was more difficult still; *have I got what it takes to be judge, jury AND executioner?*

Mother noticed the increased distance. 'Hendrik, are you in love or something, because you don't seem to be quite with us.' She sensed some schism in my psyche. It was strange, but she was not entirely wrong. My lack of concentration on the commonplace was not unlike that experienced by the befuddled in love. We couldn't drag this out too long.

While busy piecing together our plan of attack, others in CS-6 were carrying out actions of their own. The newspaper of 4 June told of the assassination of Dr. F. E. Posthuma, Mussert's 'Empowered' for agriculture and fisheries, having been carried out the day before. The tone of the reporting seemed to suggest that this was of no major consequence to the SD, but it did throw the leadership of the NSB into near hysteria and paranoia. A desired result.

Momentum was building. Towards the end of June, a Dutch lieutenant of police, a notorious betrayer and informer on his countrymen, was shot off his bicycle and killed. We knew we'd soon have to make a move ourselves. Most of the plan was in place; there were only some details of how we would make our escape out of the city that needed to be ironed out. Henk had taken sick leave from the Distribution Office from Thursday 1 July because of his tuberculosis, he said. The following Wednesday he suggested another excursion to Nijmegen for the next day. I had used up all my leave entitlements on our previous reconnaissance expeditions so was unable to go. Henk said that he'd go alone.

'Fair enough,' I said, 'But be careful and for God's sake, don't do anything stupid.' I remembered how Henk had once told me that because of his illness he wasn't expecting to live to any ripe old age.

'No, I won't. I just need to tie up those last details. I won't even take my pistol. I promise,' he assured me.

I left it at that.

Thursday morning dawned bright and mild, a balmy summer's day to be cycling to Drunen to deliver ration cards to their sub-office. Lulled by the rhythm of my pedalling and the fragrance of the morning air, I fell to musing on the fact that nature just carries on, season after season, with us or indeed, without us. She pays no heed to the uproar, hatred and violence we perpetrate on ourselves, our existence of no more consequence than an ant pissing on the trunk of some great oak. How our arrogance and egos distort and neglect the natural world, wasting the reverie and calm that is our birthright. I must remember to wear a hat though, too much sun on the brain can let one's thoughts run away with themselves.

My work in Drunen was done by about two o'clock in the

afternoon and, feeling in no particular hurry, I decided to stop off at home for a coffee with Mother before heading back to the Distribution Office. I had only drunk about half of my cup when one of my colleagues from work came bursting breathless through the front door and into the kitchen. He looked like he'd just run a marathon.

Sweating, his face red with exertion and panting heavily, he blurted out, 'Henk, Henk, you have to … they're looking …' All the while he was pointing feverishly into the distance.

'Sjaak, slow down, who is looking? What do I have to do?' I said, grabbing him by the shoulders and looking him in the eye.

He calmed down a little and said, 'The Gestapo are at the office going through Henk Romeijn's desk, and they're also looking for you. I snuck out and ran here as fast as I could.'

A lucid bolt of awareness shot through the marrow of my being. I knew instantly what must have happened. 'Sjaak, you did well to alert me, thank you, now make yourself scarce. Mother, I've got to go!' I declared as I grabbed my jacket and bolted out of the front door. I slung a leg over the bar of my bike and was about to hightail it down the cobblestones when I suddenly remembered that my pistol was still in the attic, secreted in the old stove, along with the ration cards for the Amsterdam group which I'd been planning to deliver the following week. If the Germans found these it would be curtains for my family, so I raced back into the house, bounded up the stairs and retrieved my handgun and the cards.

Mother had been watching me scamper up the staircase and on my way back down and out of the door, I stopped briefly, kissed her on the cheek and told her, 'Mother, I love you but I have to disappear.' With pounding heart, I leaped aboard my bicycle and pedalled away as if my life depended on it, which, in fact, it did.

At the end of the street I threw a quick glance over my shoulder in time to see the Gestapo pull up in front of our house. I flew around the corner, adrenaline charging through my system like steam from an overheating boiler, feet pumping pedals like the pistons of an engine red-lining, heading Christ knows where. Taking the back lanes out of town and into the polders, I tried to calm down enough to get a grip on my situation. What might be happening back at my house? What the fuck had Henk gone and done? How was I going to escape getting caught?

Priorities needed to be sorted out. I had to find a safe place to hide, and Father Sanders would have to be notified that, in all probability, Henk Romeijn had gotten himself arrested by the SD and that would have serious ramifications for the rest of the group. Riding furiously along the willow-lined lanes that cut through the low-lying fields outside of town, I remembered that I had friends in the nearby village of Harsteeg who I felt sure could be trusted to hide me for a few days.

I was still trying to catch my breath as they kindly took me in and proffered brandy and sugar as a calmative. Listening sympathetically as I explained my predicament, they offered to help in any way they could.

'Well, if you don't mind, there's an important call I need to make. May I use your telephone?' It was imperative that I ring Father Sanders to warn the group that Henk was in custody.

'By all means, you can take it in the front room,' they suggested.

I got through to the good Father and explained that Henk had travelled alone to Nijmegen that morning, had most likely shot van Dijk and must have been caught because the Gestapo had raided the Distribution Office in the afternoon and ransacked his desk. I told him that they'd then asked for me but I was by chance at home and managed to flee moments before they pulled up in front of my house. He listened calmly to my story and said to come to Amsterdam first thing in the morning and go to a particular house near his church where I was to meet with him.

OK, that was that bit sorted, but what had me really worried was the fate of my family. How had they fared with the Gestapo in the house wanting to talk to me? I asked my friends if I could impose upon them to go past the Stationstraat in Waalwijk in the morning and see if they could find out any information about what might have happened to them. I told them that I needed to go to Amsterdam first thing the next day and would ring them from there in the afternoon to see if they'd been able to ascertain anything of the situation. They assured me they would and made up a bed on their couch for me. Even with another couple of brandies on board sleep proved elusive as my mind kept spinning off at tangents, worrying for my family, thinking of what might be happening to Henk and even a little concerned for myself; how the hell was this going to play out?

I must have gotten a little shut-eye because it was soon dawn. My kind hosts were already up and about, making me a welcome breakfast of fried eggs and a cup of real coffee. They again promised to go by my house to find out what they could. Thanking them profusely, I reiterated that I would ring them in the afternoon from Amsterdam for an update and flung myself onto my bike to ride to s'Hertogenbosch to catch the nine a.m. train.

Where I could I avoided the main roads. I trundled briskly down the side roads and lanes between villages, thinking that the Gestapo must surely have decided that I was still in the area. Each encounter with a car of any kind sent my blood pressure soaring. Bloody Henk, I thought to myself somewhat unkindly, he had promised to not take his pistol or do anything rash, but he'd obviously done enough to get arrested. I shuddered to think what he might be going through at the hands of the Gestapo, the poor bastard. I managed to reach the train station in s'Hertogenbosch without any drama, bought a ticket and boarded the nine o'clock train. So far, so good. Every fibre of my being was on alert for any signal of danger, any hint of being recognised. The solid breakfast my friends had provided was doing a good job of settling my guts; I did not need to be any shakier than I already was. I was later to learn that the SD surrounded the station not long after my departure, checking every passenger's credentials, looking to apprehend me. A close call!

I kept my nose buried in the newspaper I'd bought until the train jolted to a halt at one of the platforms in the huge caverns of Amsterdam's Central Station. It was of some small comfort to be able to lose myself in the bustle of a big city morning, striding purposefully along the canals until I reached the house where I was to meet up with Father Sanders. He was already there, in mufti, having ditched the ecclesiastical garb for clobber more suited to flight. We exchanged greetings, and I gave him the ration cards I'd brought for the group, which he stowed in the back pocket of his trousers.

'Thank you, Henk,' he said, 'I hope they can still be of use, but for now, there's no telling how much the Gestapo know about our activities. A lot depends on how long Henk Romeijn can hold out in the face of what they're most likely doing to him. I've arranged for you and me to disappear and lie low in a monastery of my acquaintance, in the countryside about an hour and a half out of Amsterdam. Wait here while I go fetch my suitcase from the presbytery and we'll head off.'

I nervously ensconced myself in the front room by the window to await his return, the coiled spring of adrenaline's fight or flight mechanism buzzing through my system like a junkie's vein invasion. After some twenty minutes I began to grow suspicious; it shouldn't be taking the good Father this long to grab his valise. Suddenly he appeared coming round the corner flanked by two goons in leather trench coats, the unmistakeable stench of Gestapo. Shit! I blindly bolted in the opposite direction, out the back door of the house, across a small yard and over the back fence in a single climbing leap, landing in another street where a tram just happened to be passing. With a sprint I caught up to it and leaped onboard, mind struggling to catch up with what my body was already doing by instinct. I tried to take stock of the situation. The Gestapo would surely have discovered the ration cards in Father Sanders' back pocket, giving them the names of the other members of the group, so it was imperative I find a way, as soon as humanly possible, to warn the rest of the network. Added to that, and very much to the point, those bastards now knew that I was in Amsterdam so another urgent priority was to find a place where I could lie low and escape detection. Overriding all these considerations of course, was the sickening, disquieting thought of what might be happening to my family in Waalwijk.

Rattling through town on the tram, not even knowing where it was headed, oblivious to the other passengers, I suddenly remembered that I had a second cousin, a nun, who taught at a school in the south of Amsterdam, in the Banstraat. I was sure her Christian charity would extend to putting me up for the night. By the time I got off at the next stop, a light rain had slicked the cobblestones with a thin shine so I turned my collar up to look for a tram heading to the south of the city. I thankfully did not have to wait long as standing still made me feel vulnerable and exposed. I needed to be on the move.

Sister Bernadette was somewhat taken aback to find this damp, harried-looking distant relative of hers rapping on the convent door, eyes darting this way and that, obviously in some kind of distress.

'Henk, my God, you look terrible, come in and sit down, I'll get you some hot coffee,' she said.

I was never a very religious person but being now ushered into the confines of a convent, I had to admit to sensing an aura of protection, of tranquility, of benevolence, even if salvation seemed still some way off. It was safer for her and for the convent if she knew nothing of my plight and what had led to it. I merely impressed upon her my sincere need for a safe haven for the night. The forgiveness of the Lord shone in her eyes along with a worldliness that precluded the need to ask any questions as she said that that would present no problem. To stay in the convent was, of course, out of the question, but as the students were on summer vacation, she would make up a stretcher bed for me in one of the classrooms of the school. I was more than grateful for that and the soup and bread she brought me from the convent kitchen.

As night descended, I laid myself down on the bed, rolled and lit a cigarette and as the smoke coiled and wafted to the ceiling, let the events of the last two days replay across my mind. They almost didn't seem real, as if they had happened to someone else. For the moment, though, I was reasonably safe and felt I could give my body up to gravity and let the tension, anxiety and adrenaline that had propelled it through the day fall away for a time. I was going to need a clear head. Deep weariness descended, leaving me instantly leaden and dead to the world.

I awoke with a start as the night's darkness was beginning to melt into the cool grey of dawn, wondering where the hell I was. Opening my eyes wide enough, the sight of school desks brought it all back into focus. Sister Bernadette came in, trailing the sweet aroma of fresh coffee wafting about her person like ecclesiastical incense and asked if I'd managed any shut-eye. I nodded in the affirmative as I sipped the hot, sweet restorative and told her how sorry I was to be putting her in possible jeopardy by my presence.

'I don't know what you've done, Henk, and I don't want to know, that's between you and the Lord, but these are ominous times and my Christian faith demands that I don't judge, only practice charity. And anyway, you are family and I've arranged for you to meet Theo Kuijpers, a teacher at our school, who is happy to hide you at his house for as long as you need. He is a young man of twenty-eight, a bachelor and a man of sound principles who can be trusted implicitly.'

Sister Bernadette made the introductions when Kuijpers arrived at the school. He came across as a serious young man, but with a calm demeanour that made it easy to relax in his presence.

'I appreciate you taking me in at such short notice,' I told him. 'My situation is, how shall I put it, delicate and rather fraught with danger. I need a little time to figure out what to do next.'

Sister Bernadette offered to pray for me as I said my goodbyes and thanked her for giving me sanctuary in my hour of desperate need.

She said, 'Go with God.' However I was convinced that Our Blessed Lord had long since abandoned us to fight this out amongst ourselves.

I walked with Theo to his house. An awful feeling clung to me, like a cheap deodorant, that at that moment I was a dangerous man to know, that the very act of someone helping me could get them killed. Back at his place, Theo made us coffee with bread and jam. I couldn't tell him the whole story of course, no matter how trustworthy he might be, but he deserved to know the risks he faced in harbouring me. I highlighted the fact that members of a Resistance group within which I'd been active had most likely been compromised when yesterday the Gestapo had seized a colleague of mine who had in his possession a clutch of ration cards bearing their names. We'd been on the verge of leaving Amsterdam to go into hiding and I'd come within an angel's breath of being captured, which meant that not only were the SD and the Gestapo exceedingly keen to have me in custody, they knew I was in Amsterdam. It was imperative that I find a way to warn my comrades while at the same time try desperately not to get caught.

I had to presume that the Gestapo had by now found the ration cards in Father Sanders' possession, giving them the names of the main CS-6 members. It would be suicidal to try to contact any of them, or even show my face on the street. There was, however, a more recent associate who was not yet receiving any ration cards who might help if I could persuade Kuijpers to go and see him.

I hadn't had many dealings with Kas de Graaf, but I knew

where he might be found. He kept a room in the otherwise empty top floor of a building on the Vijzelstraat above a Chinese restaurant called Taiton. The only way up to that room was through the secret panel in back of a telephone booth in the restaurant which could be opened by the proprietor if you had the password. I knew I was testing Theo's commitment and courage by asking if he was willing to take a message to de Graaf, but there was really no other choice. To my great relief, he said he had no illusions about the possible ramifications of his acceding to my request and was happy to contribute even a little in resistance to the loathed occupation of our country. Good.

Armed with the password for the telephone booth in restaurant Taiton, he was to warn de Graaf that Father Sanders had been arrested and that, as a result, the members of CS-6 were likely compromised, as the priest had their ration cards on his person. He was then to explain that I had managed to evade capture and was lying low in his house.

I made a half-hearted attempt to peruse the many books lining a wall of the teacher's living room as I waited for him to return from the Vijzelstraat, but I couldn't distract myself from the urgency of the situation and instead plonked down in a chair by a window that afforded clear view of the street and smoked cigarettes. All manner of thoughts wafted through my mind with the inhale and exhale of tobacco breath, not the least of which was serious doubt about having sent Theo into what was to him, unfamiliar and possibly treacherous territory. I wasn't even entirely sure that de Graaf could be trusted – I had heard some disturbing rumours about the goings-on in the rooms above the Taiton, but my options were limited and I did not have the luxury of time.

After about two and a half hours that had seemed so much longer, Kuijpers appeared walking down the street, thankfully alone. He'd encountered no difficulty in meeting de Graaf who had listened carefully to what Theo had to tell him and who had passed on an address where he said I should go.

It was on the Admiraal de Ruijterweg, at the opposite end to the Boomkerk, Father Sanders' church, and home to a family by the name of Peridon. Theo gave me a fedora and an old pair of his glasses to disguise my features as I apologised for having put him in danger's way and thanked him for his invaluable help before setting off across town to find my new safe house. Was it just my paranoia, or were there more Germans about the place? The city seemed lousy with them. Whatever the case, I kept my head down and strode the streets as nonchalantly and unobtrusively as possible until I found the address.

I was expected. Johan Peridon was a clerk with the city council and lived there with his wife Petra and their thirteen-year-old son, Willem. They made me feel welcome and showed me to an attic room with a single bed, a small desk and chair and a chest of drawers of which I could avail myself for as long as was necessary. A window in the sloping roof could be set open for fresh air and a narrow door in the wall opposite the bed opened onto the flat, pebbled roof over the back part of the house, an area roughly four metres square which provided a welcome feeling of open space and even better, a possible escape route across the adjoining rooftops if the house got raided by the SD.

De Graaf arrived at the house while I was still checking out my new surroundings and brought with him a forged identity card for me, with a false name, date of birth, occupation, etc. which only needed my fingerprint and photo to pass as the real deal. It was a brilliant facsimile, right down to the watermark outline of the heraldic Dutch lion in each of the three panels, which were a feature of the legitimate ones, making the fake virtually indistinguishable. De Graaf gave me the address of a photographer in town who had done some previous work for the group and who could provide me with a headshot photo appropriate for the identity card.

But before anything else, I needed to find out what was happening with my family. The dread of what the Gestapo might be doing to them was drilling a hole through my composure that threatened to leave me dangerously adrift from the rational thought my situation demanded. Using the Peridon's telephone, I rang the friends in Haarsteeg with whom I'd spent my first night on the run. The news was not good. They'd gone past my house in the Stationstraat only to see the Gestapo still there, obviously lying in wait in case I returned home. Neighbours further down the street were able to tell them that my father and two brothers had been taken into custody by the Germans, leaving my mother and sister under house arrest. The worst possible scenario.

My heart sank as pangs of guilt rent my guts like bayonet stabs. What had I done to them?! My father and brothers were probably right at this moment being tortured because young Henk here had to play the Resistance Hero. There was only one honourable thing to do; I had to give myself up. Talking this over with de Graaf, he suggested I first go into town to get the pass photo and that he would make enquiries regarding my family's fate in the interim. He also urged me to be especially careful, a policeman who was friendly with the group knew to tell him that the Gestapo didn't only have my name, they'd also managed to find a photo of me which they had begun showing on 'wanted' posters in cinemas across the city.

I pulled Theo's fedora down over my wanted face and headed into town to the photographer's studio. He was happy to oblige and sat me down on a wooden stool in front of a large, plain paper backdrop and, after arranging a couple of lights on metal stands, took a few shots. I'm sure I must have looked spooked because that's pretty much how I was feeling, but anything except a smile would suit the purpose. He told me that they'd take roughly twenty minutes to develop so I retired to a small coffee shop nearby where I took a seat in the darkest corner furthest from the front door to wait.

I had only just gotten my coffee and rolled a cigarette when, in an extraordinary turn of fate, a young couple who lived on my street in Waalwijk and who I knew very well, happened to saunter into the cafe. Frans van Oostrum and his wife Jeanne were only recently married and had just arrived in Amsterdam for a kind of honeymoon. After exchanging warm greetings and commenting on the ridiculous coincidence of running into each other in this random cafe, I enquired if they could give me any up-to-date information of what was happening in the Stationstraat. They had left there only that very morning so they knew exactly what was taking place. My father and brothers, they said, had not been shipped off to a concentration camp as I feared they may have been, but were locked up in a cell in the local police station. They also knew that the Germans were still in our house. I told them that I was seriously considering giving myself up.

'Don't be too quick to do that just yet,' said Frans, 'while they're in our local police station they're reasonably safe. We know those constables well enough to be sure that they'll look after them. After all, we've grown up with those guys. The moment there's any move to send your father and brothers to Germany, I promise to let you know and you can decide to surrender yourself then.'

That made a lot of sense so I gave him the Peridon's address to write to if worst came to worst. I was only too painfully aware of what would happen if I gave myself up to the Gestapo, so Frans' words were of some comfort, even though, if it came to the crunch, I would have no other option.

So now with the pass photos, my new identity card could be completed. De Graaf had copies of the official rubber seals to be stamped across the corners of the photo and fingerprint and I was ready to go. Only I wasn't good to go. I wanted to go. I desperately needed to get out of Amsterdam, but despite the convincing forgery, this new card had my photo on it and I knew that the Gestapo also had a picture of me that they were widely circulating around Amsterdam. Having already captured Henk Romeijn and now Father Sanders, they would know that they were dealing with an organised Resistance cell, of which the next member they needed to seize was me and I was still in Amsterdam. Careful reconnaissance of the train stations revealed that they were all heavily guarded by the SD and that the papers of all passengers were being closely scrutinised, so I really could not move without significant risk of arrest. Luckily for me, the Peridons, good people that they were, had no problem extending their hospitality until such time as the group and I could figure out a plan to smuggle me out of town.

For a frustrating couple of weeks, I stayed out of sight, biding my time reading and playing solitaire, all the while worrying whether my dear father and Jan and Bart, my brothers, were being humanely treated by our friends in the Waalwijk police station. Listening to the radio set the Peridons had secretly retained, it seemed that the German General Christiansen's edict for all Dutch ex-military personnel to register as prisoners of war was still in effect and being systematically enforced. This decree, of course, had been the catalyst for the spontaneous, national general strike earlier in May which had resulted in widespread refusal and the going underground of thousands of affected men.

One morning, the radio broadcast the call-up of a particular battalion of ex-Army men, mainly from Amsterdam and surrounding districts, who were to assemble a few day's hence at an appointed time in Central Station to be transported to Amersfoort, a city to the southeast. A station platform suddenly swamped with a hundred or more milling men and their families should provide sufficient mayhem, I thought, to enable me to board a train without having my papers perused.

I rang De Graaf, who agreed that this would be the optimal opportunity to get me out of Amsterdam. CS-6 was, by this time, aligned with the rapidly evolving network of the LO, the National Organisation for Helping People go Underground, so De Graaf said he'd arrange, with their cooperation, a route and a destination for me to disappear to in the countryside, away from Amsterdam. The following few days were filled with a mixture of relief and apprehension. I was still somewhat flabbergasted at how my life had spiralled so swiftly into a state of mad momentum, carrying me God knows where.

CHAPTER 9

A LONG, LOUD, CRACKING SOUND rent the crisp winter air like a drawn-out thunderclap, wrenching me from restful slumber and jolting me into immediate consciousness. An attack maybe, I thought. Leaping from my cot, I darted over to the small window overlooking the lake. Through the lightly frosted pane I had a clear, one-hundred-and-eighty-degree view of the surrounding countryside but noticed nothing untoward. Relieved that I was in no immediate danger, I let my gaze linger over the expanse of the lake and came to the sudden realisation that it had completely frozen over in the night and that the rapidly expanding ice sheets, colliding and thickening, had been responsible for the alarming rumble with which I'd been so rudely awakened.

By this time I had been laying low in seclusion for several months since my escape from Amsterdam. The attic room I occupied was in the caretaker's house adjacent to a rather imposing electric pumping station which regulated water flow from the lake, the Sneekermeer, into the canals bordering the surrounding polders. The custodian, a widower who lived there with his two sons and two daughters, was a cantankerous misery guts who managed to regularly steal my cigarettes, despite the fact that he was being supplied with double ration cards and paid one hundred guilders per week to harbour me.

This bolt hole in the north-east province of Friesland had been found for me by the Shire president, a Mr. Gerbrandy, who, in addition to being the brother of our prime minister exiled in London, was a leading figure in the LO in Friesland. He had chosen the pumping station not only because of its remote location, but also because it was situated on a tiny island that could only be accessed by a metre-wide bridge which would be drawn in each evening. Gerbrandy was well connected. He didn't say how, but certainly knew about my troubles in Amsterdam and how keen the Gestapo were to get hold of me, so he as good as ordered me to hide out on the lake for at least a year and not go anywhere. He would take care of the necessary ration cards.

My new life at the lake, bordering on boredom, especially now with the winter frosts descending, could not have been in starker contrast with those last few frantic days in Amsterdam at the end of summer.

On the day that the lads of the locally based battalion had to board their train to Amersfoort, a member of our group accompanied me to the station. The platform was swarming with throngs of men surrounded by suitcases and families seeing them off, so the SD wisely decided to just hold back and observe, rather than face the insurmountable task of examining each man's credentials. Taking full advantage, my colleague and I mingled stealthily with the assembled multitudes, steering a course as far from the guns and goons as we could and ensconced ourselves unobtrusively in one of the carriages. As soon as everyone had boarded, the train chugged out of the station with no further official scrutiny. The cigarette I lit tasted all the sweeter for the relief it celebrated.

My offsider would travel with me as far as Amersfoort, where it was arranged that he would hand me over to another Resistance member from that region. In this way, my first travel companion would only know that I'd travelled to Amersfoort but would have no idea where I was headed next. My new comrade met us at the station to take over the following leg of my journey. I had no clue as to my final destination but was certainly glad to have made it out of Amsterdam in one piece. He led me to another platform where he had bought tickets for us to travel north to the city of Zwolle, the capital of the province of Overijssel. I was finally feeling somewhat safer because even if my papers might at some stage be perused, I could be reasonably certain that the Germans doing so would not have been in possession of my likeness, just my real name.

In Zwolle I was passed along to another lad for the next part of my journey. This chap had no idea where I had come from, only that he needed to accompany me to the next stop which was the town of Heerenveen, further north again into the province of Friesland. There was to be one further stage, a last train trip with yet another chaperone, to the city of Sneek. Once there, this guy led me some distance out of town, to the shore of what seemed like a significant lake. We had walked roughly half of the way along the lake's foreshore when he pointed out a building about five kilometres away. He gave me the bottom part of a torn in half playing card, the eight of spades, and said that the folks in that house where I was to go and stay had the matching other half so that they would know who I was. He left me to walk the rest of the way by myself and disappeared back in the direction of town.

About three kilometres from my destination, I noticed another smaller structure behind the one first visible. The moment it came into view a weird sensation struck me and in a flash I could see every aspect of that second house, even the far side. I saw it had one of those old Dutch wooden halved doors which led into a kitchen with a large iron stove. I saw the layout of rooms in the house. There was no way I could actually have seen all those details from where I was standing, not even with binoculars; it was just a surreal bolt of recognition that I couldn't explain and which I'll never forget.

But being now firmly ensconced on my little island, the year was rapidly turning into the winter, not so much of my discontent, but of my tedium. The family were in the habit of going to bed each night at eight o'clock sharp. In the mornings, the two older boys went to work on neighbouring farms and the youngest daughter to school, which left Janus, the widower and his second daughter Anna, to do their chores around the house.

The caretaker really was a cantankerous man with a serious chip on his shoulder with the world, a regular misanthrope who could not be coaxed into civilised conversation, so I gave up trying and we mostly sat in brooding silence.

Anna, on the other hand, had an air of alert intelligence about her that she seemed at pains to conceal beneath the outer industry of domestic duty. Janus would glower at her should her verbal exchanges with me drift beyond the merely courteous. She was a young woman of around eighteen years with clear green eyes and shoulder-length blonde hair which she kept tied back in a single ponytail, almost in defiance of the predilection of most Friesian women to wear theirs in two tight plaits. Being of slender build, I thought I detected in the way she carried herself a certain boldness of will which did not find expression in servitude to her father. She did not appear happy, nor was she, I thought, completely unhappy. Indeed, she was an appealing enigma cloaked in servant garb who, over the course of several months living under the same roof, began to take up more and more of my deliberation and not only out of boredom.

Initially she had seemed aloof, restrained, annoyed perhaps at having to feed and cater to a random stranger, an extra burden on her already significant workload. The entire responsibility of household care and maintenance rested upon her slight but sturdy shoulders. She was, in effect, the de facto mother of the house. I did attempt to engage her in polite conversation but she gave me short shrift and continued to blithely attend to her chores. This, of course, rather pleased her morose and uncommunicative father, the lazy slob. Janus was more than aware that I was totally beholden to him and had no chance to go anywhere, a fact he missed no opportunity to impress upon me. On my part, I did my best to avoid being in the same room as him and kept much to myself, although I must confess that I contrived my movements about the house in such a way as to be crossing paths as often as possible with his dutiful daughter. I'd traverse the kitchen to get to the back door just as she was in the act of sweeping, so that she'd have to momentarily pause while I passed and acknowledge my apologies. This she did without making any eye contact. A cursory nod of the head was all I got, no doubt accompanied by cursing under her breath.

On occasion I'd offer to help with the washing of the dishes after yet another meal of black potatoes and sauerkraut, no meat, no gravy, which she allowed so long as I didn't speak. If she was hanging out the washing, I'd saunter closely by on my way to look at the lake. To be honest, I was beginning to secretly enjoy this game of mildly annoying her and wondered how long it would be before she either blew up or finally spoke to me. As she became more used to me being underfoot, I think she sensed that I actually admired the inner strength she seemed so determined to conceal and possibly even found herself entertaining a scintilla of curiosity about this unknown man who had been so rudely thrust into her milieu.

Then one day as I was lazily smoking a cigarette, leaning on the railing of the pumping station, looking at nothing in particular, I experienced a sudden, vague feeling of being spied upon, an indeterminate ripple of consciousness that I was not alone. I swung my head swiftly back over my left shoulder and cast my gaze back to the house just in time to see Anna staring intently at me from the open top half of the back door. Our eyes locked for a split second, long enough to know that I had finally breached her defences and seen into her heart. She now knew that I knew that at least a small measure of interest existed between us.

From that moment on, my hitherto perfunctory hallos and good afternoons were no longer met with her previous cold indifference, but with a discernible courtesy and sometimes even an uplifted gleam from those pellucid green eyes. This thawing of relations between the two of us was a welcome relief as winter tightened its icy grip.

On a day in January when the skies were clear and the air crisp, the noontime sunshine drew me from the confines of the house to idle away some time skidding around on the thick ice surface of the lake. After a carefully accelerating run-up, I could let myself slide effortlessly along the ice. The fleeting sensation of suspension between the clear blue sky and the seamlessly melding horizon of the frozen lake brought out a boyish bravado of which I'd forgotten I was capable. On a subsequent dash my attention must have been more on the aesthetic than the athletic, for I misplaced one of my feet which slid out awkwardly in front of me, taking the other with it and dumping my derriere unceremoniously on the deck. Immediately from behind me a raucous laughter erupted at this most slapstick of moments and I turned to see Anna standing at the lake's edge, heartily guffawing into her cupped hands. Any embarrassment I may have felt at my predicament melted instantly away at seeing her reaction to my pratfall and I could do nothing but burst out laughing myself.

'Oh dear, you did look rather silly crashing on the ice like that. Did you hurt yourself?' she asked as I limped off the ice and joined her on the bank.

'No, only my pride,' I countered, 'and anyway, what are you doing out here spying on an uncoordinated dolt like me?'

She said her father was taking an afternoon nap and it was such a glorious day she just had to drink some of it in. I linked her arm in mine and walked her away from the house to a sunny spot at the back of the pumping station where we sat down and enjoyed the first real conversation to have occurred between us during my time so far on the island.

She loved her father, she said, but he was a humourless, sad and domineering man who had been that way since he lost his wife some six years before. She had died giving birth to Miepke,

Anna's younger sister and it had thrown the father into a deep depression from which he'd emerged bitter and resentful. Since that awful event, the task of looking after the family had fallen to then fourteen-year-old Anna and she had been fulfilling that role ever since. She didn't really mind, she said, but it did, from time to time, make her feel like a captive on this little island in the lake. I could relate to that, I said, eliciting from her a warm smile.

'If this war ever ends and Miepke is old enough to fend for herself, I'd really love to move from here and see something of the world. Have you travelled much, Henk?' she enquired.

'Not really,' I replied. 'Only on account of my postings with the army and then only to a few regional cities. Before that I fairly much lived my whole life in Waalwijk where I was born. It's not a bad town, probably smaller than Sneek, but I definitely enjoyed living there. Actually, talking about it now makes me fret for my family. My father and two brothers were arrested by the Germans because of things I was involved with, and they guard my mother and sisters in our house.'

I fought back tears of helplessness at the thought of what might be happening to them. Anna extended her arm about my shoulders and drew me towards her in a deeply loving hug, the first physical contact with another human being I'd had in too long a time. There was some maternal concern in her embrace, Anna the little mother, but more than that, I could feel her own longing for connection at a deeper level. I turned to face her. As soon as our eyes met all decorum evaporated and a magnetism beyond will drew us into a kiss of mellifluent mouth music, a soaring song of sex. I've no idea how long we remained locked at the lips, but a whole new world was explored in intimate detail while we did. Then when we finally came up for air, the cold, hard, familiar physical world seemed somehow altered for the better.

'Anna, where are you? Where's my afternoon tea?' Dear old dad had stirred and was bellowing.

'Gotta go,' she said, hastily planting a peck on my cheek. 'Coming, Father!' Then she was gone, leaving me sitting, smiling, some centimetres above the ground.

Dinner that evening was the usual subdued affair; they were not what one might call a garrulous family. The older boys, having been active in the outdoors all day, were simply there to fuel their bodies and get some sleep. There was no need to discuss the day's events because these were much the same as any other day. Miepke was telling father of her progress at school, which the old curmudgeon acknowledged with a few punctuated grunts. Anna exhibited her customary demure demeanour and ate silently, although now exuding, I thought, a small measure of inner joy. I hoped it was not too obvious but I could not take my eyes off her. It was to me as tunnel vision has been described; one central area of focus and clarity surrounded by an indistinct aura of fuzz and vagueness. The world that was not her lost significance. I took pains to not let Janus sense how relations had changed between his older daughter and myself, as he'd surely make life difficult for the girl if he did and she had it tough enough as it was.

After dinner – black potatoes, sauerkraut, no meat, no gravy – I chivalrously offered to wield the dish towel so that I could be close to her. During this dish-drying dance, it was possible to inadvertently brush against her arm, trusting that she wouldn't whack me in the face with a loaded sponge. I could have sworn that miniature bolts of electricity crackled between us with each slight physical contact. Far more delicious than dinner had been. By eight in the evening, Janus' invisible but palpable whip rounded the family up to get to bed. Anna managed to fire me a last mischievous glance from those intoxicating eyes as she mounted the stairs, and I was pulling on an extra jumper to go out by the lake for a cigarette.

Watching the moon play hide and go seek with the scurrying clouds had me ruminating on my own fugitive life, relatively secure for now but with a malevolent iron fist waiting just out of reach to crush me at any opportunity. The same malodorous menace that was at this very moment physically threatening my kin. I am not a man much given to praying, but I confess I did bounce a beseeching invocation off the moon.

It was getting cold, the freezing vapour of my breath now indistinguishable from the cigarette smoke, so I dragged my carcass up to my cot and laid down to see if sleep might visit. Attempting to subdue the insistent thoughts that were ricochetting off at multiple tangents like silver spheres in a pinball game, I hovered for some time between consciousness and the dreamtime, that surreal state of delirium just prior to the deep repose of sleep.

In that sentient limbo, I hallucinated a flickering vision of loveliness descending, spreading light and warmth. I sensed no fear as this wraith drew near but when I suddenly felt its touch on my arm, I shuddered awake to find Anna standing by the bed, balancing a lighted candle.

'Henk, I have come to kiss you,' she said.

'Well for goodness' sake girl, get in here under the covers before you freeze that delightful Friesian bottom off!' I exclaimed.

She blew out her candle and proceeded to light another, more passionate one, somewhere deep within my being.

Life, and the lust for it, had managed to bloom under the pall of a frigid winter, the short days and long nights now considerably brightened by the illicit joy of carnal companionship. Roughly once per week, Anna would come to my little attic room and illuminate the gloom of sleepless nights with her warm caress. I loved her smell, her taste; we sensed that it was doing us both good to live a little like this.

Then one foggy afternoon as I was leaning on the railing outside the pumping station smoking a cigarette, out of the mist materialised Mr. Gerbrandy who had just ridden up on his bicycle. He told me he had a letter that had been sent to the Peridon family in Amsterdam who managed to hand it to De Graaf, who in turn, had it forwarded by LO couriers to Sneek. My heart leaped. It would be news of my father and brothers. With trembling fingers, I tore open the envelope and studied the contents. They were home! Unscathed! A whoop of relief rent the foggy air as the stone that had been weighing on my soul disintegrated and fell away.

'Good news, I take it?' commented Gerbrandy. Frans van Oostrum, my neighbour from the Stationstraat in Waalwijk, had written to let me know that, thanks to the intercession of one of my father's suppliers, a man known for his trading on the black market, the Gestapo had released all three from the Waalwijk police station and let them return home. There would still be surveillance on our house in case I showed up at any time, but there would be no further prosecution. I thanked Gerbrandy for getting the letter to me. It had taken a couple of weeks for it to be passed along the networks.

Winter now found me with a renewed spring in my step and I allowed myself a small measure of positivity about the world. Anna continued to impress her lascivious lightness on me from time to time for which I was eternally grateful. I almost entertained pangs of guilt at how fine I was feeling, albeit mixed with a nagging premonition that it was too good to last. An intimation that proved, in time, to be on the mark.

For some weeks now, Anna had not been able to make her nocturnal visitations due to the increasing suspicions of her father. He thought he'd detected some defiant happiness in her bearing that he couldn't stomach and wished not to tolerate. Dependent on her devotion to domestic duty, he nevertheless maintained a barely conscious resentment of her being alive when his beloved wife was not. It was a feeling he could never have articulated but it certainly informed the way he treated his eldest daughter. His comfort depended on the subservient unhappiness of his housekeeper which felt now threatened, so he was keeping a close and domineering eye on her.

After two uncomfortable weeks of being subjected to this scrutiny, Anna could take no more and late one night came to my room, stripped bare, leapt under the covers and clasped me to her bosom with a ferocity of purpose that left me breathless but even more besotted. When spent, we lay spooned together and drifted off into deep reverie.

'Anna, you whore! Are you up there in that attic? Get down here now!' The shrill, hysterical howling of her father split the dawning day and shook us into instant wakefulness.

'Shit!' Anna shrieked. 'I've slept in. There's gonna be hell to pay!'

It was customary for her to be up before dawn to feed her

brothers and sister before they went to work and school and now, for the first time ever, she'd missed her morning mission. Bugger. I heard him bellowing in the kitchen below but thought it best, for her sake, to wait until later, when the boys had gone off to work and Miepke to school, before going downstairs to face the music. When I did, he was sitting at the kitchen table smoking one of my cigarettes. I could tell that the old coward had not hit her, but Anna's eyes were rimmed red with tears. He puffed out his puny chest and with a threatening finger poking the air in my direction, laid down the law according to Janus. He had sorely wanted to kick me out of his house immediately, he told me, but, being the tightwad that he was, said he needed and wanted the money he was being paid to keep me, so I was to stay. Then the threat; if I was to so much as talk to or touch his daughter again, he would unhesitatingly turn me over to the Gestapo to be taken and shot. I was, from that moment on, to keep wholly to myself and not speak to anyone in his family. Meals were to be taken in my room where I was mostly to contain myself. He then aimed a bitter barb at his daughter, saying that, if she didn't want me to die, she should have no further dealings with 'this gigolo' as he called me.

It had indeed been too good to last. I felt banished from the world and descended into something like a blue funk, sleeping each day until noon and merely moping around smoking cigarettes. Anna had taken her father's threats seriously indeed and although I knew it hurt her deeply, she was keeping an aloof distance. In a romance novel I might have rescued her from servitude and we would have eloped to some far away land to live happily ever after, but this was 1944, and we were deep into a war that was only becoming more savage the longer it endured, a deathly dangerous time of severely limited options.

The frozen lake thawed, as nature, oblivious always to the lamentations of man, followed her primeval rhythm and morphed into the promise of renewal that spring ever presents. The days grew longer. There was greater opportunity to be outdoors and shake off the claustrophobia of being cooped up in such close proximity to the one person I desired but could not have.

In a large storeroom at the back of the pumping station that I hadn't yet explored, I found a fishing rod and tackle, as well as a wooden sailboat. Sweet distractions now that the weather was slowly warming. I had fished a little as a boy so I had a rudimentary knowledge of tying hooks and the like, but found it was more the meditative aspect of sitting quietly, idly watching the line, that appealed rather than the thrill and achievement of snaring a fish out of its preferred habitat and killing it. Although to be honest, had I possessed the requisite skill to actually catch a fish, it might have provided a welcome variation to the unrelenting diet of black potatoes and sauerkraut, no meat, no gravy, that was almost as severe a punishment as the enforced prohibition of access to Anna's loving ministrations.

As for the sailboat, I never asked, just dragged it out of the shed on days when the wind was gentle and the sky unthreatening and launched it on the still water. It didn't take me long to get the hang of setting the sail properly into the wind, relishing the acceleration as it filled. There is something marvellous about movement that emanates from no mechanical source. There's little sound except for the waves slapping the bow of the boat and it was tempting to feel that it was actually the 'winds of change' propelling one forward into new horizons. One should remember to wear a hat, though. On days like this it could seem as though the war was but a distant anomaly, except for the now more frequent overpass of British bomber squadrons flying east on missions over Germany. Aware that enemy ground forces now possessed radar to track their aircraft, the British had devised a method of confounding it by dropping millions of pieces of shiny paper. I've no idea how effective this seemingly primitive enterprise turned out to be, but I was by this time so bored that I began collecting these shiny scraps as some kind of demented hobby. Sometimes on my idle wanderings around the lake, I'd encounter some of the large metal disposable fuel tanks discarded by the planes and thought they might be used as pontoons, a superfluous notion as they were too heavy to manoeuvre back to the island.

Ever so slowly, as spring begat summer, I began to see other human beings boating about the lake. Incongruous as it seemed in a time of enemy occupation, there were now holiday-makers taking to the outdoors. Friesland, except for her larger cities, was a predominantly rural province with the result of there being fewer Germans in evidence compared with more populous districts of The Netherlands, and although the privations of war existed here as elsewhere, the wind was plentiful and free.

One day a small motor boat chugged up to the island and moored to the pump house railing. A man I guessed to be in his forties came ashore and introduced himself as Harry Reeskamp. He said that he lived on his boat, a modest seven-metre long, steel-hulled vessel which he had recently anchored in nearby Sneek. With the weather improving, he thought he'd get out on the lake and take full advantage he said. He enquired as to the caretaker of the pump house. I told him the man's name was

Janus, but not to expect much in the way of joy in conversation with him. Harry laughed and said he'd better go and introduce himself and see if he could stay docked on the island for a few days. Good luck with that, I ventured.

Reeskamp emerged from the house a couple of hours later in company with Janus who was now, shock horror, laughing heartily and slapping Reeskamp on the back, suddenly transformed into a hail fellow, well met! This guy's got some serious gift of the gab, I thought to myself. Cracking the sullen misery that usually enveloped old Janus like some psychic suit of armour would take the silver tongue of a snake-oil salesman.

'What a sweetheart,' said Reeskamp as he sauntered over to join me at the water's edge. 'Guess you're stuck with me being around for a day or two.'

He offered his tobacco pouch to roll myself a smoke and asked how I liked living on the lake. I said that I'd been there for nearly a year and was rapidly going out of my mind with boredom and the futility of nothing to do. I gave him a condensed account of my dalliance with Janus' older daughter and how it had ended with being forbidden, on pain of betrayal to the Moffen, to have anything to do with her or his family.

'Oh dear,' Reeskamp muttered. 'What about hobbies or ways to pass the time?'

I said that I used to play the mandolin way back before the skies had darkened with the blood-red menace of the Germans. I had now tried my hand at fishing but was being constantly outsmarted by those scaly denizens of the deep. He chuckled and said he'd see what he could do to help alleviate my doldrums. We hung out for a couple of days, becoming relatively firm friends, smoking cigarettes and generally shooting the breeze. I was grateful for having another human being with whom to converse and was by no means averse to the partaking of a few drams of the *ouwe jenever*, the Dutch gin, that Harry had on his boat.

When time came for him to leave, Harry said Janus had told him that he was welcome to come back to the island anytime, so I'd most likely be seeing more of him from time to time. That was fine by me, anything to break the monotony of island life.

When he showed up again after about a week, he shoved an old banjo mandolin into my hands, saying he'd found it in a shop in town and thought that it might keep me amused. To be honest, it not only kept me distracted, it probably secured my sanity. As I had already told Harry, being so close to Anna and not being able to touch her or talk to her was eating me alive. The island had always been small, but it now felt as though it was strangling the soul out of me. I'd been there nearly a year and now desperately needed a change of scene. Harry threw me conspiratorial glance and said to not lose heart, you never know what's possible.

Strumming that old mandolin managed to mostly deflect thoughts of Anna, except when I played the blues. Some of those sad old American tunes had a way of wringing a tear or two from jaded eyes. I began to spend more time inside the pump house, where the mandolin's sound reverberated through the huge open cavity as if it were amplified in some grand concert hall. Music soothes not only the savage breast, but also the love-sick heart.

As summer proper set in, a boatload of holiday-makers arrived at the island keen to tie up for a week or so to relax and go fishing. It seemed fine with Janus and was probably what normally happened in summer. The two young lads and their girlfriends were university students on a break from their studies and proved more than pleasant company.

One day during their stay with us, Harry boated in to say hi and after he left, one of the girls told me that she knew who Harry was. He didn't know her, she said, but she was from the same town, Bussum, where Harry was from. According to this girl, he was a pharmacist with a wife and nine children who still lived there. Harry was widely known as a man not to be trusted, said the girl, a man with a tarnished reputation who had spent a year of his army service in jail, due to a conviction for the stealing of copper. She cautioned me to keep my wits about me in any dealings I might have with Mr. Reeskamp. I made a mental note to remain alert, but I wasn't too particularly troubled by this lass' revelations. That was until the day I accompanied Harry into town to visit a contact of his, a Sneek policeman who was active in the Resistance. While Harry had excused himself to make a toilet visit, this policeman too, quietly warned me that Harry was a big talker but was distinctly not to be trusted. There was no way I could ignore two tip-offs from two separate sources, so I resolved to remain vigilant in my dealings with Meneer Reeskamp. Caution that would, in time, prove prescient.

CHAPTER 10

A SEARING PAIN SLICED THROUGH my abdomen like an angry sabre slash. The sudden ferocity of it doubled me over, nearly tumbling me from the bed. Darting to the lavatory, I mounted the throne luckily in time to thunder an explosive bowel evacuation into the porcelain. Several more such detonations followed, thankfully not as devastating as the first. I squatted there silently for a time, hoping I hadn't disturbed anyone else's slumbers with my midnight abdominal distress.

As the pain and colonic convulsions eased somewhat, I consoled myself with the knowledge that I had a reasonably clear idea of what had initiated such an intestinal upheaval. Dinner that evening had been delicious. Grilled pork chops slathered in rich gravy, with roast potatoes and carrots. Therein lay the problem. Having subsisted for one whole year on not much more than a basic diet of black potatoes and sauerkraut, no meat, no gravy, this sudden exposure to real, nourishing food was more than my sorely deprived constitution could tolerate, resulting in the drastic reaction I'd just experienced. It took roughly a week, but gradually my much-maligned digestive system adjusted to this new regime of nutritious and tasty food. I began to feel a welcome sense of wellbeing slowly restoring itself.

A few weeks before, a boat carrying four young men had sailed up and docked on the island. I'd been belting out a couple of tunes on the mandolin inside the pumping station when I saw them approach. I instinctively knew they weren't just random holiday-makers from the district, there was an air of determined mission about them as they secured the boat and came ashore.

Muzzling the mandolin, I strode out to the lake's edge to meet them. My suspicions proved correct as they introduced themselves as members of a Resistance group from town, saying they knew who I was and why I was there. They then got straight to the point and asked whether I would be interested in joining a group such as theirs from a small village nearby who needed someone experienced in illegal activities to help carry out vital Resistance work in their area.

It was a proposition I did not need long to consider. Firstly, even though our house in Waalwijk was still under surveillance, my family was now relatively safe. Secondly, it would take considerable weight from Anna's shoulders as me being off the island might actually tone down some of old Janus' misanthropy and make her life a little more bearable. And, finally, it might give me something meaningful to do after a year merely existing. So I said, yes, you've got me. The lads welcomed me figuratively on board and said that it would take probably a week or so to find me a place to stay in the village with a family who could be trusted. That was fine by me, another week on the island was not a long time in the overall scheme of things.

THE BAKER'S SON

One day during that week there flared an intense and brutal dog fight in the air above the lake. A squadron of American B-17 bombers returning from a mission inside Germany came under attack from a swarm of Luftwaffe Messerschmitt fighter planes machine-gunning into the formation like angry, lethal hornets. The sky erupted into a menacing maelstrom of high-revving engines and loudly sputtering machine-gun fire as the bombers approached the lake. Messerschmitts arced wildly through the air, spewing deadly hail onto the lumbering American Flying Fortresses from whose gun turrets answering salvos of lead endeavoured to track and attack the enemy stingers as they looped and darted erratically through the bombers' formation.

One of the B-17s had been badly hit. Its fuselage was on fire and thick, black smoke plumed from her four engines which spluttered and coughed like emphysemic steam trains. Suddenly, the plane lurched awkwardly sideways and began to plummet from the sky like a huge, flaming brick in the direction of our little island. I took cover behind the pumping station as the roaring fireball soared directly over our house, clearing it by no more than a hundred metres. As the plane plummeted downwards, I saw one solitary parachutist leap from the conflagration to land about a kilometre away in a polder. The plane itself flew some way further before slamming into the ground in an explosion of fire and fury that echoed over the fields like a mighty clap of thunder.

I scurried across the neighbouring fields to try to locate the downed airman. I found him lying on the ground in an untidy tangle of ropes and canopy, attempting to free himself from the parachute's harness.

'Are you OK?' I asked in my best schoolboy English.

'Yeah, fine, except my ankle feels like it's been trampled by a horse,' he replied, sounding very much like a cowboy in some American western movie. I looked down to see his left foot jutting out at an awkward angle to the alignment of his leg. A rather nasty and no doubt painful fracture. I managed to free him from the tangled remains of his parachute, got him to his foot and, taking the weight on my right shoulder, hobbled him slowly back to Janus' house. That miserable cretin freaked out when I dragged the wounded aviator into the kitchen and plonked him finally down onto a chair.

'Get him out of here,' the uncharitable cur exclaimed. 'The Germans will shoot me if they find a Yankee flyer in my house!'

I told him to calm down and I would go and see Gerbrandy to find our wounded flyboy a safe house, but Janus would have none of it. By this time he was almost hyperventilating with insistence the American should not be under his roof. Anna, bless her, was tending to the lad, putting his busted foot up onto a cushion on a chair and making him a cup of tea. Janus, still fuming, bolted from the house, saying he was going to get the Germans to take this liability off his hands. The bastard, I thought, and headed out myself to see if Gerbrandy could help.

Gerbrandy was sympathetic and said he'd try to find the American a safe place to hide where one of the town's trusted medicos could tend to his injuries. I should, in the meantime, return to the island and keep the man as comfortable as possible. Cycling along the lake's edge and coming within sight of the pumping station, I suddenly noticed two German squad cars pulled up at the little bridge to the island. That bloody mongrel Janus! I scurried off the path and secreted myself and my bike low in the tall reeds that bordered the shore. Through the grass,

THE BAKER'S SON

I could make out the profiles of a couple of German soldiers carrying the wounded Yank across the bridge and depositing him in one of the cars. The rest of the Moffen then got in and they drove off at speed. The right fucking bastard! What little civility towards Janus I may have managed up to that point now turned instantly to a deep loathing for the man. As I cycled slowly back to the island, I hoped to God it wouldn't be long before those lads from the Resistance found me lodgings anywhere else than at the pumping station.

Indeed, it only took them a few more days before a bed was organised with the Altenburg family in the village of Oosterwierum about fifteen kilometres north east of Sneek. I was sure glad to see the last of Meneer Janus. He maintained his spite to the bitter end by forbidding Anna any opportunity to say goodbye, a sad end to what had been a bright and loving interlude which would replay in my mind for many months to come. I never quite got over her. I initially met her because of the war, and it was because of the war that I could never have her.

I settled into my new surroundings and became used to the real food my host family were able to procure from sympathetic farmers in the district. Then I was visited by a man who introduced himself as 'Karel' (a codename) who said he was the regional commander of the Resistance forces. He bade me walk with him a while in the countryside abutting the village. Strolling along the tree-lined lane through acres of flat, green paddocks populated with cud-chewing cattle, Karel gave me an overview of the Resistance work I would now be joining. There had been significant developments during my time at the pumping station, he said.

'You should know that your former group, CS-6, no longer exists. They were infiltrated and betrayed by people in the pay of the Abwehr, the German Intelligence Agency, plus some from their own ranks who had been arrested and forced to inform on their comrades. I know this is difficult for you to hear, but nineteen group members, including Jan Karel and Gideon Boissevain, were rounded up and shot dead in the town of Overveen on the first of October last year. Jan Verleun, who I believe you also know, was executed just this last January.'

I immediately thought of Henk Romeijn and Father Sanders who would, in all probability, have met with the same fate by now. Tears of rage and grief welled up behind my eyes as whatever impotence I may have felt in the face of such atrocity resolved instantly to a deep obligation to continue their unfinished work to prove the ultimate sacrifice of their lives had not been in vain. The fight was back. I had a job to do.

'Just so you know what we're up against, Henk,' said Karel, 'the SS and SD Chief Rauter was so incensed by the operations of CS-6 that he instigated secret-assassination squads to hunt down and kill known Resistance workers and even people known to be heavily anti-German. He was originally going to call it "Operation Blood Bath", which gives you some idea of what a maniacal psychopath this man is. He apparently backed down a little and his death squads now go by the name "*Silbertanne*", "Silver Spruce". There have been some thirty cold-blooded murders that we know of so far, and he hasn't finished yet.'

Karel went on to explain that late the previous year Rauter had also established a new national squad of Dutch volunteers and NSB'ers called the *Landwacht*, or 'Landwatch'. It was designed to supplement a police force he felt had the fatal flaw of being sometimes sympathetic to their countrymen.

'Mussert was obviously hoping to use them to protect him and his cronies from further assassination attempts, but Rauter kept them answerable only to him,' Karel told me. 'They were to wear the uniforms of the NSB with an identifying arm band and be only armed with whatever vintage hunting rifles they could rustle up. Their main tasks are to guard the transfer of distribution cards and coupons, patrol roads and perform whatever menial jobs required of them by their Aryan overlords. They have proven themselves to be self-righteous, vindictive upstarts revelling in the largely illusory power they hold over us. They are pretentious pains in the arse, and they're dangerous because of their ineptitude and idiot zeal. People have already begun to call them "*Het Janhagel*", "The Riffraff".

'The Germans are currently introducing a second identity card in addition to the one already in use and you can only get it by personally going to the local Council Chambers, which will make it bloody hard to come by for all our friends who are underground. So,' he continued, 'the new focus of our activity is the liberation of large quantities of these new cards and stamps by means of armed raids on distribution offices and council chambers where they are kept. To that end we are escalating the operations of the "*knockploegen*", or "fight squads", the KP, setting up smaller, armed units in villages across the province. Your current safe house is a transit point while the LO and the KP check your bona fides, after which you will be placed with a *knockploeg* in the town of Scharnegoutum, closer to Sneek.'

He then proceeded to give me a quick rundown of the structure of the Resistance in Friesland. 'We Friesians not only have our own language, we also feel somewhat apart from the rest of The Netherlands. We are a proud and independent people who like to do things our own way which is why we are not aligned with the RVV, the "Council of Resistance" existing elsewhere in the country,' he explained. The leadership of the Friesian LO-KP was based in Sneek, he said, but regular forums were held with representatives from Leeuwarden, the province's capital, and other districts of Friesland, to oversee and sanction operations to ensure that the Resistance, especially the KP, would not descend into banditry. Also to this end, and unique to Friesland, a sort of tribunal called a *Veemgericht* had been instituted, where three independent 'judges', not known to each other, separately deliberated on submissions placed before them by district representatives to liquidate informers or people deemed highly dangerous to the Resistance.

'I cannot emphasise enough, Henk,' he pointed out, 'the importance of maintaining utmost integrity in all our clandestine dealings so as to not lose the support and respect of the Friesian people themselves, which has been hard won and without which we cannot adequately operate. We are a mostly rural province and rely heavily on the goodwill of the people on the land to help feed us and to hide folks like yourself who are wanted by the Germans on their farms.'

Just before parting, he back to Sneek and me back to my new abode in the village, Karel told me that Mr. Gerbrandy, the shire president, had already vouched for me and that it wouldn't be long before the LO's own intelligence unit cleared me to begin work, at which time one of the lads would come by to take me to Scharnegoutum to join the *knockploeg* there.

I liked Karel. I admired the deep integrity underlying his

convictions and felt comfortable throwing in my lot with his organisation. Not only that, a renewed sense of purpose was the perfect antidote to my wounded heart and had the capacity to throw off the lethargy of the past year. It was time to get focussed; the world was a bloody dangerous place and carelessness was not an option.

Only a few days later, a man cycled up to my safe house, introduced himself as Pedro and said he'd been sent to accompany me to my new address, a farm outside of Scharnegoutum where he himself was in hiding. I thanked the Altenburgs profusely for their kind hospitality and fine food and they, in turn, made me the gift of a sturdy bicycle. I was touched. To them, giving and sharing were unconditional, no matter the danger, unlike the begrudged, mercenary shit I'd had to cop for so long from old Janus.

As Pedro and I trundled down the raised roadways and lanes along the damp polders, he told me that his real name was Pieter Glastra Van Loon, he was thirty-one years old and had been a teacher at the Christian School in Scharnegoutum before the war. He'd drifted into Resistance work with the LO, helping find farmers in the outlying districts prepared to shelter folks who desperately needed to disappear. Their ranks had swelled so significantly over the now more than four years of Occupation that a corresponding necessity for large-scale supplies of identity papers, distribution cards and coupons had seen him graduate to a more active role with the KP. The squad I'd now be joining, he told me, had originally been set up by Harry Reeskamp, a pharmacist from Bussum who had come blazing into the district like some Hollywood cowboy, full of bravado and bluster.

'He likes to pass himself off as a physician at times, gallivanting around carrying a doctor's bag,' said Pedro. 'It seems that he has left behind a somewhat dull existence as husband and father to nine children to take on the more exciting role of gangster, of a hard man living a dangerous life. To be honest, the heads of the KP consider him something of a loose cannon. He isn't Friesian to begin with, but they've tolerated his rather daring exploits on account of the care taken so far to not physically harm anyone.'

'Yes, I've made Harry's acquaintance,' I told my new friend. 'He sailed up to the island on the Sneekermeer where I'd been hiding. He's certainly some piece of work!' I added that he had indebted himself to me with the gift of a mandolin which had certainly preserved my sanity during such a long period of lying low with nothing to do.

According to Pedro, we would be having regular dealings with Reeskamp, but that he also operated independently of KP oversight, carrying out his own agenda with one or two handpicked henchmen.

In due course we arrived at our destination, an isolated farm a kilometre or so from the town of Scharnegoutum. The farm house was built in the Friesian style of a thickly thatched roof covering two levels of living area. The house commanded an open square bordered by a large cow shed and, opposite the house, a voluminous hay barn.

Pedro introduced me to the farmer, Hessel Bouma, a tall, thick-set, strong-looking man with a shock of unruly black hair and the ruddy face of one used to being outdoors. He had large, rough-hewn hands that were obviously no strangers to manual labour, the right one of which went close to crushing mine when we shook hands. Hessel in turn, introduced me to Maaike, his wife, a generously proportioned woman with a cheerful demeanour and bright, knowing eyes. They lived there with their two older sons who helped work the farm and two daughters just coming into adulthood. Another son, Jessel, had a farm of his own not too far away. I liked them. They seemed like genuine people in a world too easily corrupted by fear and self-preservation. I felt welcome as Pedro led the way across the courtyard to my new quarters in the hay barn.

The barn was an enormous wooden structure accessed by an industrial size, sliding timber door which opened into a cavernous space maybe nine metres high under the peaked roof and roughly thirty metres long by fifteen wide. Except for the narrow walk space to a door at the back of the building, about half of the barn was stacked, floor to ceiling, with hay bales. At the front of the stack, eight or so loose bales revealed between them an opening into the pile just wide and tall enough for a person to enter. Pedro beckoned me to follow him in. I ducked my head and shuffled through a two-metre-long passage in the hay to surprisingly emerge into an actual room, rectangular in shape, evidently my new home. A single, bare, electric light bulb struggled to illuminate the space. As my eyes adjusted to the gloom, I followed Pedro to a table in the centre of the room where there was seated another man. He rose as I approached, and we shook hands. Pedro made the introductions. His name was Wim Roth, and he was from the town of Enschede in the east of the country, near the border with Germany. He was thirty-two years of age, he said, and, although born in Germany, had grown up in The Netherlands. An engineer by trade, he'd nursed a deep loathing for Herr Hitler and the growth of

National Socialism in the land of his birth and when those authorities conscripted him into military service, he'd immediately gone underground here in Friesland, in time becoming an active member of the Resistance.

I sat down, rolled a cigarette, and offered my new companions one. As the smoke coiled up to dance around the light bulb, I gave them an overview of my own story. The strange thing was that it somehow felt as though I was telling someone else's tale – did all that really happen to me? Well it must have, because there I was, sitting deep inside a hay stack on some remote farm in Friesland.

I took in my surroundings. It was a space probably eight metres by five, with a height of around two and a half metres, lined, walls and ceiling, with plywood. The floor was roughly boarded but reasonably level. There were, of course, no windows, being well inside a hay stack, but there was an opening, some thirty centimetres square, about halfway along the ceiling and near the wall, above which a vent connected to a portal in the roof to facilitate fresh air circulating into the room. A similar vent had been installed above the small closet in the far-left corner which housed a wash basin and a crude, bucket and seat toilet. Amazingly, in the far-right corner of the space was parked an actual motor car. A small, two-door sedan, dusty but seemingly serviceable, it had been stashed but was obviously not being used. There were three rudimentary cots aligning the walls, along with shelving for storing clothing, books and, I noticed, pistols and ammunition. The centre of the room housed the table and chairs at which we were now seated.

My new friends had been living there for some months, they said, carrying out various activities tasked to them by the KP leadership in Sneek. The room had apparently been built late in the previous year by our host, Hessel Bouma and Harry Reeskamp who had been living upstairs in the farmhouse at the time. It had so far proven a safe and secure hideout, the flatness and relative emptiness of the surrounding countryside enabling precious time for concealment in the event of any approaching danger. The lads were full of praise for the genuine care and hospitality extended to them by Hessel and his family, keeping them well fed with farm produce and always being supportive and non-judgemental of their activities. I was assigned a bunk and some space was cleared on the shelves for my, admittedly meagre, belongings.

After a hearty meal of roast pork and vegetables brought to our room by Trijntje, one of the Boumas' daughters, Wim, Pedro and I sat a while at the table talking, smoking cigarettes and generally getting to know each other. I had a good feeling about them. They were down-to-earth, intelligent men, devoid of arrogance or overcompensated egos. Like me, they had been swept up in the black tide of history that had engulfed our nation and remained determined to preserve some dignity by doing what was right in the face of so much violence and corruption. That night, as I stretched out on the straw mattress of my cot, I let the complete silence of this hay-insulated room lull me to a deep repose, switching off, with the light bulb, any speculation as to my immediate future.

CHAPTER 11

WE WAITED UNTIL AFTER dark before setting out on our pushbikes for the twelve-kilometre ride to the town of Rauwerd. Pedro and Wim wore the police uniforms they kept hidden in our hay hole. These had been generously donated to them by two German-loving cops whom the lads had ambushed at gunpoint, forced to strip to their underwear and made to swim across a canal. A few shots were fired into the water to send them on their way. As it was now after curfew and only police were allowed on the streets, Pedro and Wim cycled on ahead, with me following a good distance behind. At the first hint of danger, they would switch off the rear lights on their bikes as a signal for me to hide until safe to continue. It was a ruse we would employ time and again.

We were fortunate that night and reached our destination without incident. The widow's house was on a sparsely populated road on the edge of town, and I secreted myself with the bikes behind a tall hedge while the two 'policemen' approached the front door. She let them in without fuss, and I waited while

THE BAKER'S SON

they did what they had come to do. This was a lady of some sixty years who worked as a clerk at the local council. According to my contact in Rauwerd, she was fiercely pro-German and had compiled a thorough list of all people being hidden on farms in the district, including Jews, Resistance workers and ex-servicemen dodging the labour camps in Germany. A downright dangerous woman. There would be fatal consequences for a lot of people if she was allowed to make use of that list and the KP leadership in Sneek wanted her taken out of action.

I had kept a sharp, luckily uneventful lookout and after about three quarters of an hour, the lads emerged from the house, and we leaped aboard our bikes and pedalled hastily off in the direction of home. As we rode, Wim could barely suppress a snigger which soon deteriorated into a hearty guffaw as he described the lady's plight. She'd turned ashen white apparently when the boys had explained the reason for their visit. They had stressed that the situation was untenable and would not be tolerated, so drastic action was called for. The widow had begun trembling uncontrollably, begging for her life and pleading remorse for her deeds. Wim had then exhorted Pedro to hold her head steady as he produced from his tunic, the instrument of punishment. Hair clippers. He shaved the woman's head completely bald and left her sobbing in a mess of detached tresses. I heard later from my man in Rauwerd that the widow had been briefly seen in the town after her night of punishment, wearing a head scarf from which protruded the stuck-on locks of salvaged curls, but that she had left the district shortly thereafter to live with family somewhere to the south.

My first task as the newest member of the Scharnegoutum KP was to cycle, once per week, around the district gathering information about German troop movements, how many, what vehicles they were using, where they were stationed, that sort of thing. I needed also to liaise with our contacts in the surrounding villages and pass on to headquarters their particular needs or observations.

This was how I had come to hear of the widow in Rauwerd, for example. This intelligence gathering was crucial, especially in respect to where in town the newly issued second identity cards were being kept and how closely they were being guarded. The SS had introduced these to thwart the now huge numbers of people going underground. You could only get one by personal attendance at a council chamber, which of course, was out of the question for people in hiding, so liberating, well, stealing them became a major focus of KP activity. Armed-guard duty for these cards was mostly undertaken by that rag-tag rabble of German-loving traitors, the *Landwacht*, so my colleagues and I thought it only right that we should relieve a couple of them of their uniforms. Our wardrobe of disguises already contained several police uniforms and quite a variety of German ones of varying rank, so the addition of some *Landwacht* outfits would be handy in any future raids on distribution offices.

In Scharnegoutum there were two of these lads guarding the Town Hall and I had ascertained that when their shift finished at six a.m., they had to cycle home some several kilometres to the north of town. Early one morning, Pedro, Wim and I hid ourselves in some bushes beside the road they would be taking and waited for them to cycle by. The land was characteristically flat, so we could see their approach from some distance, whistling and chatting together in the brisk morning air. As they drew close, we leapt onto the roadway from our hiding spot, handkerchiefs over faces and revolvers drawn, demanding they stop and get off their bikes.

One of the two began quaking uncontrollably, muttering, 'Don't shoot! Don't shoot!'

I'm glad he managed to not soil himself, because we next demanded they strip to their underwear. This they hurriedly did and stepped back keeping their arms aloft. Wim stuffed their uniforms and boots into a kit bag which he tied to one of the bikes. We then slung their rifles over our shoulders and ordered them to begin walking the rest of the way home and whatever they did, not to look back. We took their bikes and cycled smartly back to Bouma's farm where we stashed the booty in our 'cave'.

That there was an element of slapstick in watching two grown men hobble down the road in their long johns could not be denied, but it was coupled with the daunting realisation that my life had now become that of an armed highwayman, a brigand, an outlaw, with all the potential peril and consequences such a role entailed. This was a point of no return. No more lazy days fishing or sailing on the lake, I was back in the adrenaline-soaked, life-and death-momentum that had characterised my time in Amsterdam, albeit with a modicum of greater control. I'd have to keep my wits sharp and about me.

So now we had a pretty good stash of uniforms for all occasions, a couple of antique rifles and extra bicycles, but what we didn't have and couldn't easily get hold of were good bicycle tyres. These had been unavailable, even by coupon, for years. When punctured or worn out, we'd taken to stuffing them with material, old rags, holey socks, you name it, to soften the ride, even if it made pedalling so much more difficult. Bicycles were our lifeline, our only mobility. Messaging across our network was carried out by fearless, mostly female couriers, travelling by bicycle. Something needed to be done.

Wim came up with a plan. He'd noticed in Sneek, a business by the name of Knor, which dealt in retailing and fixing bikes and he was sure that it held a considerable number of bikes with serviceable tyres. If he could hide himself inside the establishment when they were locking up for the day, we could come by later and be let in. We picked a day and Wim managed to get himself locked in after closing time. At about midnight, Pedro and I approached in our socks, shoes tied behind our backs and knocked on the door. Wim opened from inside and we set to work stripping whatever decent tyres we could find from the bicycle wheels. Pedro was left outside as lookout.

Suddenly he whispered into the shop, 'Danger!'

We downed tools and noticed a Dutch military policeman coming our way.

He saw us and what we were doing, but said, 'Don't shoot. I'm a good Fatherlander.'

We kept working and ended up with a good haul of tyres to take back to Scharnegoutum. The MP had seen nothing. It was a big relief to get rid of the old rag-filled tyres and we had taken enough so that we could even supply a few of our regular couriers with new ones.

One such lass visited early one morning with the message that Karel wanted to see me as soon as possible, so I rushed off to Sneek while Pedro and Wim put new tyres on her bike.

Karel had an urgent job for me. A prominent KP organiser from the province's capital city of Leeuwarden, further to the north, had been captured by the SD somewhere in the countryside. It was known that he had significant and incriminating documentation in his house in the city which would severely compromise Resistance operations should it fall into the hands of the Germans. There was a chance that the Gestapo had not yet been there, so I was tasked to go to his house and retrieve it. Karel gave me the address and had arranged for a girl from Leeuwarden HQ to accompany me. I was to meet with her on the outskirts of the city. She was then to wait at the end of the guy's street while I did the job and if I didn't come out within ten minutes, to report immediately to HQ that the mission had failed. This was certainly no milk run, just a pure gamble that the Gestapo were not yet in the house waiting. A bloody dangerous job that I really didn't like, but it had to be done.

I packed my pistol and false papers and hurried out to cycle to Leeuwarden. The girl from headquarters was there to meet me and she led the way to the man's street where all seemed quiet and normal, no official-looking cars or untoward activity. I took a deep breath and, one hand on the gun in my pocket, entered the house. To my eternal relief, no leather-clad stormtroopers met my arrival, so I gathered up the relevant material as quickly as I could and bolted from the premises, knowing full well that the Gestapo could show up any second. I reunited with the waiting lass, and she took me to one of the KP leadership's safe houses to deliver the compromising documentation. They were as relieved to have it recovered as I was to have escaped capture and imprisonment.

Operations now came thick and fast. My regular reconnaissance runs through the districts were yielding good intelligence for Resistance actions. On a trip through the town of Joure to the south, I had noticed the imposing Drum tobacco factory, still operating only because all of its output was being shipped to Germany. This was, of course, true of all Dutch industries that were allowed to continue. Livestock, labour, agriculture, foodstuffs, the Germans were intent on robbing our country blind, no matter the cost to our own citizens.

I got talking with one of the workers from the factory who was out having a smoke on a break, just shooting the breeze. When I got the feeling he was a decent, down-to-earth Nederlander like the rest of us, I asked him whether there was any high security guarding the factory at night. He took a long drag on his cigarette, looked me up and down and, apparently satisfied that I was not a threat, told me that there was generally little if any German presence, and that the job was mostly left to a couple of *Landwacht* stooges. There were perimeter lights but no fences or gates surrounding the building. Giving me a somewhat sly look, he added that there was presently a large stock of packeted tobacco accumulating ahead of a planned shipment to Germany the following week.

I thanked him for the information and headed back to Scharnegoutum, thinking all the while that I should discuss with Wim and Pedro the notion that we may need, as a patriotic gesture, to prevent all that tobacco leaving the country. They readily agreed, and not just because we were all smokers. It would be a noble strike to deprive our enemy of the enjoyment of a relaxing toke. Reeskamp and a few of his cronies might be recruited to lend a hand so that a maximum amount might be plundered. We ran the idea past Karel in Sneek who gave us his blessing to go ahead with the raid figuring that supplying our hard-working operatives with a decent smoke would boost morale no end. Reeskamp was, of course, keen to join the heist. He seemed to thrive on the adrenaline of danger more than most, so arrangements were made to meet at our farm after curfew on the following Saturday night.

Quite a motley crew had assembled that moonless, overcast night, but with a quick change of attire into uniforms of the SD, we were transformed into an officious and legitimate-looking German outfit. Wim wore the uniform of an officer, we of regulars. Being German born, he was fluent in the language, able to converse and cuss with the rest of the *schweinhunden*, so he was to be spokesman in the event of encountering real Moffen. We would just keep shtum. Reeskamp had brought two companions so we were six in all, each equipped with saddle bags on our bikes and armed with holstered hand guns. We hit the road, pedalling in formation behind Wim, our Fuhrer.

After having travelled some ten kilometres without incident, we suddenly noticed two wobbly headlights heading our way along the road ahead. A two-man German patrol came cycling up, their rank below that of our resident 'officer', who, after the obligatory 'Heil Hitler's', engaged them in conversation of a seemingly friendly nature. We could make out the odd '*scheisse*' here and there. They exchanged cigarettes and he sent them on their way with more 'Heil Hitler's'. We hadn't been too worried, they were well outnumbered and the confrontation had occurred well away from any towns; still, hands had been kept close to holsters should they have seen through our ruse.

We reached our destination a little before midnight without having encountered any further enemy patrols and secreted ourselves amongst some trees outside the reach of the factory's perimeter lights to take stock of the situation and decide on how best to proceed. From our vantage point we could see that there were only the two *Landwachters* on guard duty. They had emerged from the building and stood for a moment smoking and talking. They then split up, each walking in opposite directions around the factory until they met up again and went inside. Through the window we could see them place their rifles against the wall in a corner of what looked like a small lunch room. One of them took a seat at the table while the other went to the bench to put the coffee on.

We decided that Wim, Reeskamp and I would make a brisk entrance into the room while Pedro and one of the others remained just outside the door. The last guy would stay in amongst the trees and cover us until we had the situation secured. As quietly as our boots would allow, we walked towards the door. Wim swung it open and we swarmed smartly in. The poor *Landwachters* didn't know whether to shit or salute. Wim, pistol drawn, demanded the keys to the factory while Reeskamp produced the lengths of rope we had brought with us. When the keys were handed over, we sat the chaps down on two chairs, tied them securely and gagged their mouths with bandannas. I motioned for the outside guys to bring the bikes around while I unlocked the door which led into the factory's store room. We left one of Reeskamp's men to stand guard on the *Landwachters* while the five of us hurriedly filled the saddle bags on the bikes to bursting with packets of fine Dutch Drum tobacco. We reckoned we must have liberated close to five thousand in all.

On the journey home we came across the same two-man patrol we had seen on the way in. We all recognized each other and merely mutually 'Heil Hitler'ed' as we passed without stopping. Back at Bouma's farm, we stashed the loot inside our hidden hay bunker and celebrated with a snort of jenever before the lads headed home. Reeskamp had wanted to take a saddle bag full of packets to sell on the black market for some spending cash but we overruled him. That was not why we'd pulled the heist. Over the following couple of days, we would ferry our booty to KP headquarters in Sneek for distribution around the squads, except of course, for the packs we kept for our own needs.

We didn't have long to rest on our laurels, because a day or two later, Harry came around to see if we could lend a hand on a fresh assignment that Karel had given him. A delegation of district farmers had let it be known to the Resistance that there was a serious problem with the provincial food commissioner's office in the town of Goenga, not far from Sneek. The commissioner was responsible for implementing German demands for quotas of beef from the province's farmers, allocations they all did their level best to evade. I mean, fuck the Germans, this is our produce, was the understandable consensus. The only trouble being, that some punctilious prick of a German-lover at the commissioner's office was now proposing to visit the farms to personally scrutinise compliance. This would not do at all. Was there anything the Resistance might do to help? Reeskamp reckoned we were just the fellows to sort the situation, a sentiment with which we readily concurred.

Late on a Saturday night, Pedro, Harry and I set out from Sneek in a sailboat down waterways that led us to just below Goenga. We had bicycles with us and were at the food commissioner's office just before midnight. Harry and I managed to find an unlocked window through which we let ourselves in, leaving Pedro, armed with a bludgeon, on lookout. Every official-looking document to do with beef quotas, milk and egg allocations, we took. And I mean everything. There was a lot. On one of the desks stood a wind-up alarm clock.

'Hey, look at this,' exclaimed Harry. 'Let's lock it in the cupboard with a warning for the morning staff.' We stuck a note on the door that read: *Achtung! Achtung, wird morgen um 12 Uhr explodieren.* Attention! Attention, this will explode tomorrow morning at 12 midday. That should put the wind up them. What material we couldn't take with us, we threw in the canal. Back on the boat, we sailed in the night to the Sneekermeer (the Sneekerlake) and burned our booty on one of its many reed-choked islands.

Having slept in the boat, by morning we were back in Sneek and had breakfast in a cafe fronting the dock. A couple of policemen, who we did our best to avoid, came in and had a great story about a break-in the night before in an office in Goenga. The manager had rung them worried about a bomb going off and had evacuated the premises. The whole town got to hear about a bomb about to explode at midday. That gave us a pretty good laugh on our way home. And of course, our farmers could now continue to operate outside of German scrutiny. A good thing as many of them were prepared to divert generous amounts of fresh produce to support what the Resistance estimated to be around thirty thousand people by this time underground in Friesland.

To say that this was a logistical nightmare would be an understatement. These folks also desperately needed identity cards, coupons and stamps with no legitimate way of accessing them. That's where we came in. Our new focus was raiding the council chambers and distribution offices where those items were kept. There had been instances where clerks employed by those institutions had pilfered ration cards and the like, as I well knew from my time in the distribution office back home in Waalwijk, but not in nearly sufficient quantities for what was needed now. Karel at KP headquarters in Sneek began coordinating such robberies in our region of western Friesland and would assign them to different squads on a kind of rotational basis.

One of the towns I regularly cycled through was Workum, about fifteen kilometres west of Sneek. Karel now suggested that Pedro, Wim and I organise a raid on that town's council chambers to relieve them not only of their supply of ration cards and coupons, but to take and destroy the local citizen's register. This was an inventory of all the town's inhabitants regularly used by the Moffen to target men to send to their labour camps in Germany. It was going to take quite a bit of planning.

Fortunately, I'd met the local KP contact man on a previous trip. Karel had given me the name of the local butcher, Hans Van Drongelen and I was to introduce myself as a KP operative by asking him the covert question, 'Are the pigs fattened at this time of year?' to which he would answer, 'Yes, if we have enough feed'. Bonafides thus established, he'd invited me into his office at the back of the shop, poured me a jenever and offered to supply any local knowledge I might ever need. Now would be a good time to take him up on his generosity.

I cycled out to Workum and found Hans at work behind the counter of his butcher shop. As I entered, he assigned one of his lads to look after the customers and waved me through to his office in back. He liked a drink, did Hans, and poured us both a jenever even though it was only eleven o'clock in the morning. Not wanting to be rude and rather fond of a snort myself, I clinked his glass and let the soothing, warming liquid do its dance on my tonsils. I told Hans what we were planning to do.

'Ah yes,' he said, 'that should be possible. It would be a pleasing slap in the face of our mayor, an NSB'er who I would describe as a pig, if that wasn't such an insult to those fine beasts from whom I make my living.'

The mayor, he said, was a tyrant to those who worked at the council and a much-disliked man in the town. His only real ally was the sergeant of police, a dangerous individual keen to be seen by the Moffen as being as ruthlessly efficient as them. The constable under him, Joop Lommers, on the other hand, was a decent bloke trying hard to use his position to help locals in any way he could. Hans suggested we plan the raid for when Joop was on armed-guard duty at the council chambers, a job he alternated with some local *Landwachters*. He would find out when that was and let me know in good time.

Another recommendation he had was that I should talk with a certain Gerard De Leijer, senior clerk at the council, a man he trusted implicitly, who could give me valuable intelligence as to the layout of the building, the location of the safe, who held the keys and so forth. He gave me Gerard's address and said he was usually home from work by five o'clock in the afternoon. Hans would have a word with him to let him know to expect me.

Just as I was about to leave, this bear of a butcher refilled our glasses, we clinked them together and uttered the mutual exclamation of 'Morgen!' This was a uniquely Friesian wartime version of 'Cheers!' that literally translated as 'Tomorrow', implying a deep wish that we would continue to have them and that they might end up better than our 'Yesterdays'. We downed the fiery nectar in one gulp.

THE BAKER'S SON

I returned to Workum on an afternoon a few days later to meet with Mr. De Leijer. He met me at the front door and led me to the kitchen at the back of the house. Over coffee he reiterated what Hans had told me about the mayor, that he was an arrogant and spiteful man who was convinced that if subordinates and employees didn't hate you, you weren't doing a good job. He always worked in the evenings, from about seven until ten p.m. to make sure all paperwork was in order for his German overlords, Gerard said, but perhaps also to avoid spending time with his dear lady wife, an apparently overbearing harridan. He trusted no-one else in the office to hold the key to the safe, keeping it on a chain in the pocket of his waistcoat.

Just inside the front door of the council building, on the left as you came in, was a side office where the overnight guards were stationed. The mayor's office containing the safe was further down the hallway. Gerard added that, alongside the normal telephone, it was equipped with a direct connection to the local police station. And speaking of police, Constable Lommers whom Hans had mentioned, was usually on the late shift every second week accompanied only by one unarmed *Landwacht* lackey. During the alternate week there would be two armed *Landwachters*. He agreed with Hans that the ideal time to schedule a raid would be while Lommers was on duty and not the two *Landwachters* who would be, due to their rank incompetence, as unpredictable and dangerous as monkeys with machine guns. I thanked him for his invaluable input and cycled home before curfew made it too dangerous to be out and about.

Back in the bosom of the hay bales on Bouma's farm, I briefed Wim and Pedro on the information I'd been able to glean so far. It was clear that we'd need one other person to successfully pull off the raid. Pedro suggested one of Reeskamp's compadres might be persuaded to accompany us. Good. We devised a ploy where two of us dressed in SD uniforms would demand access to the mayor so he could supply from the citizen's register the names of twenty men to be mobilised for a work detail the following day to fix the rail line used to transport requisitioned livestock to Germany, which had been blown up.

Wim would assume the role of SD officer, with Pedro his offsider. We were sure that the mayor, being such a German sycophant, would not hesitate to produce his key and unlock the safe. Once that was achieved, Pedro would manoeuvre himself behind the policeman, snatch the fellow's pistol and order hands to be held high while Wim severed both the telephone line and the direct connection to the police station. Because my face might be recognised from previous travels to the town, I would wait outside the council building with our fourth man until the lads had secured the scene inside and unlocked the front door. We would have enough rope with us to securely bind the hostages to their chairs. It was a plan that just might work. On one last visit to Workum, Hans Van Drongelen told me that our preferred policeman was to be on duty all of the following week, so that was when we would strike.

There was no denying the danger involved; we all felt it. All manner of things could go wrong, horribly wrong if it came to having to use the weapons we carried, but previous escapades had gone some way towards sharpening our reflexes to the point where we were confidant cool heads would prevail.

Reeskamp had happily supplied one of his co-conspirators to give us a hand and on the following Wednesday night we

THE BAKER'S SON

set out for Workum. Wim and Pedro, our two pseudo-SD'ers rode on ahead, while myself and Reeskamp's man trailed some way behind, ready to leap off the road with our bicycles should the taillights of the bikes ahead switch off at the first sign of danger. We only experienced one such incident along the way, safely negotiated except for our fourth man and I getting a little damp in the reeds beside the raised roadway, but we reached our destination a little before nine p.m.

We stashed our bikes behind Hans' butcher shop which was only about a hundred metres down the road from the council chambers. Being well after curfew, the street was deathly quiet and, on account of the black-out regulations, dark as a dungeon. My compatriot Jos and I took up positions around the side of the building as Wim and Pedro stepped up to the front door and gave it an authoritative pounding. Tension rose as the portal was opened and we could hear Wim demanding in forceful German that the policeman inside immediately let him in to speak with the mayor. He made a thoroughly convincing SD officer, did Wim, and we could hear the policeman saying to follow him to the mayor's office, after which the door closed and was again locked. For the two of us waiting outside there was nothing more we could do but trust that things would play out as planned and be ready with our ropes and gags.

Anxious minutes passed like treacle through an hourglass until at last the front door creaked open and Wim's face beckoned us inside.

'All good,' he said. 'Hurry with those ropes.'

Jos and I donned black masks and followed Wim down the hall to the mayor's office. Pedro stood with a pistol in each hand, the one he'd managed to snatch from the cop and his own, pointed menacingly at the three hostages who stood against the far wall with their hands in the air. The mayor was coming apart as we tied him to his chair. He was shaking and muttering about how he had a wife and kids and don't hurt him please, he was a good Nederlander, he loved the queen etc., the sooner we gagged him the better.

But what was that smell?! An unholy odour suddenly seeped into the room, assaulting nostrils like some foul fog from the bog. The mayor had seriously shat himself! Filled his pantaloons. Defecated in his dungarees. The tough and mighty NSB'er had soiled himself at the first confrontation with danger. Christ, he smelled worse than any beasts on the farm. This was now added incentive to get on with the job and get out of there.

As soon as the cop and the *Landwachter* were also securely tethered, we rushed into the safe and began stuffing cards, stamps and coupons into the hessian sacks we had brought with us. The citizen's register was shoved in as well. Wim, Pedro and I each carried a bag as we bolted from the building, leaving our hostages to stew in the effluvium of the mayor's soiled trousers, while Jos scattered liberal amounts of pepper in our wake to ward off any bloodhounds the SD might set on our trail. The street was still clear as we retrieved our bicycles from behind the butcher shop and took off across the polders for Scharnegoutum which we reached in good time and without encountering any German patrols.

Our haul was a good one. We counted about seventeen hundred identification cards, some five thousand coupons and roughly two thousand stamps, not bad for a night's work. Pedro produced the clay bottle of jenever he had stashed under his bunk, and we toasted another successful caper, guffawing heartily at the mayor's lack of sphincter control and imagining the scene when the rest of the council staff would arrive for work in the morning. Wim said that our becacked friend had been all too willing to obey the orders of an SD officer and had not hesitated to open the safe and produce the citizen's register, the toad. We had another good giggle, made up Jos a straw bed on the floor and turned in for what was left of the night.

Somnolent slumbers were shattered by the sound of cups and plates being deposited on our table. One of Bouma's daughters had come in bearing a pot of steaming coffee and bread with butter and jam.

'Come on you lot!' she exclaimed. 'Time to get up; it's already one o'clock in the afternoon.'

Yeah, yeah. Splashing my face from the bowl of water in our little latrine, I had another chuckle to myself, thinking that the mayor's office in the council chambers in Workum smelled a whole lot worse than this makeshift WC.

After coffee we sent Jos on his way with our thanks for a job well done, then took the citizen's register out back behind the cow barn and set fire to it. None of us had any qualms about destroying it. The SD would, in future, find it very difficult to plunder the male population of Workum because there would be no record of who lived in the area. After the war a new one could be drawn up in the 'New Netherlands' we hoped would take the place of the old regime of elitism, class distinction and rigid denominationalism of which we'd already had a gut full. We dumped the ashes of the register in the pit where our bucket latrine was emptied. The only task remaining was to ferry the cards and coupons to KP headquarters in Sneek where, it seemed, the tale of the mayor of Workum's trouser trauma was already known and gaining notoriety in Resistance circles.

I was getting good physical exercise from my ongoing cycling reconnaissance of the districts around Sneek and, still being summer, the weather was less likely to be unpleasant. It was by no means sub-tropical of course. It is said of The Netherlands that summer falls on a Sunday afternoon, but there were balmy days when the predominant grey drizzle of heavy skies held off and the outdoors were an agreeable place to be.

My contact man in Joure had some interesting information for me. He'd noticed unusual activity on the Offingawier, a large canal on the town's outskirts which was an important thoroughfare for barge traffic. Friesland was riddled with waterways, many of which serviced the shipping of freight throughout the country. Before the war, if winters were particularly severe, an annual event called the *Elf Steden Tocht*, or 'Eleven Cities Tour', would be held, in which ice skaters would race on the frozen canals in a circuit that would pass through eleven cities, an indication of the widespread web of waterways that were such a prime feature of the province. My man said that cart-loads of confiscated radios were being taken from a warehouse in Joure and loaded onto a canal barge on the Offingawier, apparently for transportation to Germany.

Earlier in the Occupation the SD had ordered all radios to be surrendered to prevent the population listening to subversive broadcasts emanating from England and these had until then been merely locked up in storage. But with the tide of war seemingly turning against them, the situation on the Russian front, and since D-Day the Allies making headway in France and into Belgium, the SD now appeared to be accelerating the wholesale looting of our country in ever more desperate haste and intensity. Since learning of the June invasion of Normandy by the Allied forces, we were keener than ever to hear of progress being made in defeating these mongrel Moffen, so the decision to steal back the impounded radios was an easy and timely choice to make.

My contact man, whose intelligence was impeccable, knew to tell me that the barge was scheduled to sail in two days' time and that it was patrolled only by *Landwachters*, not the SD. There was no time to waste, so the following night Wim, Pedro and myself set out well after dark, my two companions disguised as policemen and me trailing some distance in their wake. This time we encountered three different German patrols on the way to Joure, but Pedro had a convincing story about checking on farms in the area not adhering to the strict blackout regulations and we got by unscathed.

On reaching the radio-laden barge, we could make out two *Landwachters* sitting on the foredeck chatting and smoking cigarettes, their rifles propped up against the outside of the wheelhouse. We donned black eye masks which, despite giving us the appearance of cartoon crooks, prevented them recognising us and thereby compromising future exploits. Sneaking up the gangplank as silently as possible, we were upon them, pistols drawn, before they knew what was happening. Wim disposed of their ancient weapons in the canal while I offered them an under the circumstances reasonable choice: stay on the boat and be shot, or leap into the canal and swim to the opposite shore. *Landwachters* in general were not known for their courage, so it came as no surprise when they opted for a refreshing dip in the dark waters instead of mounting a fight.

With them gone, we rummaged through the cargo and

selected six of the more salubrious sets to take home, after which we emptied the bottle of gasoline we had brought with us over the remaining radios and set them alight. We were already some distance away when the glow of a serious fire lit up the heavens behind us, signifying that the boat was burning well and its cargo of no further use to the enemy. An enemy that, like some cornered beast, was becoming more savage and dangerous the more it was poked.

CHAPTER 12

KAREL WAS LIVID! It was mid-afternoon and I'd just called in from a circuit of the villages north of Sneek to give him my report. It had been raining and I thought that perhaps he was mad at me for dripping water onto his carpet. He said for me to take off my coat and join him in the kitchen where he was pacing the floor like an expectant father waiting for news of delivery. I'd never seen him so incensed.

'Those lame, lily-livered bastards!' he fumed. 'Just who do they think they are?' He motioned for me to take a seat and pointed at the brown clay bottle of jenever on the kitchen table. I got the gist and poured out two shots of that warm, welcoming spirit and pushed one glass along the table in Karel's direction. He pulled the chair out, sat abruptly down, picked up the glass and drained it in one gulp down his throat. Slamming the glass onto the table, he gestured for me to refill it. This I did and waited for him to calm down enough to tell me what the fuck was contaminating his composure.

Taking just a sip this time, he said he'd been in radio

contact with the exiled powers-that-be who had ordered, not suggested, recommended or proposed, but royally decreed, that all Resistance forces, and especially the armed *Knokploegen*, be formed into a single force to be called the *Nederlandse Binnenlandse Strijdkrachten*, the 'Dutch National Fighting Forces', of which the OD would assume command.

'The OD, of all people!' thundered comrade Karel. 'Christ, the *Orde Dienst* [Order Service] wouldn't know if their arses were on fire! They're nothing but a bunch of two-bit aristocrats and over-the-hill ex-army officers who've done fuck-all but sit on their arses since the Moffen invaded and who can't wait to resume their privilege as soon as this god-damned war is over.'

'What a cynical, paranoid act to put them in charge now! Even the name! How confidence inspiring does "NBS" look, when "NSB" is the most hated acronym in the country. Have they really thought this through? But of course Henk, they have thought this through, long and hard. They are shit-scared that after the end of the war they might face a country that has no more need of them, that has been run efficiently and courageously in their absence and that, frankly, has no wish to revert to the class snobbery and inequality bullshit we've already had to put up with for far too long. That is why the old-boy, officer-class elitism of the OD is their preferred option. They are desperate to preserve the rank and privilege of the ruling class come the end of the war.'

'And to add insult to injury, Henk, they've promoted that philandering fool, that lapsed Nazi, Prince Bernhard Von Lippe-Biesterfeld to the position of commander in chief. Well, they had to give him something to do. The British don't trust him, and he's been loitering around the world trying to set up business deals for himself, so now they're about to spruik him as some kind of Resistance hero for God's sake!'

'It's not common knowledge, but did you know that in 1942 he actually sent Herr Hitler a letter offering to be installed as chancellor of The Netherlands in place of the queen, so he could oversee the roll-out of National Socialism across the country? The man's a limp-wristed playboy, a gallivanting buffoon who would sell us out to the Germans at the drop of a carnation.'

'But Churchill's little "Special Operations Executive" wants to begin weapon drops into the country, so our government wants a structure in place that will ensure these don't end up in the wrong hands and compromise their continued power and relevance. Well, screw them. We are going to carry on doing our work the way we have been, and they can fuck off and play their little power games to their heart's content.' The venting seemed to have calmed Karel down somewhat, he took a deep breath, lit a cigarette and this time merely sipped at his jenever.

His contempt for the arrogance of our capitulated army's officer echelon mirrored my own deep disillusion with the military hierarchy under which I had served just before and during the start of the war. With the exception of Lieutenant Van Der Krap, all my army superiors had been hubristic, disorganised milksops who wouldn't know courage if it came up and bit them on the arse. It was fanciful to think that, after all we'd been through, we would now be taking orders from them. Well, let them play-act and stumble around at leadership; here in the real world there was heavy lifting to be done.

In mid September, we received a rather cryptic order from Piet Van Den Berg, the commander of the KP in the north of The Netherlands. He wanted as many men as could be safely spared to take as many weapons as could be carried and cycle some eighty kilometres south to the town of Vollenhove and await further orders. He didn't specify the nature of the mission but assured us that groups from the other northern provinces of Groningen and Drenthe would be joining us. KP Friesland hated the idea but reluctantly agreed to cooperate. In Sneek, Karel was of the opinion that sending too many operatives out of the district would leave it vulnerable, so he asked Wim and Pedro to stay put and sent me to join Reeskamp and a couple of his cronies cycling south.

We ended up being seven men in all, including a guy from Groningen who we'd never met. It seemed counterproductive to split up groups that were well worked in on each other in favour of clustering random men together, but we got on with it. A couple of young lady couriers from the local LO directed us to our billet on the outskirts of Vollenhove where we were to lay low until further instructed.

Well, we thought we'd won the lottery. Our safe house turned out to be a castle with an actual moat, situated in the midst of a heavily forested estate of some fifty hectares. Called *'De Oldenhof'*, it was owned by a pair of spinster baronesses named Isabella and Jeanette Sloet Van Marxveld who lived there with a minimal staff. Reeskamp, ever the silver-tongued salesman, charmed the lovely sisters into extending us warm hospitality and opulent comfort, the likes of which were well beyond our ken and certainly several steps above my own haystack home. We organised a rotating roster where one of us would stand guard throughout the night while the rest of us drowned in the feather-bed comfort that the ladies had provided. Not wanting to be mere freeloading vagabonds, we cooked meals for the spinsters and ourselves with produce from the estate and, it has to be said, we had rarely eaten better.

Guilt, however, gnawed at us as we sat in splendour with no further orders while for all we knew, the shit could be hitting the fan elsewhere. I couldn't reconcile living like some idle aristocrat when there was work to be done. After a day or so, we heard of Allied paratroopers landing in Arnhem and perhaps the same was true of Friesland, we didn't know. Our situation, however congenial, was becoming rapidly untenable so we got in touch with KP headquarters in Friesland via our wonderful couriers, for direction. They called us home.

It was too far to reach Sneek before curfew, so we overnighted with a contact of the guy from Groningen on a farm in Gaasterland. Our host was a hospitable man and over a jenever or two there was much discussion about whether the Allies could actually be making headway into our region. It was possibly mere hopeful conjecture. In the course of conversation, he happened to make mention of an NSB'er who lived nearby, an apparently hateful, self-centered German lover who had plenty of money. Reeskamp's ears pricked up and he suggested we go visit this guy and relieve him of some of his ill-gotten gains.

'Don't be stupid, Harry,' I interjected. 'Why would we go and rob some bloke just because we think he's a wanker? The Resistance doesn't need the money; we're getting enough from the NFS [*Nationale Steun Fonds*]. There are bigger targets on which to expend our energies.'

I was pleased that most of our compadres concurred, and Harry backed down. It made me think of the warnings I'd been given about him back on the Sneekermeer. Sure, he was fearless and cool under pressure, but there was something mercenary about him, some driven need to act like a gangster, to be seen as larger than life, outside of the law, a dude to be reckoned with. Any role but the reality of being a pharmacist with a wife and nine children.

Karel was as pissed off as we were when I went to see him for an explanation as to why we had needed to cycle some eighty kilometres from home, sit on our arses for several days with nothing happening only to make the hazardous journey back again with fuck all to show for it.

'I've run some enquiries,' Karel said, 'and it apparently had to do with the cunning plan devised by Field Marshall Montgomery to drop a couple of airborne divisions near Arnhem, take the bridge there and rout the retreating Germans so they could claim victory by Christmas. The arrogant bastard completely disregarded the intelligence provided by the local Resistance forces, which revealed that the area was lousy with the German Second Pantzer Corps. Through Bernhard and the B.S. [they'd now dropped the N for Nederlands to improve the acronym] he'd summoned the northern Nederlands' KP forces to confront the retreating Moffen as the British drove them towards us. What a condescending prick! Our guys, you blokes, would have been mown down in an absolute bloodbath. If I had known of this plan in advance, I would never have sent you. It was apparently called "Market Garden", a name that will stick to him like a bad smell, because from all reports it was an arrant disaster.

'And while you're here, Henk,' continued Karel, 'remember I told you that the British Special Operations Executive, the SOE, wanted to begin weapons drops in our region? Well they're starting soon. Suitable locations have been scouted by British aircraft and it's time to assign groups to each of them. Yours will have the code name "Bulldog", and will be in the fields of a farmer named Fokkema, just to the west of Oosthem village. Go and make contact with him and give him one of those radios you rescued so he can hear if the drop is going to proceed.'

I knew Oosthem well, having cycled through there on many occasions and had a very good contact man in the village who could direct me to Fokkema's farm, as well as rustle up some local muscle to help with the upcoming drops.

'Yeah, no sweat Karel, I'll get right on it,' I replied, downing the shot of jenever he had poured for me. He said to let him know how many torches we might need. One of the KP squads had recently raided a warehouse belonging to Philips, the huge Dutch electrical goods company, and made off with a large quantity of hand-held flashlights, beacons and, importantly, batteries.

Pedro and Wim were as indignant as Karel and I when told the reason for my pointless and unnecessarily dangerous trip to Vollenhove. They figured we should, as a result, remain wary in any dealings with the British if in their arrogance they had no qualms about serving up our Resistance comrades as cannon fodder in such ill-conceived and badly executed operations.

'Funny you should say that, lads. The Poms are about to begin showering us with weapons. Like manna from heaven, they're soon to start raining Bren guns and explosives down onto our little Dutch heads, so we'd better get organised and figure out exactly what we'll need in terms of manpower and logistics to get this job done.'

I'd been told that each drop would consist of around twelve large canisters of considerable weight, so we reckoned it should take a total of at least sixteen men to drag them out of the fields, get them onto some mode of transport and stash them in whatever safe hiding places we could organise. Our drop zone 'Bulldog' was some twenty kilometres from Scharnegoutum, so to minimise our presence on the road after curfew, Pedro suggested we split the manpower requirement between us and Oosthem, eight men from each district. That was a good idea. He knew our local crews well and would recruit five guys to help us. I would get my contact man in Oosthem to supply another eight from there to give us a hand.

We were also going to need some torches. We needed a signalling beacon to flash the pilot a morse code 'B' for 'Bulldog' to let him know he was flying over the right place and that we were good to go and not compromised, at least four torches to shine up and delineate the actual drop area and a couple of flashlights to not only get around in the dark, but to be used by the man on guard duty to signal danger approaching. Good. Wim would go and get those from Karel and I would travel to Oosthem to take farmer Fokkema a radio set and organise a crew there.

Anton Sleehoff, who ran a small bookstore on the main street of Oosthem, had been a knowledgeable and dependable contact man for some time. He could only sell books sanctioned by the Moffen of course but kept a clandestine stash of banned titles by various Dutch authors in the attic of his modest house attached to the shop. These he would lend out or sell to people he felt were implicitly trustworthy. He possessed a keen intelligence and had an encyclopaedic knowledge of the town and its inhabitants, traits which made him a valuable ally.

When I visited the following day, he bade me come in, locked the front door, flipped over the dangling sign to 'closed' and led me into the kitchen out back. Over coffee I explained to Anton what was soon to happen with weapons drops in his neck of the woods and what we needed from him to prepare. When I mentioned farmer Fokkema, he said he'd known him for some time as a man of integrity who would be happy to help. We'd go to meet him as soon as we finished our coffee. The farmer had two sons in their early twenties, he told me, who could also be relied upon to lend a strong hand. Other than that, another four men from the local KP group would not be a problem to organise. I told Anton that I had a radio to give to Fokkema so he could listen to the coded broadcasts from England to ascertain when drops were likely to proceed, and he said that he himself still had one which he'd conveniently 'forgotten' to hand in when the Germans ordered them confiscated.

We cycled out to Fokkema's farm. It was about three kilometres west of the town, situated off the main sealed road, at the end of a two-hundred-metre-long dirt track which was elevated above the surrounding land and lined with knot willows whose leaves were just beginning to colour and wilt in the brisk air of autumn. The farmhouse was built in the Friesian style, featuring a high, pitched roof of thick thatching. Opposite it and fronting a large quadrangle were two good-sized wooden barns, one to accommodate the milking of cows, the other to store hay, horses, milk vats and equipment. At the far end of the open quadrangle, a wide gate served to access low-lying polders which were hemmed by drainage canals. A single row of tall trees delineated a broad field at the far extremity of the farm. Drop zone 'Bulldog'.

Anton made the introductions as Fokkema led us into a large kitchen, warm with the welcome aroma of freshly brewed coffee.

He was a stout man with a rather rugged and weathered face who I guessed to be in his late forties or early fifties. He smiled broadly as I gave him the radio set and said the house had been altogether too quiet since they'd been forced to relinquish the old one. I thanked him for agreeing to let his fields be used as a site for the upcoming weapons drops, a decision that could not have been an easy one to make, given the inherent danger and logistical difficulties of such operations. He merely shrugged his shoulders with the stoicism that characterised so many Friesian farmers, saying simply that he was happy to do his bit.

When we finished our coffee, Fokkema took us out to the barn to see how suitable it would be for our purposes. One end was stacked high with hay, much like our abode in Scharnegoutum. A black, sturdy-looking horse was stalled just inside the wide sliding door. Various leather reins and rigging hung on one of the walls for hitching the horse up to the flat-bed cart that was parked in the corner behind the horse's stall. The wooden carriage with rubber-tyred wheels would be ideal for carting however many cumbersome containers from the drop zone back to the barn. Fokkema said he had two sons, both in their early twenties, who'd be ready to organise the horse and wagon as well as help with any heavy lifting. Excellent. I was pleased to note that the barn was big enough to accommodate our crew of sixteen men and their bicycles. We would have to wait in there, out of sight, until it was time to venture out onto the field and then unpack and sort the weapons after we'd ferried them back into the barn.

Fokkema then led Anton and I through the gate at the end of the yard, across the polders to the far field that was to be the drop zone, so we could see its layout in daylight. The next time we'd be out there would be in the pitch black of night. A line of tall trees separated our preferred paddock from the ones closer to the barn, good cover until the time came to light the beacons with which to guide the plane's trajectory. The meadow was roughly the size of four football pitches laid side by side, room enough for twelve or so heavy containers to plummet to earth, the only real hazard being a drainage canal along its far perimeter. We should be able to direct the plane away from there and it might only become an issue if the night was particularly windy.

Strolling back to the house, Fokkema told us that he knew a couple of farmers further down the road who could be trusted implicitly and who'd be prepared to hide weapons on their properties if needed. This was a good back-up option as we couldn't be sure how many containers would fall from the sky and the logistics of distributing them amongst the district's KP groups were daunting, to say the least. I again thanked him profusely and said I'd let him know as soon as the drops were scheduled to begin. The Oosthem end of the operation seemed well sewn up. Anton assured me he would have the necessary manpower lined up and ready to go and I said I'd leave that up to him, the less I knew of his contacts the safer it was for all of us. What you don't know, you can't confess.

Back at Bouma's farm, Pedro said there'd been no problems recruiting five men from the Scharnegoutum KP. He'd sought out Reeskamp but was told that Harry had drifted off from the main group with a couple of dodgy offsiders, petty criminals really, to begin unsanctioned actions of his own. The word was that he'd shacked up with an eighteen-year-old local girl, a fact which raised more than a few eyebrows amongst the older Friesian men in the Resistance. A Bonnie to his Clyde, perhaps. The five guys Pedro had enlisted to help us were ready to go when needed, so our team was well sorted in terms of manpower.

Wim was just back from picking up the torches and batteries from Karel. He was busy affixing cardboard tubing to the four we needed to place on the actual drop field, so that the light would shine upwards to the plane and not be seen from side on. Another larger beacon was fitted with a mechanical shutter to signal the morse code letter 'B' for 'Bulldog' to the pilot so he would know he'd reached the right field and that we had not been compromised. Because I'd been a radio signaller in the army that task would fall to me. Karel told Wim that the Brits had already completed a fly-over in Oosthem, photographing the meadow, its approaches and surroundings and had adjudged drop zone 'Bulldog' to meet their logistical requirements, so the first weapons drops would begin the following week.

Each day we were to listen to the BBC broadcast of 'Radio Orange' at midday and if a particular phrase was used, for our group it was 'the wolf has red hair', we were to be ready for a plane to come that night. Then came the tricky part. Confirmation of a drop would only come if the same phrase was repeated at eight o'clock that evening, meaning we would have to leave Scharnegoutum at around six-thirty p.m. in order to be at the farm to listen for verification at that time. If the phrase was repeated, we'd have to stay until midnight and do the job, but if it wasn't heard, it meant that for whatever reason the drop would not go ahead and we would have to cycle back home after curfew, a trip fraught with danger.

The Scharnegoutum lads Pedro enlisted had access to a radio, so he would ride out in the morning to give them the code phrase and tell them to meet us at Bouma's farm at six-thirty in the evening if they heard it broadcast. I'd travel out to inform Anton and Fokkema of 'the wolf with the red hair' code and to ensure they knew to begin listening for it the following week.

Cycling out to Oosthem and back, I was a bit perturbed by how many more Germans there were about the place. Until then they'd been reasonably thin on the ground. I guessed the inroads being made by the Alllies in France, Belgium and the southern parts of our own country were forcing them further north. German patrols stopped me four times and asked for identification. My forged papers were impeccable of course, so there was no drama, but we were going to have to be bloody alert once the weapons drops began.

The next few days felt like a calm before the storm. We thoroughly cleaned our pistols, readied ammunition, torches and batteries and prepared the police uniforms we were going to need to cover our travelling. We checked the tyres on the bicycles and lashed large saddlebags to the frames to accommodate as many guns as we could carry. My mandolin got a workout, a momentary distraction from the tension building ahead of the coming hard work of the weapons drops.

Then it began. On the Tuesday we were huddled around the radio when, just after midday, apropos of nothing, the announcer uttered the phrase, 'The wolf has red hair'. The jolt of recognition sent our adrenaline levels soaring. We were on! Luckily for us, Maaike Bouma, our lovely landlady had a big pot of vegetable soup bubbling away on her iron stove out of which she ladled three generous helpings for us haystack hillbillies, some sustenance to stick to our ribs. There just might be a long, cold, dangerous night ahead.

Wim and Pedro were already dressed in their police uniforms when the Scharnegoutum guys rode up at about a quarter past six so we could set off straight away. Our ersatz cops rode on ahead while we six followed some distance behind. Being now well into autumn, night fell early and we kept a close eye on the tail lights of the two in front. Should they be switched off, we knew to instantly get off the road and hide in the damp ditches until given the all-clear from Wim and Pedro. With ever more Germans now blighting the countryside, we considered ourselves fortunate to have been stopped only once on the way to Oosthem, a two-man patrol on the far side of Sneek demanding to know what a pair of police officers were doing on the road after curfew. Pedro gave them his tried and not quite true story of them investigating reports of illegal wood cutting in the district. We watched from a good distance as the exchange ended after a short while with the obligatory 'Heil Hitler's' and we were soon on our way again.

We reached Fokkema's farm at about quarter to eight to find Anton and his crew of four Oosthem comrades already waiting in the barn along with Fokkema himself and his two sons. Our friendly farmer had rigged up the radio in the barn so that we could all listen for the code to know if the operation would proceed. Eight o'clock came and went with no mention of any red-headed wolf. Half past eight and still nothing. Just a barn full of sixteen fidgeting, idly pacing men listening in silence to a lone radio. To be totally sure, we waited until after nine o'clock at which time it was clear that, for whatever reason, the plane was not coming that night and we would have to negotiate curfew and cycle back home again.

At least we were sure we had a complete crew that would

show up the next time we got the call. In the pitch black of night, we again took off following two distant twinkling tail lights, riding silently, not smoking, knowing well that light and sound carried uncommonly far across the polders when the day's air layers had settled. On the way home this night we were pulled up four times by various German patrols, each time scattering off the road and into the reedy ditches besides the paddocks to wait while Wim and Pedro talked their way out of danger. There were distinctly more Moffen about the place.

Our total focus was now on the weapons drops, all other activities fell by the wayside. We would routinely sit by the radio from eleven o'clock in the morning listening to the broadcast of Radio Orange from England as if waiting eagerly for the next instalment of our favourite serial. Only our real life was becoming more dramatic than any radio play.

Then a couple of days later, there it was again. In amongst commentary on totally unrelated matters, the announcer snuck in the phrase 'the wolf has red hair'. If you weren't listening for it, you'd have missed it. An innocuous remark to be sure, but one which instantly elevated the tone inside the hayloft to a state of high alert. We began to busy ourselves checking torches, cleaning and loading pistols, pumping up bicycle tyres etc. and when that was done, tried to pass the next several hours as best we could before heading off to Oosthem. It felt a little like being a boxer in his dressing room, pacing and waiting to be summoned to the ring to defend his title. Wim was reading a magazine, Pedro writing in his notebook while I tried for some moments of shuteye on my bunk. If the plane came, it was going to be a long night of hard work.

We set off as soon as the lads from Scharnegoutum got to

our farm so that we would have enough time to cover any interruptions from German patrols. But we were lucky this night and reached Fokkema's farm without having been stopped even once. Anton and the crew from Oosthem arrived shortly after and we all huddled in the barn to listen to the eight o'clock broadcast from Radio Orange. At about five past eight the announcer suddenly said 'The wolf has red hair' and an instant, almost visible spark of realisation charged around the room. This was it. The plane would come at midnight, time to get organised.

Fokkema's sons had the task of hitching the horse to the wagon. They would stand by in the barn until the plane had discharged its cargo, at which time we would summon them to the drop zone by shining three long torch beams in their direction. Anton designated one of his men to be our lookout at the farm's front gate, keeping a sharp eye on the road in case of German activity. Wim handed him one of the torches and spelled out the code to use to signal danger. One flash was to signify that there were Germans on the road, two flashes meant the Germans had noticed something was not right and shining his light in a circular motion meant they were coming, and everyone was to scatter and hide themselves.

Another guy was nominated to be his 'buddy', that is, from out in the field, he would constantly keep his attention focussed on the lookout so that the rest of us could concentrate on retrieving the containers. I would take the beacon with the shutter mechanism to guide the pilot to our paddock. I was to flash him the letter 'B' in morse code: 'dash, dot, dot, dot' from the middle of the field, indicating drop zone 'Bulldog' and our preparedness to receive the weapons. Wim, Pedro and two of the Scharnegoutum crew each took one of the torches that were modified to shine only upwards. These were the lights needed to delineate the actual drop terrain and to indicate wind direction. This was crucial, as we'd been told they'd be flying in at an altitude of no more than a hundred metres to evade anti-aircraft fire and German radar, and at that minimal height needed all the lift they could muster by flying straight into the wind.

Another two of our men were issued with shovels. The containers would be equipped with parachutes which needed to be buried as soon as they could be untied from the canisters so as to leave no evidence of a drop having taken place. The rest of the lads were to wait in amongst the tree line bordering the field.

I was sure none of us had any illusions about how bloody dangerous this job was going to be and how much heavy lifting was involved, but I deemed it still necessary to articulate strict instructions for us all to follow for the duration of the drop. These rules were: no gathering in groups, no smoking and no talking. Lit cigarette ends could be seen at night for quite some distance and sounds carried remarkably far across the flat polders. Let's not bring any unwanted attention upon ourselves, I said. For the moment we relaxed in the barn as best we could, just smoking cigarettes, chatting quietly and making sure everyone was clear as to their roles and responsibilities.

Then, just before eleven, we set out from the barn to take up our respective positions. Once away from the farm buildings, out on the fields it was dark as a coal mine. I was glad to have been there before in the daylight so that I had some idea as to the geography of the terrain. A cold, light drizzle was slapping us in the face and dampening our clothing.

Apart from the wind, no sound pierced the gloom, only the

distant lowing of some shivering cows. We moved silently out to the drop field. Most of the guys huddled in close to the trees that lined its border, trying to stay out of the misty rain that showed no signs of abating. The wind was blowing from the north, meaning that the plane would have to approach from the south, so we manoeuvred our signalling torches into an upside-down 'T' formation with Wim and Pedro stationed about fifteen metres apart on an east–west axis at the far southern end of the paddock. The other two torches were aligned north to south, the first one two-hundred metres north of Wim and Pedro's bottom line and the other one a further two-hundred metres to the north. In this way the pilot could tell to make his approach from the two closer parallel lights and head north into the wind to make the drop. I stationed myself between the north–south guys.

That done, like shadows of a moon that wasn't there, we waited, silently, in the murk of midnight, hands in pockets, marching on the spot to pump blood to lower limbs threatening to go numb with the cold. I wished my breath condensing in the frigid air was cigarette smoke. Surely there were better places to be than loitering in a damp, chill paddock waiting on a plane that may or may not come.

Then suddenly, some thirty minutes after midnight, from the west came the low thrumming of distant engines. The plane. Time to switch on the torches and shine them up into the air as the rumble of propeller motors grew ever louder. We could see nothing in the inky blackness until the crescendoing growl of the approaching aircraft grew to a cacophony of epic proportions and the lumbering, four-engined British Bomber emerged from the gloom a mere eighty metres directly above the field. It flew over and banked hard left in the sky to circle round for its money run from the south. I'd given the pilot the morse code flash of dash-dot-dot-dot as the plane passed and prepared to do so again as we heard him manoeuvre a tremendous arc across the firmament to line up his approach.

As once again the aircraft's din grew to fever pitch, I noticed small green lights being activated on each wing tip, presumably signifying it was all systems go. When it was close enough to just make out its formidable profile, the bomb bay doors flew open and an indeterminate number of sinister shapes tumbled out into the void as the pilot gunned his engines to full power, rising sharply into the sky to swerve hard left and disappear into the direction of England. Despite being fitted with parachutes, the canisters came hurtling to earth with a ferocity of speed that was truly frightening. They were thudding into the ground all around us, and we had to dodge the bloody things as best we could; you wouldn't survive one landing on you.

With the aircraft's drone fading into the night, the men in the tree line came bolting across the polder to begin retrieving our payload. The lad we'd assigned to keep an eye towards the guard by the road, now signalled Fokkema's lads to bring up the horse and cart. The guys with the shovels began digging a hole big enough to accommodate the parachutes of what turned out to be eighteen containers spread over about a hundred metres of field. They looked like overgrown metal cheroots about two metres long and sixty centimetres across. Christ they were heavy, probably two hundred kilos or more, but thankfully had sturdy handles attached so that at least four men could, with some difficulty, carry them.

As the horse and wagon rolled onto the paddock and we

began loading the containers onto the dray, it became obvious that it was going to take at least two trips to move them all into the barn. With eight canisters the carriage was at capacity and had the poor horse working hard to pull it over the spongy ground. We sent half of our men back to the barn with the horse and cart to begin unloading, while the rest of us stayed out in the field to gather up the remaining cylinders. It was bloody hard work, but better than just standing around getting frostbite and pneumonia.

But now time was getting tight; we'd have to get all the canisters into the barn, unloaded and well hidden, then ride home, all before dawn. The only way to get the last ten back to the barn in one trip would be to transport just the contents and not the containers, so we set about emptying them onto a couple of spread-out parachutes to await the wagon's return. As each drum was unpacked, a few of the lads took the casings over to the drainage canal and flung them in so they wouldn't be found. By the time one of Fokkema's sons returned to the field with the horse and cart, we had emptied nearly all of the remaining canisters and began loading the rifles, Bren guns, pistols, boxes of ammunition, gelignite, detonation cord and whatever else, onto the back of the wagon as silently and quickly as we could.

Back in the barn, we hit a problem. There were just too many weapons to safely conceal. Fokkema suggested we take the load that was still on the wagon to his friend's farm half a kilometre further down the road. He was absolutely trustworthy, he said, and would not object to stowing a load of guns in his barn for a short time. Not a bad solution; we were running out of time and the weapons would only need to be there for a few days while we sorted transportation out to KP headquarters. A couple of us got busy shovelling turf over the parachute covering the load so as to camouflage it, while one of Fokkema's boys proceeded to tie hessian bags around the horse's hooves to dampen the sound they might make on the roadway. We delegated six men to accompany Fokkema and his son, stressing again that there was to be no talking, no smoking, just get the guns there, stash them under the hay and get back as soon as possible.

Fokkema's farm was primarily a dairy operation, liberally provisioned with the metal milk tuns used to transport milk to the factories and he had put a significant number of these at our disposal. They were of an optimum size to accommodate most of the weapons, grenades and ammunition that had been dropped, only the Bren submachine guns, of which there were four, were too long. Those we hid, for the time being, deep inside the hay at the back of the barn.

We now filled twenty tuns to the brim with Sten guns, their detachable magazines, rifles, grenades, sticks of gelignite, fuse cord, etc. From my friends in CS-6 I had learned to be careful in handling the sausage shaped sticks of gelignite, as the tarpaper casing was prone to sweat traces of the explosive, which, if you got some on your hands, could be dangerous. One of Anton's lads found that out to his detriment, suffering a substantial headache after scratching his forehead with a gelignite-smeared finger. The most prized part of the haul was the inclusion of a couple of dozen English automatic pistols, far superior to the antique revolvers we'd been used to, so we each rewarded ourselves with one of those, slipping them into our belts and stuffing our overcoat pockets with ammunition. Of almost equal value were the many packets of Woodbine and Players Navy Cut cigarettes the thoughtful Tommies had seen fit to include.

Next we crammed as many weapons as we could into the saddle bags slung over the rear wheels of our bicycles and when the boys returned from down the road with the horse and cart, having thankfully not encountered any German patrols, we loaded the tuns onto the wagon. The plan was that Wim and I would return the following day to accompany one of the Fokkema lads in taking the load to Sneek, as if ferrying milk to the cheese factory there, and deliver the weapons to a safe house that Karel had arranged. Anton and his crew would retrieve the stash left at the farm of Fokkema's friend and distribute that in their district.

It was nearing dawn when we got ready to saddle up and ride home. What a night! I think we may have underestimated just how much stuff was dropped and what sheer, physical labour was involved in retrieving it, because we were all about spent. Still we needed to stay alert to not get caught with sacks of illicit weapons strapped to our bikes.

Goodbyes were exchanged and we eight from Scharnegoutum set off in our usual formation of Wim and Pedro, still in police uniforms, up front and the rest of us, heavily laden with weapons, some way behind. It was tough going. Five times on the way home we encountered German patrols, each time the six of us scurrying off the road to hide bodies and bicycles in the ditches while our 'policemen' talked us to safety. I was never so glad to pedal up to Bouma's farm, just as the sky was reddening with the dawn as that morning. We didn't bother unloading the saddle bags, just herded the bikes into the barn, bid adieu to our comrades from the village, flopped down fully clothed onto our cots and surrendered to the welcome delirium of sleep.

It was just as well that the hard work of recovering and

sorting a large load of weapons took such strenuous effort as it countered to some extent the emotional and mental strain of just how dangerous the exercise was. Discovery or betrayal would precipitate a very nasty death indeed. The deep fatigue enabled me to sleep for quite some hours, a feat rarely managed in those treacherous times.

The next day, as had been organised, Wim and I cycled back to Fokkema's farm where his lads had already hitched the horse up to the wagon load of weapons-grade milk cans. We threw our bikes up on top of the tuns and joined the elder Fokkema boy on the front of the carriage. He declined to be armed, but both Wim and I carried one of the new automatic pistols, locked and loaded, in the pockets of our overcoats. This was no milk run. We all agreed that if challenged to expose our cargo, we would shoot while young Fokkema geed the horse up to full gallop to make an escape. We simply could not let ourselves be captured or have the weapons fall into the hands of the SS. It was all or nothing.

As it turned out, we were stopped about five kilometres out from Sneek by a two-man German bicycle patrol. But our papers were particularly convincing fakes, and they readily accepted our story of taking a consignment of milk to the cheese factory and let us proceed without wanting to verify the cargo. I guess they felt secure in the knowledge that the cheese, like most Dutch produce, would end up in Germany anyway.

Breathing a sigh of relief and relaxing the vice-like grip on the pistols in our pockets, we clip-clopped on up the road and reached Sneek without further ado. We found the warehouse that Karel had organised, drove the wagon inside and helped the fellows waiting there unload the guns as quickly as we could.

Young Fokkema was thanked and sent back to Oosthem with his empty milk tuns. Wim and I rode back to Scharnegoutum at a leisurely pace, smoking a celebratory cigarette for a job safely accomplished.

We kept up our daily vigil of listening to Radio Orange at around midday and, three days later, again heard the red-headed wolf mentioned in dispatches. Now that we had a good idea of what to expect, we readied ourselves through the afternoon hours with a lot more confidence. As soon as our comrades from the village showed up at the farm, we set out for Oosthem.

Expectations of a smoother run this time were soon dashed, however, due to a greatly increased presence of SD about the place. We were stopped three times before even reaching Sneek and once again in the town itself. The latter incident proved rather awkward as the six of us lagging behind Wim and Pedro needed to find places to secrete ourselves in the streets and laneways. With the aid of blackout regulations and a lack of moonlight, we stayed hidden in the yard behind a cafe until our 'policemen' managed to talk their way out of trouble and we could all proceed. Another two confrontations with German patrols had us scurrying off the road and into the polder ditches before we finally reached Fokkema's farm, just in time to hear our code repeated at eight-thirty, meaning we could again expect a plane sometime around midnight.

Following the same procedures and protocols as the previous time, we were all in position on the drop zone by eleven o'clock.

The wind was not so much blowing as howling from the east, so we set up our signal lights accordingly, hoping that, despite its ferocity, it would not affect the drop going ahead. It had better, because this field at midnight was about the most miserable and uncomfortable place one would hope to be. Not only was the hammering wind cold and intense, it carried a lacerating spray of fine rain that threatened to flay like a watery whip the very skin off one's face. At least the guys in the tree line could huddle behind the trunks but out in the middle of the field there was no deflecting its onslaught. Minutes trickled by like a footrace in quicksand.

One a.m. came and went and still no plane. Maybe it had been blown off course. Maybe shot down. We couldn't know. Just when I was thinking about packing it in for the night, through the whistling wind came the unmistakeable drone of aeroplane engines heading our way. Torches were hurriedly switched on, and I began signalling the morse code letter 'B' from the middle of the field. The huge bomber suddenly filled the sky above us, then flew off in a deafening roar to line up its drop run. As it again approached and was nearly on top of us, I could see its wings wavering wildly in the strong headwind as the bomb bay doors opened, spewing out its cargo of dark projectiles into the void, before the pilot gave her motors full throttle to arc through the maelstrom of angry air and disappear.

The rapidly plummeting canisters were making erratic trajectories as the savage wind tore through the parachutes, scaring the shit out of those of us on the field beneath them. We ducked and weaved and ran to avoid being impaled by the two-hundred kilo projectiles raining down like boulders spat out of a volcano.

As the lads from the tree line came bounding onto the paddock, we tried to take stock of just how many containers had been dropped and, more to the point, where they had landed. Indeed, they were strewn widely over the terrain, one had landed in the drainage canal and another, its parachute collapsed by the wind, had fallen nose first to the ground at great speed and was buried about a metre deep in the turf, the rest of it poking out of the soil like a tilted gravestone. We deployed the shovel brigade to dig this one free before going on to bury the parachutes while four of us headed to the canal to see if we could retrieve the sunken one. Fortunately, its parachute lay slumped over the bank on our side of the stream and, using the ropes still attached, we managed with some effort to fish the drum out of the water and onto the sodden bank. The extra time it took to salvage this wind-dispersed drop meant that we would not have time for more than one trip back to the barn so we took a gamble that all twelve containers could be taken in one go and that the horse would cope with the extra load and the wagon would not get bogged in the rain sodden soil. With literally all shoulders to the wheel, the cargo made it safely back to the barn and was unloaded and stashed before dawn so that there was still time to cycle home in the dark.

We were all tired. The night had not gone at all smoothly, what with the extra patrols on the road and the wind-ravaged drop, but if we somehow thought things might improve, we were to be sadly disappointed. Entering the town of Sneek, a car full of German officers pulled to a stop at the far end of the street along which we were cycling. It was closely followed by an armoured personnel carrier and a truck full of soldiers. In the dark they hadn't seen us and we managed to sprint away down a side lane. There was now no chance of riding through Sneek and getting home by dawn. Luckily we knew the town well and were able to circumvent the street where the Germans were gathering, thinking our best bet might be to make our way to the warehouse where Wim and I had brought the milk tuns on the drop before. With the amount of weapons we were carrying, we had to get off the street and somewhere safe, fast! An armed stand-off with that many Germans would end in a bloodbath and none of us had the appetite for that.

Our Resistance comrade who lived on the premises was roused and he led us with our heavily laden bicycles into the huge warehouse space. When we told him of the considerable German patrol disembarking a couple of streets away, he said he was not surprised, that it had become a more regular occurrence of late. He reckoned the SD were getting mightily pissed off at the increase in illegal activity in and around Sneek and were clearly flexing their muscles to intimidate the populace.

'You're going to have to lay low for the day,' he told us. 'Wait until nightfall before trying to get home. Luckily you've come to the right place.'

From in amongst a jumble of hand carts and delivery bicycles, he produced a mobile gantry two and a half metres high which he rolled over to the centre of the vast room. It was equipped with a steel hook suspended on a block and tackle. In the middle of the dusty floor, he uncovered a small square hatch, which he lifted up to reveal a metal eye bolt. Snapping the gantry's metal hook through the bolt, he began tugging on the block and tackle's rope. Ever so slowly, a large section of floor, probably four metres long, two metres wide and hinged at the far end, lifted to reveal a ramp leading down to an ample, cavern-like expanse beneath the warehouse.

Before the war, he said, the warehouse had accommodated a business importing various goods from across Europe, including, ironically, from Germany. One of the main commodities had been wine and this cellar had, in its time, stored ten to twelve large oak barrels filled with quality product. Only four now remained, filled with German Pinot Noir, the rest of the vault serving as a well-camouflaged repository for weapons.

'You'll all be safe in here; the Germans won't find it if they come looking. Help yourselves to some of the wine but please don't drink it all, I'll come back after nightfall and let you out again. There are some kerosene lanterns and plenty of straw on the shelves so you should be comfortable enough to get some sleep. You all look like you could use some.'

We ferried our bicycles down the ramp and settled down to while away the hours until night as the trap door was lowered shut behind us.

The air in the cellar was of a musty, mouldy consistency, leavened with the sweeter smell of straw and a backing note of fermenting grapes, so not altogether unpleasant. It was also not cold, allowing us to shed overcoats and use them to stretch out upon. There was enough wide shelving along the brick walls of the crypt for the eight of us to be quite comfortable. One of the Scharnegoutum lads found a stash of tin wine-tasting cups and we deemed it only polite to take up our host's offer to sample the tipple from the imposing wine barrels. A couple of snorts of what was a most agreeable wine followed by a soothing cigarette and it was easy to let sleep revive our tired bodies for a while.

The sensation of Wim tugging on the sleeve of my shirt snapped me to instant consciousness. I must have been out for the count because in the disorienting gloom it took me some seconds to remember where I was, all I could see was Wim's face with a raised finger over his mouth warning me to silence. Although the cellar was well insulated, we could hear footsteps and muffled talking coming from above our heads. It was difficult to make out the content, but there was no mistaking the terse, insistent tone of German being spoken. We quickly doused the kerosene lanterns and huddled quietly in the subsuming dark, pistols at the ready in case the big trapdoor into the cellar was uncovered and raised. Agonising moments passed with only more indistinct speech and footfalls filtering through the warehouse floor, our ceiling. And then, nothing. It seemed the SD had come, found no trace of anything untoward and left to search more of the town.

We relit the lanterns but no-one felt much like sleeping; the adrenaline still coursing through our systems put paid to any easy repose. Had the Moffen discovered that hatch in the floor of the warehouse, we would have been trapped like rats in a sewer with no hope of escape. It did not bear thinking about so we instead toasted our good fortune with another round of wine and spent the rest of the day smoking cigarettes and chatting idly as we waited for nightfall to cover our interrupted journey home.

Finally, a little after seven p.m. the great door to our tomb was hoisted slowly open and we could manhandle our heavily laden bicycles up the ramp and into the warehouse where we profusely thanked our comrade-in-arms for successfully hiding us from what had been, by all accounts, a significant Gestapo operation. He told us that the large contingent of soldiers we had seen arriving that morning had spent the entire day systematically searching the town, house by house, until finally clearing out at five in the afternoon. Their visit to his warehouse had yielded nothing of interest to them; they'd accepted it was a defunct business of no consequence and had moved on to the next place.

It was a wary band of brigands that cycled through the streets of Sneek after curfew that evening and out across the polders towards Scharnegoutum, but finally luck rode with us and we reached Bouma's farm without any further enemy entanglement. Although too late for dinner, a pot of stew was still simmering on the farmhouse's stove from which Maaike ladled each of us a big bowl full, accompanied by a thick slice of home-baked bread. An after-dinner slug of Pedro's jenever and it was off to sleep, for early next morning there was a load of explosives and weapons to be accompanied from Oosthem to Sneek.

In the shrill light of day, we relied on the precision of our forged papers and the successful camouflaging of our illicit cargo to pass muster in any encounters with SD patrols. Capture could not be countenanced; it was out of the question. Just like the previous time we all understood that if the Moffen discovered our subterfuge the only option would be to abandon all pretence and shoot our way out of the confrontation, hoping our booty could be sped away in the ensuing firefight. These weapons runs were not for the fainthearted. The onerous nature of the next day's delivery was dialled up even higher when Pedro and I arrived at Fokkema's farm to find that the cargo had been loaded onto the wagon and liberally covered with a large consignment of cow manure, a popular and widely traded fertiliser, great for the soil but savage on the olfactory equipment of humans. It radiated an aura of effluvium a good several metres around the cart, to the point where we decided to just ride our bikes in front of the load instead of joining the driver on top of the carriage. We hoped that it would also prove to be a strong deterrent to any closer SD inspection.

Not much information had reached our ears on the advance of the Allied forces across Belgium and into the southern regions of our own country, but it sure seemed as though a lot more Germans were being squeezed north into Friesland as a result. On this particular run we were halted and asked for identification no less than twelve times. Our documents were of course, impeccable, but it was more the sight and smell of our cargo that saw us hastily waved on each time. We were going to need a damned good scrubbing when we got back to our barn.

While the stench was relatively easy to eliminate, the increased SD presence in our neck of the woods was something we were going to have to seriously address. We'd been lucky the other morning to have found a safe hiding place, but it was now clear that travelling home through Sneek from another weapons drop would be out of the question, the odds of getting caught were just too great. We would have to find an alternative route.

Talking it over with Wim and Pedro, we agreed that the safest way would be to cycle through the quieter farmlands north of the town and join the Scharnegoutum road on the other side, the only drawback being a fairly wide canal devoid of bridges that we would have to find a way of crossing.

'You've been covering that area fairly regularly in your reconnaissance trips, haven't you, Henk?' said Pedro. 'Are there any farmers you can think of who might be not only sympathetic but also own some kind of boat or punt that will get us across the waterway?'

As it happened, I did know a dairy farmer whose smallholding fronted the canal and who had a punt to ferry his milk to the butter factory in Sneek. A solid and upstanding Fatherlander, he'd been harbouring two Resistance colleagues from Amsterdam who were wanted by the SD, for whom I'd been supplying him with extra ration cards and coupons.

The following day, I cycled out to see if he might be persuaded to help. This was, of course, a rather delicate business. I would need to explain, at least to some degree, what we were up to, acutely aware that the information I was imparting could, far too easily, get him killed. He listened quietly as I explained our dilemma after which he put a match to his pipe, blew a billow of fragrant smoke across the room and said he'd have no qualms about putting his punt at our disposal. I admired the unflappable cool with which he agreed to help us out, fully aware of the dangers involved, yet happy to come onboard. It was true of so many Friesian farmers without whose goodwill the Resistance would find it nigh impossible to function. This was why it was imperative to maintain absolute integrity in all our activities so we didn't jeopardise their continued respect and support.

'With how many men will you be travelling?' he asked.

I told him there'd be eight of us on bicycles.

'Well my punt should hold four at one time so we'll have to make two trips,' he replied.

I made it clear that we would not know there was a weapons drop planned until we listened to the radio at midday, so if it was on, we would just turn up at his farm at around seven p.m., use his services to get across the canal and he would then know to expect us the following morning before dawn for the trip back. We shook hands and I told him he would likely be seeing us within the next week.

It seemed that Churchill's Special Operations Executive was in somewhat of a hurry to arm the Resistance forces here in The Netherlands, for not two days passed before we again heard our code broadcast at midday on Radio Orange. We were by now quite used to the routine, but that didn't make it any less daunting, especially now that we had a whole new route to travel to bypass Sneek.

The farmer whose help I had solicited wasted no time guiding us across two of his fields to where his boat was hitched to a sturdy tree on the bank of the canal. It was a flat-bottomed, wooden punt a couple of metres wide and probably six metres long, big enough, as he had told me, to hold four of us with our bikes. The canal at this point was fairly wide but not deep and with only a lazy flow so he was able to propel the boat across by means of pushing a long pole off the bottom. It made for quite slow progress but was desirably noiseless.

Along the far bank ran the road we needed to take to bypass Sneek and reach Oosthem. The first four to go across waited silently and without smoking for the rest of us to catch up. We thanked our farmer friend and said we'd return around six in the morning and would signal him with a torch when we got to the far bank. He'd be there, he said.

It was by now nearing winter and becoming decidedly colder so we kept up a brisk pace of pedalling to try to retain some warmth in the crisp night air. Of course, that would be instantly undone every time Wim and Pedro in their police uniforms were halted by yet another SD patrol and we stragglers behind had to swerve off the road and dive down amongst the damp reeds and bushes adjoining some field until they'd again talked their way out of trouble. But by eight o'clock we were in the relative comfort of Fokkema's barn when confirmation came over the wireless of an imminent midnight drop.

We had evolved into quite a slick team, everyone knew their

job and did it with precision, speed and above all, silence, so when that roaring, lumbering British bomber rained a massive twenty containers down around our heads, we swung into action and had our saddle bags loaded and ready to head home by five o'clock in the morning. It hadn't been easy; the empty canisters were now needing to be dragged further because the drainage canal was beginning to fill up with them and a whole wagon load had to be taken down the road to the farm of Fokkema's friend, but we got the job done.

Weary, damp and cold, we reached the rendezvous point on the canal a little before six a.m. having had only a couple of SD patrols to contend with, fortunately without drama. It was too dark to see if the farmer was waiting on the opposite bank but we flashed a torch in that direction. Anxious minutes dragged their feet as we waited to cross, the eight of us standing exposed on the bank of the canal, bicycles straining under the weight of automatic weapons and our usual ploy of Wim and Pedro as just two policemen out after curfew having no credibility at all.

Just when the punt heading to our side of the waterway was coming into view, the headlights of a fast-approaching car screeching to a dusty halt in front of us rooted us to the spot. We had no option to run for cover, so we let the bicycles drop to the ground and gripped tight to the loaded automatic pistols in each of our pockets. Four heavily armed German soldiers and one officer leaped from the automobile and lined up opposite us in the headlight's beam. The time that had been limping along now froze in its tracks. It stood still. There was suddenly only this moment and it contained the world; its beginning and, quite possibly, its end. The very air crackled with menace as language was dispensed with and anything that needed to be said was conveyed in eye-to-eye contact with the officer opposite. His men were nervous empty vessels awaiting direction but you could almost see the cogs of his own brain whirring wildly, weighing up the odds. Yes, they were the power, the Fuhrer's chosen ones, but they were outnumbered and the desperate-looking men facing them were bulging with weapons. Christ, they even had pistols sticking out of their rain boots. None of us batted an eyelid, staring them out with a look that said, make one move and you're all dead. Behind us the punt had reached our shore so we spread out, four of us slowly but deliberately edging backwards towards the boat, all attention still focused on the Germans. The lads boarded the punt and, never turning their backs on the enemy, quietly slipped away to the far bank.

We still on the bank held our nerve as the Moffen remained rooted to the spot. Any lapse now would be lethal. Any sudden move would detonate a firefight. The punt returned. The four of us slowly, calculatedly manoeuvred our bicycles and ourselves aboard, never once taking our eyes off the nervous Moffen. They, in turn, must have decided that discretion was the better part of valour and stayed stunned on the bank watching us drift out of sight to the other side.

Regrouping, we each took a deep breath that kickstarted time and brought us back down to earth. What the fuck had just happened? Did we really stare down a heavily armed German patrol? Sniggers of laughter grew to hearty guffaws as the reality of what had just occurred hit home. Our friendly farmer led us across the fields and beckoned us into his house.

'That was close, lads; too close for comfort,' he said. 'I think you've got time for one of these before you continue home.'

From the pantry cupboard he produced a clay bottle of jenever which he proceeded to pour into nine glasses. *'Morgen'* came the chorus as we all downed the satisfying spirit in one gulp, feeling its radiating warmth spread through our bodies like a revitalising tonic for the soul.

There was no let-up in activity. In between each weapons drop came the dangerous task of distributing the guns and explosives around the district. It was tiring, demanding work, fraught with peril at every turn but it had to be done and we were the guys to do it. There was simply no time to reflect and put all this into perspective; it was a runaway train and we had little choice but to ride it and hang on.

Indeed, the next weapons drop followed only days later, we'd barely had time to deliver the guns from the last one. Another bitterly cold, damp, dark night on the field behind Fokkema's farm had us stamping our feet and blowing into our hands to stave off what felt like potential frostbite, until at ten minutes to one, when we'd almost given up hope, came the familiar drone of an approaching British bomber. We turned on the torches and I began signalling our code into the sky as the plane flew over to ascertain wind direction and circled round to make the drop.

From what we could make out in the dark, there seemed to be a comparatively minimal number of containers falling to earth, but in amongst them was a more slowly descending parachute from which dangled the unmistakeable silhouette of a man. Well that was different. We counted only six barrels, and our men began the task of retrieving them while Wim and I approached the guy who had landed a small distance away and was busy disentangling himself from the ropes of his parachute.

He was bound to be one of us, but we kept a firm grip on the pistols in our pockets, just in case.

He greeted us in Dutch and introduced himself as 'Jaap', his codename. He told us that the recently established *Bureau Bijzondere Opdrachten* (Office of Special Assignments) that worked closely with the British Special Operations Executive had sent him to instruct our Resistance members in the use of the weapons and explosives we'd been retrieving. We introduced ourselves, welcomed him aboard our little outfit and, dragging his parachute behind us so that it could be buried with the ones from the containers, set about helping the others load the wagon that had just been brought up from the farm.

'We can talk when we get back to the barn,' we told Jaap as he pitched in with the work of unpacking the containers and ditching the empty barrels in the canal.

Once inside the relative warmth of the barn, Jaap expounded on the agenda behind his unannounced visit. The plan of the SOE, he said, was to have an armed and organised cohort on the ground in The Netherlands to supplement the slowly advancing Allied forces and to sabotage German troop movements from behind enemy lines. Hold on. Where had I encountered just such a scheme before? Oh, that's right, when our absent 'powers-that-be' sent a significant cohort of KP fighters on a wild goose chase to Vollenhove to fight retreating German troops. Those same 'powers-that-be' that had decreed all Resistance forces be under the centralised command of the useless and arrogant *Orde Dienst*, a decision obviously intended to cement their continued relevance and thwart any chance of the armed Resistance taking control in the confusion following eventual liberation. Well screw them; for us it was business as usual so we might as well learn as much as we could from this explosives guy from the sky.

He knew his stuff, did Jaap, and in the following few days staying with us on Bouma's farm, he showed us the tricks of the trade, like how to connect fuse cord to sticks of gelignite and work out sufficient burn time to retreat and not get blown up. He demonstrated the idiosyncracies of the Sten guns that made up the bulk of the armaments in the weapons drops, warning that, although popular due to their simple construction and compact shape, they required particular care as they were prone to fire if dropped. Their thirty-two round detachable magazines had a regrettable tendency to jam, due to problems with the mechanism that fed the rounds into the firing chamber. These shortfalls had earned them the nickname 'Stench gun' amongst members of the British army, he said, but they weighed only about three kilos and their short and simple shape made them easy to carry and use in battle conditions. He added that they were accurate to about one-hundred metres but it was important they be held like a rifle, not grasped by the protruding magazine, in order for them to operate to their full capacity.

Having gotten us up to speed in weapons training and explosives, Jaap moved on to the other northern provinces of Groningen and Drenthe, leaving us with the added errand of organising nocturnal tutoring sessions with the various KP factions scattered about our neck of the woods to pass on our recently gained knowledge. This again was no picnic due to the disturbing escalation of German activity. For this task we decided to dust off the SD uniforms in our wardrobe of disguises, Wim, being fluent in the Hun vernacular, donning officer's garb, Pedro and I dressing as soldiers. It was a ruse that worked well, thankfully, managing to safely negotiate numerous nighttime enemy encounters as we travelled to instruct Resistance comrades in Scharnegoutum, Oosthem, Joure, Sneek and Leeuwarden.

CHAPTER 13

It was by now coming into November and winter announced its intention to be particularly harsh and bitter by lashing out with earlier than usual frosts and snowfalls. Luckily for us, the thick hay-bale surrounds of our bolt hole in Bouma's barn continued to act as effective insulation, and we could face the extremes of the season with minimal heating.

It seemed the Germans too were feeling the cold. In their case it was the bitter, creeping wind of defeat blowing them back to their glorious *Vaterland*, a loss of face that manifested in an intensifying brutality and ruthlessness they unleashed on the people of The Netherlands still under their control. Word reached us that the KP group operating weapons drop zone 'Wardrobe', outside the town of Tijnje, had been compromised and betrayed to the Germans, resulting in eight of their members being arrested and summarily executed, without trial or due process, in a field not far from the town centre. This was a sobering recognition that the high wire we walked every day without a net was as friable as rust and ever susceptible to sabotage.

Karel paid us a visit. The weapons drops were beginning to taper off, he said and the KP were now well armed and trained, so he had new tasks for us. He stressed that these jobs were distinctly not sanctioned by the B.S., our ostensible, royally endorsed, new national military leadership.

'Don't worry about those posturing, elite pricks in the B.S. demanding their moment of glory. They've done bugger-all this whole lousy war, so we'll leave them to their play-acting; there's work to be done.

'We've had intelligence that the council chambers in the town of Mantgum to the north east have taken delivery of a large number of identity cards and distribution coupons meant for their surrounding districts. With so many Moffen now underfoot, there are going to be a lot more people having to go underground, so, Pedro and Wim, I want you to check the place out and come up with a plan to steal them.

'As for you Henk,' he said, turning his attention to me, 'the KP chiefs in Leeuwarden have a job for you. They need someone from outside of the city to help organise a plan to potentially spring Resistance prisoners from the notorious *Blokhuispoort* jail in the centre of town. They're afraid that with the Moffen stepping up operations there will be a greater possibility of key KP personnel being captured and tortured for information that would compromise the entire Resistance network. Am I right in assuming that from your previous reconnaissance trips to the area, you already have a trusted contact there?'

I told him that indeed I had; she was a nurse who used her profession as cover for extensive courier work in and around the city.

'Good,' said Karel. 'She can introduce you to Piet Kramer,

head of the Leeuwarden KP who'll fill you in on what he wants you to do.'

I liked Karel. He was a hell of a good operator who managed to stay well grounded and not lose the human touch despite all the shit and danger that daily flew around him. And he always had jenever. From the saddle bag on his bike, he produced a clay bottle of the finest, poured us all out a decent dram and said, 'Keep the bottle, lads; there's more where that came from.'

Mies Dekkinga was a slender woman of about thirty years, who had been a nurse since leaving high school. She'd seen a lot of life and death in that time so wasn't easily fazed by the hazardous courier work she carried out for the Leeuwarden KP. The leather case with the white cross she carried on the back of her bicycle would often contain highly sensitive and incriminating correspondence beneath the stethoscope, bandages, scissors and other accoutrements of her trade as she rode, sometimes great distances, delivering them to outlying groups. She knew the lie of the land.

I visited her in the house in Leeuwarden she shared with her elderly mother. Her father had died some years before the war and Mies herself had never really found the time to marry and have children. She was a good-natured person, possessed of a ready wit and the black humour so often characteristic of those in the medical profession. Over coffee, the ersatz kind unfortunately, I explained that I'd been tasked with meeting Piet Kramer and asked if she would be prepared to introduce me. She knew me reasonably well by this time, well enough to know that I could be trusted.

She looked me in the eye and simply said, 'Why don't you and I take a refreshing bicycle ride into the countryside?'

Refreshing? A cold drizzling rain had been falling all morning.

About three kilometres out of the city, we turned off the sealed road onto a rather muddy cart track that snaked through a grove of sapling trees to meet up with a reed-choked canal. Roughly five-hundred metres along, we stopped beside a barely discernible gang plank parting the more than head-high bullrushes. Mies whistled a few bars of that popular song of the day, *Wie heeft er suiker in the erwten soep gedaan* (Who put the sugar in the pea soup), obviously to announce our arrival as friendly, before leading me across the cleated boards onto a small houseboat moored there which had been all but invisible from the path. Beyond the small aft deck, a narrow wooden door opened onto a ladder leading down into the bowels of the boat. The space was divided into two rooms. In the bow, a low-ceilinged cabin contained a bed, while the main area had a bench with a two-burner kerosene stove on one wall and a table flanked by four small chairs in the middle. Seated on one of them was Piet Kramer. In front of him lay a pistol alongside a cup of coffee and a pack of British cigarettes. He motioned for us to sit down as Mies made the introductions.

'Thanks for coming, Henk,' said Piet. Then, looking me square in the eye, he added, 'Karel speaks highly of you, and we need someone trustworthy and resourceful, preferably from out of town, to help prepare a plan to spring Resistance comrades from the *Blokhuispoort* prison here in town, before the bastard Moffen torture information out of them that could conceivably jeopardise the entire network. We'd like you to try to make contact with one of the wardens from the jail who might be sympathetic to our work and get information from him as to the layout of the building, the various protocols, where the keys are kept and by whom, that sort of thing, so that we can knock together a plan to free any of our guys that might be arrested.

'You'll notice that the director of the jail, his admin staff and all the wardens are Dutch, but the SS very much run the joint, so I don't need to tell you how careful we have to be. Across the Oosterbrug bridge near the jail and a little further along the canal is a bakery called *De Korenaar*, run by one of our top men, Taco van der Veen, who'll be able to give you the names of some of the wardens. Go into his shop and ask him if he bakes raisin bread on Sundays and he'll know that I sent you.'

With that, he produced three small glasses and a bottle of jenever. 'Courtesy of some nocturnal warehouse shopping,' he said with a sly grin. I thought for a moment how similar this Friesian hospitality was to that of my own southern region of Brabant, but there was, of course, little time for sentimentality, so I flung the fiery spirit down my throat and got on with the job at hand. Piet said to report back to him on his boat as soon as there was anything to work on. We said our goodbyes and Mies and I headed back into the city.

The following day, I cycled back to Leeuwarden to initiate contact with baker van der Veen, who proved to be a most helpful man. As his shop was situated so close to the *Blokuispoort*, many of its staff were regular customers and he knew quite a few of them by name. Heavily involved in the Resistance himself, he'd so far had no reason to investigate the loyalties of any of the jail's employees, but thought that Dirk Jellema, the head warden, seemed an honourable man and solid Friesian who might be of a mind to provide inside information about the jailhouse. He told me where Jellema lived and that he normally worked late shifts so was likely to be at home as we spoke. I thanked van der Veen and rode off to find the head warden's house. Pedalling through the city, I pondered over the best approach to take with Jellema. I mean, this was not exactly cold calling an address to try to sell the occupants something; there was a hell of lot more at stake. I decided to just be up front with him, if he was at all sympathetic he might hear me out, and if not, slam the door shut in my face, either way, I'd have my answer.

The man answering the doorbell looked me quickly up and down after I'd introduced myself as working for the KP and had asked for a few minutes of his time. He made no move to close the door on me, just glanced over my shoulder left and right into the street to make sure I was alone, before inviting me into his house. I guessed him to be in his late forties and he had about him an air of alertness to be expected from someone whose job it was to be constantly on guard. Sitting down at his kitchen table he asked me what it was I wanted from him. I told him that the KP leadership was becoming concerned, not only at the surging SS presence in our region, but also the spiralling brutality with which they were clamping down on any defiance of their authority. They had tasked me to investigate the possibility, should it become necessary, of breaking our men out of the *Blokhuispoort* before they could be tortured to reveal what they knew of the Resistance network. We needed information as to the jail's layout, the protocols in place, SS presence and so forth and would he be prepared to help.

Jellema lowered his gaze, pondering the pros and cons of acceding to what was, in effect, a deathly dangerous request. I let him think. There fell between us an uncomfortable silence I thought it best not to break.

After several intense minutes had passed, Jellema looked me in the eye and said, 'Mr. Vos, the jail's adjunct director is a man not to be trusted. He is a "yes" man keen to curry favour with the SS. Our previous director, Mr. Bakker, was an honourable and compassionate man, currently in jail himself in Amersfoort, for daring to speak up against the barbaric torture being perpetrated on prisoners under his jurisdiction. What do you need to know?'

Back on the boat, Piet Kramer offered me a cigarette from the packet of Players Navy Cut that lay on the table in front of him and reached across to light it for me. They'd been a welcome inclusion in many of the weapons drops, a fact which made smoking them in public a rather dangerous luxury. It would be like waving a Union Jack at a German bull. As a private indulgence behind closed doors, they felt like a breath of freedom.

I'd come straight from my meeting with Jellema to Kramer's boat to report the head warden's readiness to help our cause. He had explained to me that the jail was divided into two blocks, separated by an open-air quadrangle, the front one being the detention centre where more short-term political prisoners were held and towards the rear of the complex was the maximum-security wing where long-term, usually mainstream, prisoners were locked up. He had stressed that with water bordering the jail on three sides and impossibly high stone walls surrounding it, a straight-out assault from outside would be out of the question. He added that all doors into the campus, including the one between the two blocks, could only be accessed from inside, but he knew of one portal, a no-longer-used coal delivery door that could be unlocked from outside of the wall. He had a friend, he said, an elderly clerk who worked in the administration office, who had access to the keys and who might also be persuaded to provide a blueprint copy of the jail's layout. Jellema would, that very evening, make wax impressions of the key to the coal port, the door from the quadrangle to the detention centre and one for the front door. I could pick them up from his house the following day.

Kramer agreed with me that this seemed a most promising plan and gave me the address of a blacksmith who had done work for the KP to whom I should take the wax impressions of the keys as soon as I got them from Jellema. The jail's blueprints would be invaluable in deciding how to proceed once inside the building. I should liaise with the blacksmith and get the duplicate keys to Jellema as soon as possible to ensure they worked in the jail's locks.

'Good work, Henk,' said Kramer, pouring us both a warming shot of jenever.

Our blacksmith worked tirelessly through the night after I had given him the moulds of the keys we would need and had them ready to be collected the following day. I picked them up in time to get them to Jellema before he left for work that afternoon. He would try them out during his shift, he said, and I should call on him tomorrow for the verdict as to how they performed.

The report the next day was not good. The key to the coal port had broken off in the lock, rendering it useless as a way to get inside the jail's confines. And not only that, the SS had ordered that the door from the detention centre into the quadrangle be barred at night with a solid wooden beam.

'Shit!' exclaimed Kramer when I imparted the bad news. 'We're going to have to completely rethink our strategy if we're to come up with a workable plan. And now there's a new urgency: two of our top men were captured yesterday, men who know too much. They'll be locked up in the *Blokhuispoort* where the SS is not going to go easy on them. We have to get them out before they break.'

I tried to think. There was no way of going over the walls and now no way to sneak through them, the only option left would be to find some ruse by which we could be let in to the complex from within. On a few occasions when cycling past the Blokhuispoort along the Keizersgracht, I'd seen Dutch police officers delivering prisoners to the narrow double doors set in the building's imposing stone walls. If we could figure out the protocols involved in such an exchange, it might be possible to actually get inside the jail and liberate our comrades. I ran the idea past Kramer. Something resembling a smile cracked his facial features with the imagined glow of a lightbulb going off in his head.

'You know, that just might work. There's a cop from the local Leeuwarden police station who we've had to send into hiding as he'd been about to be betrayed by this lowlife *Landwachter* in town. He's been a good friend to us for quite a while and I'm pretty sure he would have taken quite a few prisoners to the jail. There's no way I can be seen on the streets during daylight, Henk, so you go and see him to find out what we need to know. I'll give you the address of the family who are hiding him.'

The man of the house was wary and suspicious when he opened his front door to a stranger standing in the street. When I asked if he knew who had put the sugar in the pea soup, he recognised that Kramer had sent me and motioned for me to follow him into the house. He sat me down at the dining room table and walked to a tall bookshelf lining one of the walls, rapped a little percussive tune on the wood with his knuckles and disappeared into the front parlour. The bookcase swung a little away from the wall and from behind it, a man stepped into the room and sat across from me at the table. We didn't exchange names, the less we knew the safer it was, but I gave him a brief outline of our plan as it stood and asked if he thought it could be feasible. I could see him weighing up the implications of my request. He was obviously already in great peril should his whereabouts be discovered and was now being asked to disclose dangerous information. I offered him a cigarette which he gladly accepted, gave him a light and let him think.

Having smoked half the cigarette, he tapped the ash into the ashtray, looked me in the eye and said, 'I've done several prisoner transfers to the Blokhuispoort and this is what happens. To begin with, the police station places a call to the administration office of the jail to let them know a delivery of detainees is imminent. In turn, the jail then telephones the captain of the watch house to confirm the previous message and awaits the prisoners. When the policemen arrive at the jail, they ring the bell and wait for a warden to come to the door and open the small security hatch situated at eye level in the right-hand door, through which they would ask to see an *insluitingsbevel*, the 'custody order'. This is then taken to the jail's admin staff for verification and, if in order, the front door would be unlocked and the police officers and their prisoners would be let into the jail.'

I asked him where those 'custody orders' were kept and could we get our hands on one.

'They're on a shelf in the outer office of the police station's chief constable,' he told me. 'But it would be tricky to take one because they're numbered and controlled, so a discrepancy would be easily noticed.' He did think, though, that one of his previous colleagues by the name of Spoelstra was trustworthy enough to approach to help. 'If you need to speak to him, he's easily recognised by the way he always wears his policeman's hat at a jaunty angle on the back of his head.'

Kramer liked what he heard when I related the information gleaned from our underground policeman friend and thought it had the makings of a doable plan.

'Can you be back here by ten o'clock tomorrow morning, Henk? I'll have a good think about it overnight and figure out what else we need to do to make it work. Go and see van der Veen at his bakery before you cycle home and ask him to also be here in the morning and to bring Jan and Theo from the PTT with him.'

I'd heard of those guys. They were employees of the National Telephone Company who'd been responsible for rigging up the clandestine phone lines that kept the Resistance network operational and out of the reach of SS scrutiny.

The next morning, Kramer's little boat felt as crowded as the machine room of a Roman slave ship. Five of us were huddled around the table drinking coffee, the air thick with cigarette smoke, as Kramer addressed the baker.

'Taco, if we go ahead with this, can we use the workroom of your bakery to assemble and prepare for the raid?'

'Sure,' said van der Veen. 'There's plenty of space there with access from the lane behind the shop and there's room to store weapons and the like behind the bread ovens.'

'Good. Now, Jan, Theo, is it possible to redirect, for a short amount of time, all calls into and out of the jail to the telephone in the work area in back of Taco's shop? We'll need to pretend to be the police watch house and intercept the call the jail will make to verify the imminent arrival of a couple of prisoners.'

'Yeah, we can do that,' said Jan. 'You just need to let us know exactly when to switch the line over to the bakery and the exact time to change it back to normal.'

'OK. Henk, can I rely on you to approach the policeman Spoelstra and persuade him to smuggle out a custody order form? We can't just take one and use it as they are all numbered, so we have to copy it and put the original one back so that it won't be missed. I've got a man who is amazingly good at forgeries. He just needs to get his hands on one for about an hour so he can make a copy that'll pass for real. I'll leave that with you.

'I'm going to start recruiting comrades. I figure that all up, we're going to need around twenty-five of us to carry this off successfully. I'm meeting with all the district commanders to decide how many prisoners we can practically and safely spring from the jail. There are more than two hundred men and women locked up in there so it's going to be bloody difficult to decide who to take and who to leave behind. Do you think, Henk, that Jellema could provide us with an up-to-date list of inmates and where they're kept, cell by cell?'

'He's been more than helpful up to now, Piet,' I replied. 'I'm sure that between him and his old colleague in the admin office they can supply us with just such a list.'

'That'd be great. I'm also going to have to find plenty of addresses of people willing to take in escapees and hide them for a while. There's lots to do chaps, but I think it's beginning to feel like a viable operation. As always, keep this very much to yourselves. Let's meet back here in a week's time to see how we're progressing.'

Jellema had no qualms about smuggling out a list of the detention centre's inmates. He said to come and see him in two days and he'd have it ready. Spoelstra was also willing to snatch a custody order out of the chief constable's office on the proviso that I would return it to him within the hour so that it would not be missed. I'd loitered outside the police station as unobtrusively as possible waiting to identify the policeman who wore his cap back on his head instead of forward over his eyes as most of them did. It took a while, but there was no mistaking the cop who almost danced down the stairs at the front of the building, cap set back at a rakish angle, more Fred Astaire than Mr. Plod. I followed him down the street to a neighbourhood cafe, heart beating in my chest like an overwound clock.

Confronting a lawman I didn't know and soliciting him to perform a highly dangerous, illegal act bordered on lunacy; if he was sympathetic he might hear me out, if not, he would likely arrest me on the spot and hand me over to the SD, end of story. Turned out to be the former. Phew!

Generally speaking, our Dutch police force during the Occupation consisted of two factions: those happy to go to bed with the Moffen to make themselves feel superior, and those who specifically remained in the force so they could better protect their communities from the worst excesses of the SD. Spoelstra, thankfully, was one of the good guys. I arranged to meet him on an afternoon when he would hand me one of the forms to rush over to Kramer's boat where Piet's counterfeiter would be waiting and then return it within the hour.

When I went to Jellema's house to pick up the promised list

of inmates and their cell numbers, he had an urgent message for me to take to Kramer. Dreeuws and Leijenaar, the two high ranking KP men in custody in the *Blokhuispoort*, had been moved to the maximum-security wing at the back of the jail complex and were being viciously interrogated and tortured. He told me the SS had brought in one of their most notorious inquisitors nicknamed 'The Butcher' to squeeze them for information. Dreeuws in particular had already lost several fingers in sessions of unspeakable savagery and the bastards were about to begin on the slow, wire-twisting amputation of his ears unless he surrendered names and addresses. He had confided to one of the sympathetic wardens that he was beyond breaking point and could not last very much longer. I assured Jellema I would get the message to Kramer without delay.

Piet was pissed off but remained composed when I passed on the bad news from the prison. Level heads were needed. It was now imperative that these guys be sprung. The SS were sadistic bastards adept at keeping prisoners suffering just this side of death until they cracked and spilled whatever information the mongrels wanted to hear. If it came to that, the entire network would be in danger. There was no time to waste. Fortunately, most of the planning elements had been sorted and Piet was already busy mobilising the team that would carry out the raid.

He poured me a jenever and said, 'Henk, you've done a hell of a good job, thank you, but you've been too visible in town to include you in the squad going into the jail, so after you finish getting the custody order from Spoelstra, I want you to go back to Scharnegoutum and help Pedro and Wim with the raid on the Mantgum council chambers. We're going to need those identity cards and coupons.'

'Affirmative, chief,' I replied as I downed the shot.

We hadn't seen much of Harry Reeskamp for a while; word was he'd seduced an eighteen-year-old girl and was living with her on a farm just the other side of Scharnegoutum, a fact which had not gone down well with the local KP leadership. He seemed to believe he was living his 'finest hour'. But a married, forty-something year old man who wasn't even Friesian, shacking up with a teenage girl from the province was not a situation these mostly conservative and god-fearing men could easily swallow.

'I don't know, Henk,' said Pedro when I suggested we recruit Reeskamp to help us raid the Mantgum council. 'There's a lot of talk that he and a couple of his dodgy young sidekicks have been staging unsanctioned hold-ups claiming to be raising money for the Resistance.'

'Yeah, I've heard that too,' I replied, 'but we need a quick in and out for this job and you and I both know that Reeskamp with a gun in his hand can be a most persuasive presence. Harry is one hell of a fearless bastard.'

'I suppose you're right, but after this stunt I don't want anything more to do with him; he's becoming a liability and a dangerous one at that.' Pedro could not hide his distaste at Reeskamp's antics.

Wim was likewise sceptical about Harry's involvement. 'This guy's ego is giving the Resistance a bad name around here and that is something we can ill afford,' was his assessment.

I had to admit that I wholeheartedly agreed with them, so suggested we use Harry for this final job and then let him know we would no longer need his services. He'd be pissed off, but we'd feel a whole lot better about it.

THE BAKER'S SON

The lads had done a meticulous job of planning the Mantgum raid. They'd had a tip-off, more than likely from someone inside the council offices who was sympathetic to the Resistance, that a considerable supply of identity cards and stamps had been delivered to the Mantgum council on 4 December for distribution to the surrounding villages. The mayor, a Meneer de Vries, was a rabid NSB'er whose office in back of the building apparently boasted a large framed portrait of Anton Mussert, his hero and mentor. He was not a man much respected by the community he purported to serve. The lads had ascertained that late mornings seemed to be a relatively quiet time with not too many locals having business at the council chambers. Good. We contacted Reeskamp and got ready to go for Wednesday 6 December.

The day was a fresh one, only three or four degrees, fortunately no snow or rain, when we four cycled out to Mantgum. Keeping up a brisk pace to stay warm, breaths condensing in the cold air like snorting steam trains, we reached the town around eleven-thirty a.m. As arranged, I went straight to the post office while the others continued on to the council building. There were no other customers waiting to be served as I approached the counter window, drew my pistol from my overcoat and pointed it squarely at the head of the clerk facing me.

'Hands up!' I demanded. 'Let me through to the back of your office, now!'

The poor woman's face drained in shock, but she managed to maintain enough control to let me in behind the counter.

'Face the wall, keep your hands up, shut up and we'll get along fine,' I ordered as I found the main wire connecting the telephone switchboard. Just as I severed it, cutting all phone communication in and out of Mantgum, two locals walked in the front door. At gun point, I made them join the clerk behind the counter, facing the wall where I kept a close watch on them. The other lads should be inside the council chambers by this time, so it was now a waiting game.

After only about half an hour, Wim stuck his head in the front door to announce, 'All good, let's go!'

I gave my hostages one final command to stay where they were and not to move, then ran outside, straddled my bicycle and pedalled furiously away with my three compadres. Like cowboys galloping off the adrenaline rush of a successful bank robbery, the whooping shouts and beaming faces of my gang mates told me that the raid had gone well. As indeed it had.

The sudden apparition of three gun-wielding desperadoes in their office had the desired effect of producing from the council secretary, the key to the downstairs cellar where important archives and files were kept. It was also big enough to accommodate the front-office staff and the two locals who happened to be there at the time. Wim had bundled them up and locked them in. Reeskamp had then proceeded down the hall to the mayor's office, bursting through the door, pistol in each hand like some American movie gangster, ordering the quaking chief councillor to open the safe containing the identity cards.

When the mayor seemed to purposely fumble and take his own sweet time acceding to his order, Reeskamp said he had told him, 'Don't hurry on my account Mr. Mayor. When the Germans show up in a minute, you will be the first one I shoot.' A sudden urgency saw the mayor open the safe for the lads to take what had amounted to seventeen hundred and nine new identity cards and six hundred stamps, a massive haul.

THE BAKER'S SON

The atmosphere in our hay-bale home on Bouma's farm was buoyant as Pedro poured us all a celebratory glass of jenever. It was Wim who thanked Harry for his camaraderie but added that we would no longer seek to involve him in any of our future actions. That we seriously questioned the legitimacy of many of his recent stunts. With this, the 'hail-fellow-well-met' persona of the Reeskamp we thought we knew, cracked and shattered like a clay mask to reveal a cold and vindictive man who was convinced he'd been betrayed.

'Suit yourselves, chums,' came his chilling reply, 'but if you're not with me, you're against me!' And he stormed out into what was left of the afternoon.

I rode up to Leeuwarden the next morning to deliver the cards and stamps to Kramer. He was delighted.

'We're going in tomorrow,' he informed me. 'We're aiming to take out around fifty Resistance people if all goes well. Those identity cards will come in very handy indeed once we get them all underground. Pass on my thanks to Wim and Pedro for a job well done.'

He offered me a cigarette, reached across to light it and poured us both a shot of jenever. 'Your input has been much appreciated, Henk. You should probably now check in with Karel in Sneek to see what tasks he might have up his sleeve.'

"Ah, you're back Henk," said Karel when I called on him a few days later, "your mates in Leeuwarden have sure made an impression! Apparently the Gestapo are livid. Fifty three resistance comrades sprung from a prison across the road from their headquarters without a shot having been fired and they've yet to recapture even one of them. This will go down as one of the Friesian Resistance's boldest and most successful raids. Piet

Kramer has nothing but praise for your role in setting the whole thing up even though you couldn't be there on the night. Job well done, my friend."

CHAPTER 14

No-one was much looking forward to Christmas that year. Sure, it was going to be a white one, but a frigid, biting white, not the cute, nostalgic one of carols and story books. It was already the coldest winter of the five so far under Occupation. Folks in the big cities of The Hague and Amsterdam were suffering badly due to acute shortages of food and any sort of fuel for heating. The plundering of our country had continued unabated for years. In Friesland, our predominantly agrarian economy afforded at least better access to food, as well as the fact that, on the whole, farmers here did what they could to help their communities.

Karel had encouraged me to continue my regular visits to our contact people in the outlying villages to keep abreast of changes, dangers and possibilities, which I did when the weather allowed. On a few such rounds I began to hear disturbing stories of the exploits of Harry Reeskamp and a couple of his cronies. We'd heard rumours, but I was now getting confirmed reports of Harry robbing well-to-do farmers and even wealthy black marketeers at gunpoint, claiming to be raising money for the Resistance. This was a blatant lie. The Resistance in Friesland did not need to solicit money. Like other partisan organisations across the country, the Resistance was being financed by the NSF, the National Fund for Assistance to the Underground, a scheme set up by Walraven van Hall, the man they called 'The Banker of the Resistance'. Even more to the point, our Resistance forces were organised under a tight hierarchical regime that oversaw and sanctioned all activities with the implicit aim of preventing any descent into what they called 'banditry'. Harry's actions were not only dangerous and corrupt, they risked forfeiting the goodwill and trust of the people, a situation that could not and would not be tolerated. I passed this information on to Karel who, predictably enraged, said he would meet urgently with the other district commanders to decide how best to respond.

Their ruling, when it came, was swift and resolute. They kicked him out. Forbade him to take any action under the auspices of the Resistance and terminated any funding and support from the organisation. He was cut loose, a dangerous situation in my view, seeing as how he was such a volatile character who definitely knew too much. He really was now a lone wolf, discredited and looked down upon. There was no telling how he might react to such a major slap-down.

Pedro, Wim and I felt vindicated in our decision to have nothing more to do with him. But of course, like any other silver-tongued con man, Harry had an ace up his sleeve. He went straight to the leadership of the B.S., the *Binnenlandse Strijdkrachten*, or 'National Fighting Force', and bullshitted his way into them appointing him D.O.L., District Operational Leader for the area surrounding Sneek. In his eyes, it was a deserved promotion. In our opinion, it was a cynical and self-seeking grab for legitimacy and power when he'd lost both by being booted out of the only genuine Resistance movement, the KP.

We hated the BS. They were composed mainly of upper-class members of what was called the O.D., the *Orde Dienst*, titled and entitled ex-career army officers who had sat on their privileged arses for the duration of the Occupation and were now to be the officially sanctioned representatives of the old, pre-war order. The OD had been initially set up only to stave off anarchy in the immediate aftermath of Liberation but our exiled royal family and government had now decreed they should head up and control all Resistance groups in the country. What a moronic idea.

What had made our KP groups so successful was exactly that we operated in small units with no knowledge of the activities of the other factions. To lump all of these into one central command was not only counter productive, it was suicidal. And insulting, when they promoted that useless ponce of a prince, Bernhard, the husband of Crown Princess Juliana, to supreme commander, selling him as some kind of Resistance hero. We had dared to think that things might be different after the war. Fairer. More equitable. But it was becoming clear that the old powers had no intention of giving any ground, they were only scheming to keep their old turf. Reeskamp, of course, had no qualms about throwing in his lot with them, as long as it profited him and deflected any scrutiny of his nefarious dealings.

I continued with my regular reconnaissance trips around the district, liaising with our contact people in the villages around Sneek. One afternoon in the lead-up to Christmas, my last call was at the house in Oosterwierum where I had stayed when I first moved from the pumping station on the lake. The Altenburgs were about to have dinner and invited me to join them. I very gladly accepted. It was bitterly cold out and I knew from previous experience that the lady of the house had quite a flair for concocting delicious dishes from the sparse ingredients available.

After dinner, as I was about to take my leave, my vision suddenly blurred, everything turned yellow, the room began to spin and a searing pain shot through my abdomen like a lightning strike, knocking the wind from my lungs. I collapsed to the floor like a man whose legs had been cut from underneath him. Barely conscious and unable to move, I could faintly hear the family fretting as they picked me up off the floor and laid me down on a sofa. They were astute enough to know that I couldn't possibly be taken to the hospital in Sneek but that I was in need of urgent medical attention. Wiebe Altenburg, my host and contact man, was well connected in the village and knew a local doctor who could be trusted.

Near delirious and wracked with excruciating pain, I had no idea how long I laid on that couch in an almost foetal position before I became aware of a man examining me and trying to tell me things. The good doctor had been summoned and had cycled through the freezing cold with his black bag of tricks to come and check me out. I could only make out snippets of what he was saying as I teetered on the verge of blacking out.

'Burst appendix … Not good … Can you get him up to bed?'

I had a vague feeling of being carried up the stairs and put into a bed.

'I'm going to give you a shot of morphine,' I heard the doctor say. 'It will help with the pain and allow you to sleep.'

I had no sensation of a syringe being inserted into my arm and soon felt myself drifting up beyond the confines of my pain-wracked body to a more peaceful and bearable comfort. I felt myself relaxing into a tranquility I almost didn't believe, not convinced it was something I'd ever experienced. It seemed not so much a state in itself, more a sudden absence of the adrenaline-fired dread that had constricted my innards for these past three long years. It was a little as if I'd broken through to some other dimension, one without logic or rational thought, where merely being seemed meaningful and enough. A holiday from pain. A time-out from the effort of living. I floated there in sensory limbo, oblivious to the passage of days and nights, for what might have been an imagined eternity but was, as it turned out, roughly two weeks.

Some days into the new year my drifting consciousness began its descent from the ethereal to again connect with the body I'd left on the mere material plane of existence. Despite some pain and certainly weakness, I was becoming slowly aware of my surroundings and the situation in which I found myself. My hosts welcomed me back with a bowl of thin, warm soup, happy to see me re-enter the land of the living. Apparently, the doctor had been by every day since my collapse, dosing me with morphine and successfully staving off sepsis which, had it taken hold, would have been the end of me. I couldn't thank them enough and indeed, lacked the energy to do so, but I'm sure they could feel my gratitude.

Recovery was painfully slow. I couldn't yet get out of bed but was beginning to tolerate small amounts of food which served to bring a little colour back to my rather cadaverous features. The first time I looked at myself in the mirror shocked the bejesus out of me. Who was that bearded guy with the sallow complexion, racoon eyes and sunken cheeks? He looked like he'd had a tug-o-war with death for the past couple of weeks and only just pulled through. To have been at death's door only to find it jammed.

Wim and Pedro began coming by to check on my progress and fill me in on all the latest from the real world, a place still of spiralling danger and dirty deals. Some of the more sadistic and bloodthirsty of the SS commanders in our country were being chased north due to the advances made by our Allied forces in the south. According to the lads, they seemed to be making it their mission to eradicate any resistance to their rule, lashing out with all the homicidal desperation of the cornered rats they were. Another weapons drop crew from one of the outlying districts had apparently been betrayed by some local German lover and had been summarily executed in a field. There was no longer any question of proper process or rule of war; the Moffen were now shooting first and asking questions later.

Wim had news of Reeskamp. Since his banishment from the KP, he told me, Harry had done anything but tone down his banditry and plundering of wealthy farmers and was instead strutting around with new-found bravado as the empowered District Operations Leader of the B.S. If he thought he was pretty hot shit before, he was now hot shit with a title and rank.

'Worse than that, Henk,' said Wim. 'I've had it on good authority that he's now bad-mouthing the three of us to the leadership of the B.S., saying we were troublemakers who refused to obey his orders. He's worse than a woman scorned.'

'Yes, and now about as dangerous,' I sighed. 'Keep your cards close to your chest, lads. Meneer Reeskamp is proving to be a fickle and erratic friend.'

I was in a hurry to get my strength and vitality back. A burst appendix is a life-threatening condition, but although that danger had been successfully averted, the damage to my body was such that time was needed to get it fully functioning again. The good doctor who had saved my life returned every couple of days to check on my progress and of course, my host family could not have done more to ensure I was safe and recovering. The frustrating part though was waiting for my body to catch up with where my mind needed it to go.

By mid-January I could still only get out of bed for a short hour at a time, after which I needed to again lie down. On 18 January, Wim and Pedro came to visit with the alarming news that a well-to-do farmer by the name of Hantje Zijlstra from Wolsum had been shot and robbed on the way back to his farm from selling cattle in the livestock markets in Sneek. He'd been taken to hospital with a serious bullet wound to the head after being found lying unconscious in the snow beside the road where he'd been attacked. There was already talk that it had been a Resistance hit on a traitor but Wim was convinced that Reeskamp had a hand in it as a pure and simple robbery at gunpoint. Zijlstra had actually been a good friend to the underground, he said, secretly butchering some of his cattle to provide meat for folks in his district and hiding people wanted by the SS. He'd heard that Reeskamp, dressed as a Nazi Officer, had previously sought to extort money from Zijlstra and threatened to shoot his cattle, but the farmer, a stout, strong, ox of a man, had failed to be intimidated and had instead given Reeskamp his own ultimatum that he would take him apart if he ever set eyes on him again.

I couldn't tell if it was the long tail of the morphine still in my system or some pre-cognition of misadventure, but for whatever reason, the Zijlstra shooting had a disquieting effect on me. This feeling only escalated when a week and a half later, Pedro and Wim came by to tell me that Hantje Zijlstra had succumbed to the injuries from the bullet wound to his head and the pneumonia he'd contracted from lying in the snow for as long as he did. It was now a case of cold-blooded murder. My friends were still in contact with the KP which now monitored not only SS activity, but also the dealings of the B.S. We were convinced the B.S. saw us as nothing more than communists and anarchists and a possible threat to the old order. Wim and Pedro's sources within the B.S. told them that Reeskamp, as District Operational Leader, had been tasked to investigate the Zijlstra shooting and that he had, of course, cleared himself and his cronies of any involvement. Worryingly, he then claimed that Wim Roth had been overheard saying he hated that rich bastard Zijlstra. What a scumbag! It became clear to us that Reeskamp was capable of any treachery when it came to covering his guilty arse.

'Watch your backs, lads,' I advised them. 'The B.S. can't be trusted, and it seems we have made an enemy of Harry Reeskamp.'

By early February I was still not well but had recovered enough to go back to Bouma's farm and join Pedro and Wim in the hay barn. I needed to be doing something, some task, something other than just lying around. It was all I'd been capable of just a few weeks earlier, but now that my strength was returning it was time to go back to work. I was going to leave on the night of 7 February but a storm of epic proportions blew in over the polders, dropping the temperature to well below zero. With blizzard conditions, it would be insane to cycle through. Well, one more night in relative comfort wouldn't hurt. I'd go the following day.

Each morning, Wiebe Altenburg, my landlord, needed to travel to Sneek and back, I've no idea why and didn't think it prudent to ask. When he returned home on the morning of the eighth, he burst through the front door with the urgency of a man being pursued by demons.

'Henk!' he yelled up the stairs. 'Henk, wake up, you need to hear this.'

I came running downstairs as fast as I could to find Wiebe ushering me into the kitchen and motioning me to sit at the breakfast table.

'I've just cycled past Bouma's farm,' he gasped, 'and it's overrun with SS. There's an officer's staff car and a truck spewing out machine gun wielding uniforms taking up positions all around the farm house and barn yard!'

'Fuck!' I shrieked as a bolt of adrenaline rifled through my body and slapped me hard across the face. 'We've got to do something!' My immediate instinct was to race out to Sneek and muster a posse of Resistance comrades to come fight it out with those bastard Moffen.

'It would be a bloodbath, Henk, think about it,' came my landlord's voice of reason. He was right of course, but the impotence I felt at not being able to do anything to help Wim and Pedro who would have most likely been at the farm was draining all commonsense from my galloping brain, leaving me clutching at useless straws.

'Tell you what, I'll ask one of my daughters to cycle carefully past Bouma's farm and give us an update on what's going on,' Wiebe said. 'And we'll take it from there.'

I reluctantly agreed it was probably the best we could do for the time being.

When she came back, the news was not at all good. The SS were still there, now pulling apart the hayloft in the barn, the bolthole with all our earthly possessions, clothes, weapons, uniforms, false ID's, everything. The jig was up. What really hurt was not knowing whether Wim and Pedro had managed to escape or had indeed been captured. The state of play, which was by default highly dangerous, had suddenly turned catastrophically deadly and left me fighting a strong urge to grab my pistol, ride out to the farm and have it out, do or die. My host, a sensible and intelligent man, sensing my anguish, suggested I stay put, at least until we got a better picture of the outcome of the raid.

'The SS will most likely take anyone they arrest to the police station in Sneek,' he said, 'which is a minor bonus in that one of the constables there is a very good friend of the Resistance, so we should at least be able to find out who they've taken prisoner and if Wim and Pedro are amongst them.'

Late that afternoon, my landlord's daughter again cycled past Bouma's farm and reported back that the SS seemed to have left but had stationed a deployment of *Landwachters*, those Dutch collaborating bastards we called 'the riff raff', to keep watch and guard the place. I didn't know what to do.

My still shaky constitution was wracked with wildly conflicting emotions. Hovering above and around more obvious 'fight or flight' instincts, I was shocked to find stabbing pangs of guilt gnawing at my composure like rats attacking garbage.

THE BAKER'S SON

Why had I been merely loafing around, killing time while my comrades remained in the firing line? How come, when the hayloft got raided, I was somewhere else warm and comfortable? The sensible answer, of course, was that a burst appendix could be no more foreseen than a water main bursting or a volcano erupting, a fact that did nothing to dispel my nagging feelings of blame. I decided the best course of action would be to lay low where I was for another day and then go see Karel, trusting he might have information as to who had been arrested and locked up in the Sneek police station.

Karel knew to tell me only Hessel Bouma and his eldest son had been taken into custody but that there'd been no sign of Wim or Pedro. I allowed myself a glimmer of hope that they may have escaped the raid and were hiding out somewhere, a small positive to cling to.

'Listen Henk,' Karel lowered his voice and looked me square in the face, 'no-one can prove a thing, but we've got a strong suspicion that Reeskamp's fingerprints are all over the raid on Bouma's farm. He implicated the three of you to the B.S. in the Zijlstra murder in order to cover his arse and seeing as that organisation is more than likely compromised, there's every chance Harry's accusations ended up being filtered through to the SS. Now you don't need me to tell you that the SS are more dangerous and brutal than ever,' Karel continued, 'there's no longer even any pretence at restraint. Along with the Bouma's they've got twenty resistance comrades currently locked up in the Sneek police station. We're going to get them out. You know we've got a sympathetic constable there and with his help we're planning a raid like Piet Kramer's on the Blokhuipoort in Leeuwarden, for the twelfth to get them all out. I know you'll find this frustrating, if not damned well impossible, but the best thing you can do is stay out of sight in Oosterwierum and check in with me after that.'

Confirming I had a fully functional handgun, he loaded me up with ammunition and bade me adieu. My holiday from pain was decidedly over and being rapidly overtaken by a sobering dose of betrayal with the life-threatening side-effect of persecution. I may have still been weak, but the gravity of the situation snapped me back to full alert, total engagement. A situation I would not recommend as a method of recovery.

On the morning of the twelfth, my landlord, returning from his daily run to Sneek, said he'd seen an SS squad car pull into the yard of Bouma's farm. He'd naturally not stopped to see what was happening, but something must have brought them back; the *Landwachters* must have reported something untoward. The signs were not good. I knew that this was the day of the planned raid on the police station in Sneek, so I refrained from going anywhere near the town, deciding to wait a couple of days before checking in for news of what may have gone down on Bouma's farm. Sleep, now without morphine, proved elusive. There was too much at stake and the dice were rolling inexorably towards a dangerous and unpredictable outcome.

I met with Karel on the morning of the fifteenth. He sat me down and poured us both a shot of jenever. The raid on the police station had gone well, he said, all twenty prisoners, including Hessel Bouma and his eldest son were liberated and now ensconced in safe houses across the district and, much like the breakout at the Blokhuipoort, not a shot had been fired and no-one was injured. It had, predictably, stirred up a hornet's nest of SS outrage, but so far, not one perpetrator or ex-prisoner had been tracked down.

'But on the same day,' said Karel pouring me another shot, 'the *Landwachters* keeping guard on Bouma's farm summoned the SS because they'd apprehended Wim and Pedro.'

Fuck no! The worst possible scenario! What hope I'd cultivated that they might be alright vaporised like a desert mirage.

'It seems that on the day of the raid,' continued Karel, 'the lads had been able to escape the hayloft and reach a crawlspace above one of the wardrobes in the farmhouse. They'd lain there for four days and nights without light, water, food or sanitary provisions until Wim had fallen unconscious. Pedro had then decided to give himself up so that Wim could get medical help, only to be arrested by the 'riff-raff' and handed over to the Gestapo. They were then taken by the SS to Christ knows where. From pulling apart your hayloft, Henk, they knew that there were three people hiding there, of which they have only two in custody. They are determined to get the third. Already they are combing the district, showing your picture to people in their zeal to track you down. You don't need me to tell you what danger you are in. All I can suggest is that you try to alter your appearance and use your many contacts in the province's underground to stay out of sight. It would be wise if you didn't stay long in any one place but tried to keep moving. A moving target is more difficult to hit. You're a highly wanted man, Henk, it's time to use all you have learned to stay one step ahead of the mongrel Moffen. I'll put the word out to our Resistance colleagues to give you every assistance they can. Try to stay alive; we need you.'

With that, he pressed a wad of banknotes into my hand,

we both downed another shot and I hit the street feeling never more alone and vulnerable.

And cold. Colder than just winter. I felt as though my heart had been ripped out, taking with it all the warmth of the life I'd known. What was there left? My closest companions were more than likely, at this very moment, having their fingers chopped off or ears severed while being interrogated as to my whereabouts; my family were unreachable, as if extant on some distant planet and I had the breath of baying hounds cold on the back of my neck. I was no more than an empty shell of a man driven only by a spark for survival emanating from somewhere deep within my humanity. That spark of the species that demands we must endure. If it had previously seemed that life was accelerating too rapidly, it was now careening out of control, down a mountainside, with the steering gone.

I cycled back to my kind hosts in Oosterwierum to collect my rather meagre belongings, some clothes, water-tight boots and, most importantly, the automatic pistol from the weapons drops. My landlord gave me a fur-lined hat that had the benefit of covering part of my face and suggested I wear a pair of his old spectacles to further disguise my features. A thick woollen scarf to compliment my overcoat and I was off. The Altenburgs had been more than kind to me, to stay any longer would have put them in a deathly dangerous situation they did not deserve. In fact, it dawned on me that I was now little more than a pariah, a persona non grata, someone with whom it could be potentially fatal to have any dealings. A disturbing thought, especially in the light of Reeskamp's recent betrayal. Who to trust? There were no longer any certainties. No landmarks or valid compass points. No safe harbours in which to ride out the tempest threatening to engulf me. The only plan was to keep moving, cycle by day and call on my various Resistance contacts each evening for a place to sleep.

The reconnaissance work I'd done in what already felt like another life, another time, stood me in good stead. I knew all the back roads and lanes to take to avoid contact with German patrols and my Resistance comrades were, I must say, extremely supportive in offering me a place to crash and sharing what little food they had. In order to not bring down any unnecessary danger on their doorstep, I mostly stayed only one night and then moved on to another village. Sleep, if it came at all, was lacerated with visions of death and dismemberment while my pistol was always either in my hand or under my pillow.

I went to Joure where we had previously raided the Drum tobacco factory. To Workum where we had robbed the council chambers, where Hans van Drongelen, our butcher friend, was happy to put me up for a night. I cycled to Oosthem, the scene of our recent weapons drops, where Anton Sleenhoff let me sleep in the room behind his bookstore and farmer Fokkema opened his barn to me. I circled round to Leeuwarden and contacted Mies Dekkinga, my nurse friend, who made me feel welcome. I even spent a night on Piet Kramer's boat where he plied me with jenever and recounted the story of how the raid on the *Blokhuispoort* had gone down. Mantgum, Bolswaard, I visited all manner of villages where I had contacts before I moved on again come daylight. I must have looked a sight to them, some kind of crazy man, unshaven, with pale skin and anxious, suspicious eyes staring from sunken sockets.

Around the middle of March, I was in the vicinity of Sneek and thought it safe enough to make a quick call on Karel. It would be good to get his take on the latest developments in the province.

'You look like shit,' he said, pouring us both a bolt of warming jenever.

'Yeah, well, my regular hairdresser is out of town,' I replied, 'so I have to make do. Anyway, what's been happening since I've been on holiday?'

Karel took a deep breath and looked me fair in the eye. 'Henk, I have news of Wim and Pedro. I don't know where they were taken, but they were certainly tortured for information. On the eighth just gone, they were marched onto a field near the town of Dongjum with three other prisoners and shot. The fucking Gestapo left their bodies lying on the ground under police guard for two days, as a warning to the population. I'm so very sorry. They were good men.'

I couldn't speak. A leaden weight fell to the pit of my stomach, taking the wind clean out of my sails. My useless existence suddenly felt superfluous. I had nothing left; I couldn't even cry. Those guys had been closer than brothers; there beside me throughout all our perilous exploits, always having my back, always fully committed, totally dependable. We'd been through so much. I had to admit it to myself; I loved them. And now they were gone. And I wasn't. I felt like something of a fraud; how dare I go on living when my friends were dead? Why should I be the one to survive when they had been tortured and shot? What was the fucking point?

I spent the next three weeks roaming the countryside like some bug-eyed zombie, hand never far away from my pistol, snatching feverish slivers of sleep on the couches or in the hay barns of my Resistance comrades, wolfing down what food they could offer me, all the time on edge, alert for that knock on the door that would seal my fate. I was no more than a hunted animal running from the baying hounds close on my trail. What little sleep I did manage was rent with vivid nightmares of German Shepherd dogs with blood-smeared muzzles and otherworldly howling tearing apart our haystack to attack my friends and me. I was running a maze, barely functioning, not game to stop, paranoid and almost delirious.

The morning of 15 April dawned grey as usual. The icy fingers of the coldest winter of the Occupation still streaked the fields with frost as I wrapped my overcoat tight around me to face another day. My hair was matted and littered with bits of straw from the haystack on which I'd tried to sleep and the stubble of beard on my chin itched as if beseeching a razor to come and remove it. I splashed my face into the present with the bracingly cold water from the cow's drinking trough that was up against the wall of the barn. I was bloody hungry but the farmer who'd allowed me to overnight in his haystack was already out in the fields so I rolled a cigarette that would have to do for breakfast. Throwing a leg over my bike, I cycled briskly to town, keeping up a steady pace to try and stay warm.

I was only just pedalling up the main street of Joure when a roar of heavy engines came suddenly up behind me. They caught me up before I'd even had a chance of scampering off down some side street and my body shuddered with the thought that this is how it would end. That all the luck that had kept me alive until then had been used up. No more use running. But the lead vehicle, a squad car, instead of cutting me off, drove right on by and as it did I thought I must have been hallucinating, because from the front of its bonnet fluttered, not an iron cross, but a

Canadian flag. An unmistakeable maple leaf led a column of tanks, personnel carriers, troop-laden trucks, motor bikes and cars. The Canadians were here; we'd been liberated.

My mind, which had for so long been hardwired to expect danger at every turn, to be ready to run or fight it out with each sudden move in my periphery, now seriously struggled to process the scene before me. It was too unreal and took some moments to sink in. When it finally did, an emotional dam deep within my being suddenly burst apart with a shuddering ferocity that knocked me to the ground and all I could do was to sit there in the gutter and cry like a baby. All the tears I'd been unable to shed for too long, now filled my eyes and ran in rivulets down my sunken cheeks. I just sat there sobbing, blubbering, oblivious to the real world. What price freedom, I thought. Only three weeks ago, the best friends I had in the world had been lined up in a field and shot to death like dogs. And now, it was over.

I've no idea how long I sat on that stoop, but while I did, the street started filling up with jubilant, singing burghers, streaming out of their houses to form a gauntlet of joy around the Canadian column pouring through the town. Colour burst through the air as the red, white and blue of hundreds of Dutch flags, suppressed and hidden for so long, were unfurled and enthusiastically flapped in a hysteria of final deliverance from the ills of Occupation. Blazes of orange, representing the House of Orange, were given an overdue airing on the arms and lapels of exultant citizens. Spontaneous singing of '*Het Wilhelmus*', the National Anthem, broke out all over town as the realisation hit the populace that the five long years of brutal occupation had finally come to an end. Crowds of people were linking arms and dancing like drunken sailors as the Canadian conquering heroes drove slowly through the throng, being pelted with petals and love. The feast of Liberation.

I just slunk away. I couldn't take it. Having death breathe down your neck for so long eats away at the marrow of your being and rips your soul out from underneath its rightful place at the centre of things. There had been no let up. My finest, truest friends had been captured, tortured and shot and I'd had to keep running, with no time to assimilate the calamity of their loss or any chance to properly grieve for them. There was just no way I could face the exultant, partying pandemonium of my fellow citizens. I was spent. Spiritually, emotionally and physically. I had no more to give. I just slid away.

CHAPTER 15

The back of the truck reeked like Hell's halitosis. It was as if Satan had been eating roadkill, which wasn't really that far from the truth as I was squatting on a pile of dead, flat animals, cattle hides to be exact, recently skinned and soaked and being transported to Waalwijk to be tanned and turned into shoes. It stunk, but hey, I was finally heading home.

Back in Joure, I'd had to pull myself together and push through the heaving throngs of dancing and singing citizens like a salmon swimming upstream. Women were flinging themselves at the Canadians and men were getting seriously drunk on jenever liberated from hibernating cafes. I couldn't face it. As soon as I got clear, I leaped aboard my bicycle and headed to Sneek to get the paperwork needed to travel south. All I really wanted was to just go home. On the outskirts of town I was pulled up by some idiot with a Sten gun hanging off his shoulder, demanding to know who I was and where I was going. He was a member of the BS, Prince Bernhard's little troop of pretend soldiers who'd sat on their comfortable arses for the duration of the war and had now been put in charge of the country. A pack of pathetic, posturing wannabes poncing about like they owned the joint. They'd wasted no time taking over and sidelining 'the Communist KP' who they perceived as posing a threat to the smooth reassertion of power by the royals and the government in exile. I was in no mood to take any shit from this Boy Scout, so I shoved him aside and told him that that Sten gun had very recently cost some of my best friends their lives. The snivelling little turd had the audacity to tell me that it had nothing to do him, that they were now in charge and that I needed to forget my 'terrorist' ways and do what I was told. I should have smacked his head, but he wasn't worth it.

The council chambers of the town had been given over to the administration of the district's affairs. Canadian army officers mingled with BS, overseeing the transition to post-war governance. As I passed by the open door of one of the offices, I was startled to see my old comrade and KP chief Karel seated behind a desk piled high with paperwork.

'Christ on a bike!' he exclaimed. 'If it isn't the living dead. Come in, Henk. You look like shit.'

'Yeah, I've been hearing that a lot lately, but bloody hell Karel, what are you doing mingling with this high-class crowd?'

'Well, someone has to have some sense and organisational skills,' he said. 'These BS buffoons are as useless as pockets in underpants. They're mainly in charge of preventing looting and policing traffic, so some of us have stepped in to help with the fair distribution of food and generally making sure that our citizens are looked after. You'll find a couple of our old KP comrades working here, although the BS seems rather keen to distance itself from what they call "The Illegality".'

'Yeah, I noticed that on the way into town when some pipsqueak with a Sten gun told me I had to give up my terrorist ways. But really Karel, all I want to do right now is to go home. I'm tired; I've had enough.'

'I hear you, Henk,' he replied. 'Leave it with me and I'll organise all the documentation you need to travel.'

With that, he opened a drawer in the desk and produced a bottle of jenever and two glasses and poured us both a shot. 'To absent friends,' he announced, clinking our glasses together.

'To absent friends and a better life. May they not have died in vain,' I chimed in.

After we'd downed the shots, Karel reached out his hand to shake mine and pressed a wad of money into my palm. 'You'll need that.' My travel papers would be ready first thing in the morning he said, then gave me an address where I could spend the night and freshen up. 'Get rid of that growth on your face, Henk. You look like a caveman.'

The next morning, feeling at least a bit more myself, I cycled south to Enschede, a city close to our border with Germany. It was heavy going at times, long convoys of Allied tanks and trucks snaked their way along our roads, and there were throngs of people making the most of being finally allowed out of doors. There was a discernible atmosphere of a great weight having been lifted – of a malevolent presence having been driven off. Unfortunately, such elation did not extend to what I needed to do in Enschede, which was to call on Wim Roth's parents. They were understandably distraught. I only hoped that my account of him having been the most loyal, decent and fearless friend I could possibly have had was of small consolation to them in their grief. Heartfelt tears were shed, and not only by them.

I was invited to have dinner with them, and a bed was made up for me on their couch. It was a sad and heartbreaking visit but did help me mourn the loss of such a fine man as Wim and aid in bringing at least some closure to what had been the absolute darkest period of my life.

The following day, my travels took me through the city of Arnhem, the stage upon which Field Marshall Montgomery's folly, Operation Market Garden, had died an undignified death. Where he'd summoned our KP forces to make an appearance as 'extras'. I could hardly believe the devastation, there wasn't a single building left untouched by the artillery fire that had been unleashed on the city. Not a soul stirred, the entire population had been evacuated leaving only piles of stinking rubble and skeletal ruins where once there had been a thriving community. Here and there, stray dogs scurried and sniffed amongst the detritus, following various scents of decay. The wind whistling through the bones of broken buildings echoed like ghostly wails of the souls of the thousands who had died there. It was an unworldly tableau that I was glad to put behind me.

Travelling further south, I needed to cross the river Ijssel but there were no bridges left intact. The destruction of infrastructure was almost total, testament to the ferocity of the fighting this part of the country had seen as the Allied forces had advanced. I cycled along the riverbank until I finally encountered a farmer with a small punt who was happy to ferry me across. Disembarking the boat on the far bank unfortunately put me over the border into Germany, it seemed. And when the road I followed took me back across the border into The Netherlands, I was promptly arrested by American MP's manning the crossing checkpoint. They'd been stationed there to capture any Nazis attempting to escape punishment for their wartime sins. They couldn't make up their minds whether I was one of those or who I said I was so they loaded me onto a Jeep and drove me to their headquarters in Nijmegen, a city all too familiar to me from the many trips Henk Romeijn and I had made there in preparation for shooting the police commissioner those couple of years before. Ah Henk, my impetuous comrade, he surely would be dead by now, most likely after unimaginable torture, poor bastard. And here I was, still breathing, tears welling up behind my eyes not only for my friend, but also the pang of a decent dose of survivor's guilt.

The gum-chewing Yanks took me to the desk of a higher-ranking officer who demanded to see my paperwork. I wasn't too worried; I knew Karel's work was impeccable and would bear any scrutiny. It took this lieutenant several hours to verify it before he let me go. I spent the night with a niece who lived in Nijmegen, the first enjoyment of family I'd had for quite some time. In the morning I had breakfast in a roadside cafe where I got chatting with a truck driver who, as fate would have it, was on his way to Waalwijk with a load of cow hides.

He dropped me off in the Stationstraat, in front of number ninety. I was happy to see that all the street's trees had, like me, survived the war and were in the first blush of budding, a symbol, I dared hope, of new beginnings, of a fresh spring rising from the death and decay of our just won fight with the Devil. In the front window my mother sat knitting, calm and serene, as if nothing had happened. I felt like I'd been marooned on some island underworld and was now suddenly washed up on a friendly shore.

It had been almost two years since I bolted from my house

seconds before the SS pulled up at the front door, although it felt like almost a lifetime ago. I was a different person than I was back then, irreversibly changed by the dread and gravity of my recent past and yet to fully recognise who I had become. To my family I looked the same, if somewhat gaunt; they were simply overjoyed to see me alive.

My mother hugged me and simply said, 'Hendrik, you're home!'

My father, finding sentimentality difficult as always, remarked, 'Bloody hell, son, you smell like you've been rolling in cow dung.' It must have been heartrending for my mother to not have had any contact with me for all that time. I spared them the gruesome details of my life in what everyone now called 'The Illegality' and just took succour from their love. I was going to need it. The transition to civilian life was going to take some doing, I needed to give myself time to adjust.

What really helped was reuniting with my good friend Tom Brokken who, I was relieved to see, had also survived the Occupation. The last I'd seen of him was when he'd gone underground in Ijsselstein to avoid being shanghaied into the German forced labour camps. He had arrived back in Waalwijk a few weeks before I did and, like me, was nursing a badly shell-shocked psyche as a result of what he'd gone through. We met in the Hotel Royal where all those years before we'd sat and discussed the then growing danger of Germany's belligerence. We now knew how that had played out.

Over (quite) a few *borreltjes*, he told me that he too had drifted into activities with the KP in his area, so we had much common ground to discuss. I found it therapeutic to talk about these things with someone who had actually lived through similar experiences, most anyone else would simply not understand. Worse than that, those of us who'd been active in the armed Resistance were now being actively branded as 'the Illegality' or 'terrorists', not only by the BS in their haste to establish themselves as holier than thou, but also the rapidly re-establishing old order, hell-bent on the re-imposition of pre-war power and privilege.

Tom felt, as I did, that the solidarity and like-mindedness we in the Resistance had felt so strongly that had transcended class, religious differences and regional hubris was now seen as a serious threat to the continued reign of the House of Orange. We were being actively discredited as 'illegitimate terrorists', as armed communists who might conceivably stage a coup to overthrow those who God himself had appointed to rule. This deliberate exaggeration was clearly designed to sideline any scrutiny of their activities and was something we found deeply insulting to the memory of all those exceptionally courageous men and women who had paid the ultimate sacrifice for the freedom we now enjoyed. My friends Wim Roth and Pieter Glastra van Loon amongst them. It was an affront we would never forgive or ever forget. We found little joy in liberation.

Mother, of course, did enquire about my time in hiding, I simply told her that I lived for quite a while in a secret room built into a haystack on the farm of a fine Friesian family who had looked after me very well indeed. She in turn told me that Waalwijk had been gradually returning to some state of normality: the cinemas had begun limited showings of mostly American films, minimal rail and bus travel had been restored, people were now able to leave and come into the town without the special permits of the previous months, oh, and Jan Vermeulen from around the back had started keeping pigeons again.

She said that the shoe factories were only very slowly beginning to operate again. A lot of the machinery had either been stolen by the Germans or else sabotaged and of course, the widespread plundering of our livestock had had the obvious result of there being a scarcity of cow hides to be tanned. A few firms had retooled to manufacture synthetic leather and had managed to keep a reduced workforce employed, but new job opportunities were few and far between.

It was difficult to adjust to having nothing of substance to do. I was sleeping badly. Each night as I closed my eyes, my mind would replay films of my various close encounters with death and project them through a prism of wild association onto the screen of my dreams. Henk Romeijn and Father Sanders would appear to me, wanting to know what we were doing to keep from getting arrested. I would regularly be hiding from German Shepherd dogs baying for my blood. It was taking its toll. I decided that as the trains were running again, I should go to Amsterdam for a change of scenery and see the city without the veil of impending doom that had clouded my previous visit there.

Unlike Rotterdam, Amsterdam seemed to have escaped significant bombardment. I was pleased to see that the cobbled streets, the canals and hump-backed bridges, the stately canal houses all still exuded an almost medieval charm. Wandering leisurely around, I found myself in the vicinity of the Admiraal de Ruijterkade and decided to drop into the Catholic Church for old times' sake. I am distinctly not a religious person, no benevolent deity would have tolerated the carnage of the previous five years, but I did allow myself some moments of quiet reflection in front of the statue of St. Anthony, to mourn the loss of friends such as Henk Romeijn and Father Sanders with whom I had visited this church in times gone by.

I had just lit a candle to their memory when I was suddenly confronted with an apparition of almost mystical import. From out of the sacristy door to the right of the altar appeared, to my amazement, Father Sanders himself! I rubbed my eyes to make sure I wasn't hallucinating, but no, it was him alright!

'Jesus Christ Father!' I blurted out involuntarily. 'Pardon the blasphemy, but I'm amazed and delighted to see you alive.'

We hugged and shook hands there on the altar steps.

'Ah Henk, good to see you too. You look terrible. Come and let me buy you a coffee,' he said. And with that, we wandered down the street and into a most agreeable cafe where we took a booth and began to talk.

One of the things I wanted to know was what had happened with the ration cards of most of the CS-6 members that the good priest had in his possession when the Gestapo arrested him. He told me the story. They'd been in the back pocket of his trousers when he'd left me to go back to the rectory to fetch his suitcase. As he entered, two Gestapo goons were waiting inside and arrested him. Thinking quickly, he explained that he was a diabetic and would need to take with him the insulin and syringes which were in his upstairs bedroom. They acceded to his request and accompanied him up the narrow staircase to the bedroom on the third floor. The Germans preceded him back down the stairs and on the way down they passed an open room where his housekeeper was standing. Father Sanders managed to surreptitiously take the cards from his back pocket and throw them into that room so the Gestapo never found them, thus, for the time being at least, sparing quite a few people their lives.

He'd been taken to one of the concentration camps inside

THE BAKER'S SON

The Netherlands where, by coincidence, Henk Romeijn was also incarcerated, so he had come to know of my friend's fate. Father Sanders had been locked up a couple of cells away from where Henk was kept and, when it was safe to do so, had loudly enquired as to his situation.

Henk had replied, 'The armoured car will be destroyed.' It was a rather cryptic answer that the good priest had not understood, but which to me, was chillingly clear. During our time working at the Distribution Office in Waalwijk, Henk had bought an overcoat made from a composite material which included wood fibre. It was all you get in those days but did make it somewhat stiff. We had joked that the coat would stand up by itself and had nicknamed Henk 'the armoured car'. Father Sanders told me that the Gestapo had brutally tortured Henk, twisting wire ever tighter around his ears until they'd fallen off and beginning to smash his fingers one by one, but he'd held on and told them nothing to give me time to figure out what had occurred and flee. They shot him a few weeks later. I couldn't control the flow of tears from my eyes at the telling of this woeful tale, what a true hero he'd been, what strength of character he'd displayed, how much in his debt we remained.

Father Sanders had survived his imprisonment, he said, to some extent on account of his diabetes, but for a large part down to the benevolent intervention of a certain Admiral Canaris, the head of the German Intelligence Service, the Abwehr. They'd met secretly before the war and again as late as 1943, when the admiral, who was fiercely anti-National Socialism and who feared Hitler was leading Germany into total destruction, had travelled abroad contacting local Resistance groups to try to facilitate a separate peace with the Allies.

In the late 1930's, Canaris was already plotting to overthrow Herr Hitler, with support from General Hans Oster whom he had appointed second-in-charge of the Abwehr. It was Oster, claimed Father Sanders, who had leaked Hitler's plans for the invasion of The Netherlands, including the exact dates it would begin, to the Dutch Resistance. This intelligence had not been believed by our government and royal family with the devastating result that as a country, we had not been ready when Germany came storming in. Canaris had ensured that Father Sanders was transferred to a less heinous facility where he was able to continue his insulin regime and survive the war.

Talk then drifted to the demise of CS-6. 'You and I are about the only associates of the group to have made it through the war alive,' said the good Father. 'You and I and Kas de Graaf. I don't know if you're aware of this, Henk, but that man is a German agent who managed to get to England and boast about his Resistance exploits with CS-6 to the Special Operations Executive in order to wrangle himself a lucrative job with Prins Bernhard. He is currently heading up an office of the Bureau *Inlichtingen* [Office of Information] in Tilburg in charge of intelligence and espionage, can you believe that? Have nothing to do with him, Henk; that man is poison.'

I told him there was no chance of me going anywhere near anyone associated with the Prins, that philandering, front-line tourist who was being sold to us as a war-time Resistance hero but whose only aim was self-enrichment. The man made me sick to my stomach. We finished our coffees, shook hands and said our goodbyes, my heart heavy with the memory of my impetuous friend Henk Romeijn and his cruel demise as I rode the train back to Waalwijk.

CHAPTER 16

After a thunderstorm the world feels, smells and looks entirely refreshed and renewed; it has been cleaned and once again shines. But after the tempest of death, destruction and duress of the previous five years, nothing had changed. The pre-war era of egotism, rigid denominationalism and class division had been restored in full. Greed, self-interest and power had once again trumped concern for the nobility of people and the promise of a more egalitarian and fair-minded Fatherland. The old regime had been resurrected, not by means of the peoples' mandate, but by self-appointment. No elections had been held.

Then, on a day when the summer sun, shining through the green canopy of the old trees that filled my street, cast dancing shadows on the road and footpath below, I received my call-up papers for re-enlistment into the army. Really? Only two months since the end of the last war and I was being ordered back into uniform? I was not impressed.

Here I was, twenty-eight-years old, still striving to adjust to civilian life and needing to figure out what to do with myself in terms of employment and career, being suddenly shanghaied into the role I wanted most NOT to do, that of becoming uniformed canon fodder for a queen and government with whom I was utterly disillusioned.

At the barracks in s'Hertogenbosch, our nearest city, I passed the physicals and some inane written tests before being summoned to the office of the recruiting major. When he informed me that because of my record of Resistance work during the Occupation I was entitled to be promoted to the rank of lieutenant, my heart lightened somewhat. A lieutenant's wage was actually not too shabby and if I was going to have to be in uniform for the next two years, I might as well make some money while I was at it. But when he gave me that crap about never forgetting I was only a baker's son, a fact that might put me at a disadvantage in dealing with my fellow officers, my blood boiled and I saw red. I only just managed to restrain myself from leaping across the desk, grabbing him by the lapels and punching him in his privileged face. Instead, I simply stood up, turned around and stormed from the room without saluting the arrogant pig.

After two cups of coffee and a couple of shaky cigarettes, I calmed down a bit and came to the conclusion that what I had seen of the officer class of the Dutch army at the start of the war, actually made me glad I was not destined to be now amongst them. They had bickered, quarrelled, panicked and fled when the shit hit the fan and scurried off to hide under some rock until the worst was over, leaving the men in their care to basically fend for themselves. Models of leadership and courage they were most emphatically not. So now, even the powers that be had to admit that there was a dearth of men blooded in battle who could instil the discipline and spirit in a rebuilt national fighting force that were surely prerequisites for a cohesive and effective military. They decided to rent such qualifications from the British who were only happy to help. After all, had the House of Orange fallen to the anarchy of the Dutch Resistance, surely the Windsors' demise would not be far behind. Unthinkable. As a result I was shipped out to England, to Catterick Garrison in North Yorkshire for retraining.

I'd been there for quite some months when, in October 1946, as I sat drinking coffee in the canteen, two Dutch military policemen strode up to my table and asked if I was Sergeant Henk van Iersel. When I answered in the affirmative, they said they had a warrant for my arrest and were to immediately escort me back to The Netherlands.

I nearly snorted my coffee through my nose and gasped, 'Arrest? What do you mean? Under what charge?'

They said they couldn't tell me as they didn't know; their orders were only to bring me to Leeuwarden in Friesland. As soon as they mentioned Friesland, a sobering jolt, like a sudden recollection of unfinished business, sent shivers down my spine and I knew it must have been to do with the robbery and murder of Hantje Zijlstra back in January of 1945, about which Wim and Pedro had told me as I was recovering from being bed-ridden with a burst appendix. We were certain at the time that Reeskamp had been involved, the KP hierarchy had recently kicked him out and it hadn't been long since we'd severed ties with him for exactly those sorts of stunts.

After Zijlstra died, I vividly remembered Wim telling me he was convinced the BS was going to lay the blame on us. Maybe those fears had now come to fruition. The two MP's turned out to be decent blokes and in the three days' travelling it took to return to Friesland we became quite friendly. I convinced them to detour past Bouma's farm in Scharnegoutum on the way to Leeuwarden so I could leave my kit there and pick it up the following day. Or so I thought.

Hessel and Maaike Bouma were more than happy to see me again. They had become like family to me back when we were busy with so many dangerous stunts. It was of course a bittersweet reunion, with the memory of Wim and Pedro's executions still fresh in all of our hearts, especially those of the Boumas' two daughters who had been in love with my comrades. There had even been the birth of a son named Pieter Ane in honour of Pedro, his father. Showing compassion and commendable fair-mindedness, my MP chaperones didn't rush my visit with the Boumas and allowed us plenty of time to just sit and chat.

'I'm still not clear why I have been implicated in the death of Hantje Zijlstra, because that is what I think this is all about,' I told Hessel.

He lowered his gaze as if formulating a train of thoughts before answering, 'Henk, after Zijlstra died, the BS asked Reeskamp, as District Operations Leader, to investigate the incident and report back to them. It came as no surprise that he found his crew clear of any involvement, but in order to divert closer scrutiny, added that you three, Wim, Pedro and yourself, had to be under suspicion since making the decision, in December 1944, to have no more dealings with himself and as such, the BS.'

Well that put Wim's comment of the 28 January that the BS was going to blame us into clear context.

'It gets worse,' he continued. 'After Pedro and Wim were

executed and could no longer defend themselves, Harry had even been heard to suggest that Wim, in particular, had a hatred of Hantje Zijslstra, a blatant and cruel lie. After all we did for him, this is how he treats the Bouma family to shit on us to save his own skin. Be careful of him, Henk, that man is nothing but a glib-tongued con man for whom loyalty and integrity are as disposable as the lives of those he deems to be against him.'

The following day, in an irony of cosmic proportion, I was delivered into the custody of the director of the *Blokhuispoort* jail in Leeuwarden, the very institution for which I'd helped organise a break-out back in December of 1944. And, blow me down with a feather, the head warden leading me to my cell was none other than Dirk Jellema, the sympathetic jailer who had not hesitated to supply keys for duplication and blueprints of the facility to aid the Resistance's plans. He was evidently still in the job and recognised me instantly.

'Jesus Christ, Henk, what have you done now?' said Jellema.

'Well, I think I'm being implicated in the robbery and murder of a farmer named Zijlstra that happened in January of 1945,' I told him.

'Oh that,' he replied. 'A local detective by the name of Aukema has reopened an investigation into that incident after he found a bullet casing at the scene of the shooting. He drinks at my preferred watering hole and seems to think he's onto a career-defining case. After a couple of *borreltjes* he becomes quite passionate about how it's progressing. I can't get you out, Henk, but am happy to keep you up to speed with what Aukema is up to. It's the least I can do.'

I always liked Jellema.

Army barracks are notoriously spartan but now seemed like a luxury resort compared to the bare, stark, uncomfortable lodgings of my cell in the *Blokhuispoort*. I could not have been more grateful for the hearty meal and warm hospitality the Boumas had provided the previous night. An old jail like this clangs and chimes, not only with the lamentations of current inmates, but also, it seems, the distant echoes of unhappy history. Sleep did not come easily.

In the morning I was led to an interrogation room in the administration block where detectives Aukema and de Jong were waiting to interview me. After establishing who I was and who they were, they moved onto the subject at hand.

Was I aware, that on 16 January 1945, a farmer named Hantje Zijlstra had been shot and robbed on his way home from the cattle sales in Sneek?

Well yes, I told them, my friends Wim Roth and Pieter Glastra van Loon, known to me by his code name Pedro, had come by to give me the news.

'And did you know that Meneer Zijlstra had died from his wounds on the 27th of January of that year?'

I proceeded to explain to the detectives that I had been struck down with a burst appendix just before Christmas of the previous year and had been laid up at the home of friends of mine where I'd been kept sedated until well into the new year. I had been gradually convalescing when, on 28 January, my compadres came by to inform me that the farmer had died.

Aukema then said something that sent a chill through my bones: 'You, Mr. van Iersel, are reported to have said that "he was killed by us". What did you mean by that?'

Who the fuck had this guy been talking to? 'Well to begin

THE BAKER'S SON

with, I never said that we'd shot him,' I retorted. 'What I meant was that the Resistance was likely to get the blame.'

'Mr. van Iersel,' he continued, ignoring my answer, 'is it true that you and your accomplices Roth and Glastra van Loon were kicked out of the *Binnenlandse Strijdkrachten*, the BS, in December of 1944, for insubordination?'

He had been talking to people. Unfortunately, it seemed the wrong ones.

'Detective Aukema, let me enlighten you, we were never in the BS. When the decree came, in September of 1944, that all Resistance forces were to be placed under the jurisdiction of the then *Orde Dienst*, the OD, with His Royal Philandering Fool, Prins Bernhard at the helm, the KP refused to acknowledge their pathetic play-acting at power and just continued with the work we'd been doing for the previous so many years, at which we'd become very organised and very good. What was true, was that in December of 1944, the three of us had informed a certain Harry Reeskamp that we would no longer be prepared to work with him on account of his repeated, unsanctioned robberies on black marketeers and wealthy farmers which he had portrayed as being for the benefit of the Resistance, but which had instead been perpetrated for his personal gain. When, as a result, the KP kicked him out, he'd wrangled himself a rank as district operations leader with the BS and informed them we'd refused to obey his orders.'

Aukema was scribbling in his note pad at an alarming rate to keep up with what I was telling him. After a bit, he looked up from his writing and said, 'That is all for the moment, Mr. van Iersel. We'll keep you confined here for the moment until we need to speak with you again.'

It was Jellema who led me back to my cell. With a metallic clunk that bounced off the unforgiving bare walls of the jailhouse, he unlocked the door and pointed me to my bunk. Instead of banging the door shut, he followed me in and sat on the cot opposite mine. He offered me a cigarette and reached across to light it.

'I'm sorry that it's come to this, Henk,' he said. 'I always respected the work you did for the Resistance. It's a pity the same can't be said for the current guardians of our community. I'll try to keep you informed of the direction of Aukema's investigation. He doesn't seem to have much to go on besides hearsay and that bullet casing he found where Zijstra was shot. Let me know if you're running short on tobacco. I'll make sure you've got enough and also get you some chocolate and fruit to supplement the god-awful swill they're going feed you in here.'

The next couple of weeks were like an enforced meditation camp, little sensory input, strict routine and too much time alone to think. Instead of sleep, my nights consisted of all too vivid meanderings through the collected fragments of recent memory that had either been too rushed or too painful for me to properly process. Surviving the annihilation of Rotterdam in May of 1940 played out in my mind as if I was scampering across a chessboard with a malevolent God shooting lightning bolts that splintered everything around me. Escaping German custody had me confronting a snarling, frothing German Shepherd dog at the end of its chain, two centimetres from my face. A desperate tram ride in Amsterdam had the track collapsing just behind the carriage into a creeping abyss. I saw myself buried under manure and straw as grotesque farm animals were gorging themselves on my slim disguise. Military tanks and armaments rained from the sky as my feet sank into mud and refused to move. A faceless doctor shot me in the arm, as through a window I watched Wim and Pedro get shot in the head. With a sharp intake of breath, I'd lunge awake, bedclothes dripping with sweat.

Lack of sleep and the absence of progress in any direction combined to gnaw holes in my composure and I could feel myself becoming rattled and angry. Not only had I been unceremoniously dragged back from my platoon in England and thrown into jail without any charges having been laid, but legal representation had been denied me.

On 6 November, I was again summoned to the interrogation room to be questioned by detective Aukema and his side-kick.

'Ah Mr. van Iersel, a few more questions for you.' I was becoming rather fed up with this whole charade. 'You told us previously that you had been laid up with, eh,' he rustled through some pages in the file on the table in front of him, 'a burst appendix I think you said. Can you offer us any corroboration of that story?'

The smug prick, I thought. 'Well yes, detective, I can tell you exactly where I was. It was at the home of the family Altenburg in the village of Oosterwierum where I collapsed just before Christmas 1944. These good people summoned a doctor who kept me sedated until well into January of the following year. It was not until early February that I was at all able to get around. I'm sure you're clever enough to find and interview those folks so they can confirm my story.'

'Oh we will,' he said sarcastically, 'and in the meantime, don't go anywhere.' Asshole.

Jellema stopped by my cell later to give me a packet of tobacco and some rolling papers.

'Dirk,' I told him, 'I'm going crazy in here. If there's anything you can do to find out what the hell Aukema is up to, I'd be forever grateful.'

He assured me that he had some reliable contacts in the Leeuwarden Police Department and would pull some strings to see what they knew. He returned the following day with some interesting news. 'Apparently Aukema and de Jong travelled to the Army barracks in the town of Eelde two days ago to interview a certain 2nd Lieutenant whose name would not be unfamiliar to you, Harry Reeskamp. It seems that Reeskamp confirmed he knew that you Henk, had been laid up with a burst appendix, but then implicated Pedro, and particularly Wim Roth, as having been heard to say derogatory things about Hantje Zijlstra.'

'The lying scumbag!' I interjected, 'What kind of lowlife, sleazy Judas puts the blame on two comrades he knows were executed by the Germans so they can't defend themselves, purely to distract scrutiny of the blood on his own hands.'

I'd known that Reeskamp was pissed off when we refused to have any more dealings with him on account of his dodgy robberies, but I certainly did not think him capable of the depth of betrayal he was now exhibiting. Hessel Bouma was right when he called Harry a glib-tongued con man devoid of any loyalty or integrity.

Being left to stew on these unpalatable truths, over the following few days I thought back over the many stunts we'd undertaken with Harry. There was no doubt he'd been full of bravado, almost to the point of recklessness and enjoying the outlaw lifestyle perhaps a little too much, as if starring in his own gangster movie. That's all good and well, but even gangsters operate with strict codes of loyalty. I could never forgive him. As far as Aukema's investigation was concerned, I reached the conclusion that I had told the detectives all I was going to and anything more about Reeskamp was for me to know and them to find out.

And find out they did. About a week later, Jellema let himself into my cell and closed the door behind him. 'Henk, there's been developments,' he said, offering me a cigarette and sitting on the bunk opposite to look me in the eye. 'Aukema and de Jong went back to Eelde barracks on the ninth of November to have further discussions with Harry Reeskamp who happened to have had a Mauser pistol lying on his bedside table. When asked if they could take it with them for examination, he gave it to them, obviously unaware that Aukema had found a bullet casing where Zijlstra had been shot. My source in the police department said that it was confirmed that the casing could have come from a bullet fired from that pistol. From reading the post-mortem report, Aukema realised that since there was no exit wound, the bullet must still have been lodged in Zijlstra's head and he managed to get a coronial order to exhume the body. They extracted the bullet and upon forensic examination, determined that it had come from the Mauser pistol that Reeskamp had given the detectives. A military magistrate by the name of Beekhuis was consulted and presented with the evidence, who told Aukema that if they could establish that on the 15th of January 1945 that pistol had been in Reeskamp's possession, they could arrest him. To cut a long story short, they did and he's now here in solitary confinement while being interrogated.' Bloody hell, I thought, what a turn of events.

'I guess I could expect to be released soon Dirk, do you think?' I asked hopefully.

'Well maybe not Henk, Harry has admitted the gun was his but maintains that he lent it out to Wim Roth who, he says, thought Zijlstra a black-market profiteer and an enemy of the Resistance. I know for a fact that Aukema has already checked on Zijlstra's bona fides and been satisfied that Hantje was a good friend of the Underground, supplying meat and hiding people wanted by the SS on his farm, so it'll only be a matter of time before Reeskamp shoots himself in the foot, as it were.'

'That's an incredible story, Jellema,' I said to him, 'but I'm still caged in this damp cell freezing my arse off.'

'Hang in there, Henk,' he assured me, 'it's obvious to anyone that you couldn't possibly have had any involvement in Zijlstra's death, but I think they're going to hang onto you until they can definitely charge Reeskamp. I'll keep my ear to the ground.'

'You're a good man, Dirk,' I said. 'I do appreciate you looking after me.'

It became clear that the investigation had moved on because I'd had no more visits from Aukema and de Jong. While a relief, it did nothing to alleviate the time-dragging tedium of being still cooped up in a damp cell. Apparently Reeskamp was likewise confined and had time to ponder his position, because according to Jellema, in early December he had requested a formal hearing. After it was held on 14 December with the military magistrate Beekhuis presiding, Dirk knew to tell me that Harry had significantly changed his tune and now blamed a couple of his more disreputable associates, Tinus Pieters and Charley Bosga.

'Yeah, I've heard of those guys,' I told Jellema. 'They weren't part of any KP group. They were just ne'er do wells used by Reeskamp to do his dirty work.'

'Well,' said Jellema, 'Bosga is by all accounts in Indonesia so they're bringing him back for interrogation while Pieters is being brought in for questioning as we speak. These development have got to be taking the heat off you, Henk.'

'I certainly hope so,' I muttered. 'Nothing against you, Dirk, but I've had more than a gut full of this bloody dungeon.'

CHAPTER 17

'**My friend over there** informs me that you're from Waalwijk, is that true?'

I couldn't immediately tell if the rather fetching young woman quizzing me was about to deride me as being a yokel from the provinces or expressing a genuine interest in my background.

Before I could answer in the affirmative, she added, 'Because if you are, can you get me a pair of shoes?'

I burst out laughing at the mercenary cheek of this girl, the mischievous damned attractive sass with which she'd confronted me and merely replied, 'Would you like to dance?'

Back in Leeuwarden, Tinus Pieters had, under interrogation, confirmed that Reeskamp had indeed ordered him and Bosga to rob Hantje Zijlstra with Harry's Mauser pistol. That left Aukema with no more reason to keep me confined and I was released back into the army. About bloody time. Had I remained with my regiment in England I would have eventually been posted to the city of Grave in the east of The Netherlands, but because the incarceration in Leeuwarden had interrupted my posting, I was sent to The Hague. It was there, at a social dance on the army base that I met and fell in love with Josephine, the girl I would marry.

I happened to be in the city one day when by chance, I encountered Lieutenant Van Der Krap walking towards me. We recognised each other instantly. He was that 'Black Devil' marine officer who had so bravely led us through the fraught battle in the Maas Railway Station in Rotterdam at the outset of the German invasion of our country all those years before.

'Lieutenant Van Der Krap,' I exclaimed, 'so good to see you and that you have survived the war. You must surely be a general by now.'

'Henk, it's good to see you too, but,' and here he pinched up the brown-hued, Indonesian skin of his forearm between thumb and forefinger, 'this is what prevents me from being ever considered good enough to join the ranks of the elite in this country.' And there was the reality of the new, post-war Netherlands; nothing learned from those five long years of Occupation and the sacrifices people had made, just a headlong, ego-driven rush to maintain all the power and position of the old Netherlands. A war hero such as Lieutenant Van Der Krap could not advance in society because of his racial origins, and I was destined to remain a sergeant because I was only a baker's son.

POSTSCRIPT

On 4 October 1985, my father, in a letter to Jack Didden, author of the book *Provincial City During Wartime, Waalwijk 1939-1945* wrote: 'Most of my Resistance comrades were deeply disappointed with what happened after Liberation. You see, we had an incredibly strong bond with each other and often discussed how things might be if we survived. With the deep solidarity we felt at that time, we were convinced that things would be different. I don't wish to be judgemental about everything that happened after the end of the war, but I and many others were so disillusioned that we decided to emigrate. End of rant.'

Our family settled in Australia in 1961 and became Australian citizens. In 1979, someone in The Netherlands sent Dad a pamphlet about Dutch military pensions. He said later, writing to Jack Didden, that, 'Seeing as we don't belong to the "rich folks", I thought there may have been something in it. I applied but was of course, rejected.' Despite their records showing he'd indeed been in military service for significant amounts of time, he was deemed to have been conscripted and therefore ineligible.

The Dutch Defence Department then apparently passed on his information to what was called The Resistance Remembrance Cross Committee, because they contacted my father in 1981 and sent him an application to apply for said Cross. Now, a sceptical person might question why it had taken the Dutch Regime nearly forty years to come around to awarding citations to Resistance fighters who had risked life and limb for the Fatherland so long ago. Might there have been repercussions in doing so earlier, relating to compensation and, indeed, pensions? Were there secrets that the passage of time had now rendered irrelevant? Whatever the reason, the Resistance Remembrance Cross wasn't even a Military Distinction, merely a Parliamentary decree of Remembrance.

Dad filled out the application with only his name and address, then added the following comment: 'Because of my statement of Military Service from the Record Office of the Dutch Ministry of Defence, the Australian Government has granted me a small Veteran's Affairs Pension, despite the fact that I've never done anything for them. Around here we call that "Funny".'

ACKNOWLEDGEMENTS

The genesis of this book was the hand-typed, twenty three page story entitled 'One Man's War' that my father wrote in 1980. It was the English language version of a piece he composed, in Dutch, in response to an enquiry from author Jack Didden to contribute his war experiences for a book Didden was writing about their mutual home town of Waalwijk in the south of The Netherlands during its occupation by the Nazis in World War II from 1939–1945.

In 2022 I was contacted by Ineke van den Houdt of the historical society 'De Erstelinghe' in Waalwijk for permission to use my father's story as a two-part article in their quarterly magazine 'De Klopkei'. Her meticulous research uncovered many hitherto unknown details, including the initial correspondence between father and Jack Didden which shed much light on how 'One Man's War' came to be written. She also shared numerous instances where some of my father's war-time exploits appeared in other authors' published works. This convinced me that the time was right for Henk van Iersel's story to be told in full and that I should be the one to write it. I am deeply indebted to her for the interest she showed and the effort she put into researching the story.

My three daughters, Zoe, Mikahl and Erin each have varying depths of memories of their Opa and it is to them that I dedicate this book.

COVER IMAGE CREDITS

Front cover image:
Henk van Iersel from the SS archives of wanted Resistance operatives.

Back cover images:
Source Amsterdam City Archives: 010164033285.jpg
Wilhelmina, Queen (1880-1962)
Collection Atelier J. Merkelbach, 1948 ca.
http://archief.amsterdam/archief/10164/35423
Copyright free
Image file 010164033285

Netherlands food distribution coupons for items including butter (boter), potatoes (aardappelen), and fish (visch).
Dutch Food distribution coupons dating from WWII. Image by Sander van der Molne. Wikipedia commons
https://commons.wikimedia.org/wiki/File:Voedselbonnen-01.jpg

Allied planes over Haarlem, Holland by J. van Rhijn
Nationaal Archief, Set 72157623679366297, ID 4481068617.jpg
Original title WWII Allied aircraft over the Netherlands during liberation. People waving.
https://www.flickr.com/photos/nationaalarchief/4481068617
Nationaal Archief / Spaarnestad Photo, SFA001015927
http://spaarnestad.pictura-dp.nl/
This image was originally posted to Flickr by Nationaal Archief at https://flickr.com/photos/29998366@N02/4481068617. It was reviewed on 27 November 2016 by FlickreviewR and was confirmed to be licensed under the terms of the No known copyright restrictions.

Members of the Dutch Resistance with troops of the 326th Medical Company (101st Airborne) in front of the Lambertus Church in Veghel during Operation Market Garden in September 1944
Nederlands: Leden van het Veghels verzet samen met de strijdkrachten van het 326th Medical Company (101st Airborne) voor de Lambertuskerk in Veghel gedurende operatie Market Garden in September 1944
By unknown author. – Public Domain, https://commons.wikimedia.org/w/index.php?curid=122889

www.ingramcontent.com/pod-product-compliance
Lightning Source LLC
Chambersburg PA
CBHW060551080526
44585CB00013B/529